D1564186

THE GREAT
AMERICAN
SYMPHONY

THE GREAT
AMERICAN
SYMPHONY

MUSIC, THE DEPRESSION, AND WAR

NICHOLAS TAWA

Indiana University Press

Bloomington & Indianapolis

This book is a publication of

Indiana University Press
601 North Morton Street
Bloomington, IN 47404-3797 USA

http://iupress.indiana.edu

Telephone orders: 800-842-6796
Fax orders: 812-855-7931
Orders by e-mail: iuporder@indiana.edu

The paper used in this publication meets
the minimum requirements of American
National Standard for Information
Sciences—Permanence of Paper for
Printed Library Materials, ANSI
Z39.48-1984.

Manufactured in the United States of
America

Library of Congress Cataloging-in-
Publication Data

Tawa, Nicholas E.
    The great American symphony : music,
the depression, and war / Nicholas Tawa.
        p. cm.
    Includes bibliographical references and
index.
    ISBN 978-0-253-35305-4 (cloth : alk.
paper)
    1. Symphony—United States—20th cen-
tury. 2. World War, 1939–1945—Music
and the war. I. Title.
    ML1255.T39 2009
    784.2'18409730904—dc22
                                   2008042162

1 2 3 4 5 14 13 12 11 10 09

CONTENTS

PREFACE

This study discusses works that I have lived with and enjoyed for years. It is meant to establish the importance of the American symphonists active in the years extending from the mid-thirties to the end of the forties. It holds that they have contributed some of the most vital artistic works of the twentieth century to the world's culture. Indeed, several respected writers on music have designated these fifteen years as the "Golden Age" of American music. When you include swing music, popular songs, and Broadway musicals in the American musical equation, the United States stands alone among nations in the fertility and diversity of musical accomplishment during this period.

Classical music was well represented on the radio throughout these years. The National Broadcasting Company and the Columbia Broadcasting System even had their own symphony orchestras, led by outstanding conductors. It was in fashion then to build movies around classical music and its musicians. In addition, symphony orchestra concerts were made available to the public at little or no cost, owing to initiatives carried out by the federal government. This is not to say that everyone loved classical compositions. As always, such music occupied a cultural niche. However, that niche grew to be a large one during this time.

Among the most worthy of the era's musical contributions are several symphonies of significance. These orchestral compositions managed to attract not just a select few but a large portion of the music-loving public. Various knowledgeable Americans of the era hoped for or thought a native composer might possibly produce "the Great American Symphony."

Some insisted this designation should go to at least two works, Roy Harris's Symphony No. 3 and Aaron Copland's Symphony No. 3.

Because several American artists of the time succeeded in composing symphonies of extraordinary power and unusual merit, because I have a great regard for their achievements, and because much of this symphonic music has been either put to one side or forgotten, I have decided to bring these compositions to the perceptive reader's attention.

This is not a book primarily about other books or other secondary studies—that is to say, about what one author or another has had to say on the subject. Nor is it about the nitty-gritty questions that researchers ask and try to answer. These approaches have been the grist for a great deal of academic writing. Valuable as they may be to the specialist, such methodologies can get quite deadly for the usual music-lover and leave him bored silly. I prefer to write so as to hold the reader's interest and, at the same time, contribute to the knowledge of the music created in the Depression and World War II years. My focus is as much personal as learned and has grown out of my own listening experience and regard for the literature. In short, this book is a labor of love about artistic works that I prize. My aim is to bring these symphonies to life again and call them to the public's attention. My hope is to win new adherents for them.

Over the years I have explored and written about every aspect of American music, especially as it relates to American society. Several books and numerous articles attest to my efforts. In the past my writings have employed the term "art music" to distinguish the formally and artistically more sophisticated and enduring types of music from those of popular music. In the pages that follow, I have decided to use the term "classical" instead of "art," since the term "classical" to most of my potential readers means a body of works from all ages of history that require thoughtful listening, some reflection on what is heard, and other additional efforts for appreciation. Scarcely any "classical" compositions are commercially viable, and they are not composed chiefly for financial profit.

On the other hand, "popular" indicates music intended for immediate and widespread acceptance. The term is applied to compositions that are generally less complicated, instantaneously enjoyable, and, for the most part, disposable. Its composers, its performers, and the music industry regard their contributions as open to commercial exploitation.

I do not desire to get stuck in the quagmire of what music—classical, popular, folk, or ethnic—is valuable and what is not. Every sort of music exhibits its own unique qualities, fulfills specific needs, and addresses its own constituency. People may remain with one genre, or cross over also to enjoy another. However, education, social class, economic status, and cultural upbringing can determine how freely they move. I know that I myself never hesitate in my listening to go from one style or type of music to another. Nevertheless, I am also aware that the symphonies that I wish to write about need someone to bridge the gap separating them from their potential audience. The problem is not that they are unloved but that they are unknown to most Americans.

Originally, "Classical" music came from one brief era in Europe, from the mid-eighteenth century to the beginning of the nineteenth century. However, most people today do not separate one period from another—whether the time is that of Bach, Mozart, Beethoven, Berlioz, Brahms, Tchaikovsky, Mahler, or Shostakovich. It's all "classical music" to them. So it is with the American symphonies I wish to take up. The American music public also thinks of them as "classical."

My plan of action is, first, to fill in the reader on the American society of the Roosevelt years—its cultural values, attitudes, and needs; and second, to consider the symphonies of the prewar, war, and immediate postwar years, in that order. I try to orient the reader through what was going on in the world while the music was being written. The impact of world events on the composers' creative efforts is sometimes direct, sometimes indirect, and sometimes difficult to establish. However, all the composers were impacted by their era—first its economic and social crises, and later its involvement in world war.

The book will provide a brief biographical sketch of each composer taken up and an explanation of how he fits into the era. It will then reflect on his style in general and the kinds of compositions he wrote during the years under consideration. One symphony of each composer will normally be singled out for special discussion, though other symphonies that a composer has written will also receive attention.

When we contemplate the eminence of the most renowned classical musicians of the thirties and forties, we should keep in mind that the consensus of cultural leaders was not challenged but accepted and even approved by the average citizen. Leaders and citizens found orchestra conductors such as Toscanini, Stokowski, and Koussevitzky praiseworthy not just for their musical talents but for their opposition to German and Italian fascism and their representation of ideals that Americans valued. Artur Schnabel, Yehudi Menuhin, Fritz Kreisler, and Pablo Casals, the great virtuosi of their day, dazzled audiences with their performances and won additional admiration for refusing to knuckle under to dictators. A number of refugee composers fled to the United States from Europe. Among the greatest were Igor Stravinsky, Arnold Schoenberg, and Béla Bartók.

The unusually favorable reception of classical music by the many members of the mid-twentieth-century public had an idealized component. These men and women still saw symphonies as something to aspire to. They often viewed their contents as having exalted moral and mental characteristics. The music could embody the most elevated principles for them.[1] From this viewpoint, symphonies "provided an avenue, in heightened measure, to a social life pregnant with meaning other than the mundane." They

> embraced an entire society, not just the artist, and embodied both the creative individual's and the society's profoundest expressions. Music thus understood included the modes for dealing with and explaining reality, the special mind-set for interpreting the circumstances of human existence, and the artistic institutions that made available this interpretation to the community. In this way individuals could direct their thinking to matters beyond and above themselves.[2]

With the arrival of World War II, the perception was also that several music compositions represented the worldwide yearning for liberty and justice. The opening motif of Beethoven's Fifth Symphony symbolized victory for the democratic nations. The message of freedom from oppression permeated Chopin's stirring *Revolutionary* Etude. Russia's Dmitri Shostakovich drew attention to a people's will to endure and struggle on to triumph over adversity in his Fifth Symphony and *Leningrad* Symphony. America's Aaron Copland evoked the democratic spirit throughout the world with *Fanfare for the Common Man* and reminded Americans of what their country stood for with *A Lincoln Portrait.* Country after country found Samuel Barber's *Adagio for Strings* to be a fitting memorial for those who died for the cause of freedom, whatever their nationality. Naturally, the struggle to achieve liberty and justice would also imbue the symphonies written in the war years.

In short, the music of mid-century was expected to have a meaningful expressive component. Composers intended to communicate with audiences in their own time, not just the future. If a symphony failed to take emotional hold of listeners, it failed as music. The first work taken up, Barber's First Symphony, contains great imaginative and emotional appeal. It is at one moment heroic, at another mysterious, and often sings with an ardor to melt the heart. At the same time, it exhibits impeccable craftsmanship. Each symphony that follows Barber's harbors its own individual expressiveness and reveals the sure hand behind it. One may sound sublime; another may be militant, or joyous, or physically strong, or rapturously excited. Each has something different to say and tries to say it well. The structures are solid; the musical argument is set forth with assurance. From the high-minded assertions of Howard Hanson's Third Symphony to the dizzying gyrations of Roger Sessions's Second Symphony, there is music for every taste.

The one thing this book cannot do is play the music. Yet without the sound of the symphonies in the reader's ear, my words have diminished effect. Therefore, the music lover is urged to hear these works in concert, in recordings, and over the air.

Finally, I should disclose that as a student at Harvard, I personally knew three of the composers to be discussed—Aaron Copland, who held evening bull sessions with students when he came to Harvard College to deliver his Elliot Lectures in 1951–52, and Walter Piston and Randall Thompson, who were two of my teachers at Harvard.

THE GREAT AMERICAN SYMPHONY

1

PRELIMINARIES

The decade and a half starting around 1935 holds major significance in America's cultural history. Most composers, artists, and intellectuals would agree with Arthur Schlesinger Jr. when he writes, "The Great Depression and the Second World War showed the desperate necessity of national cohesion within the framework of shared national ideals."[1] Necessity led to realization. A huge number of creative people's artistic works changed to reflect this cohesion. Artists, like others of the work force, found themselves without incomes. The federal government came to their aid monetarily. The government also acted to facilitate not only the production but also the performance of new musical compositions. Moreover, it provided the means for the music public to grow to a number greater than before.

It was not long before there emerged a cultural unanimity of opinion in contemporary American classical music that had not existed before. (Regrettably, this direction toward consensus would quickly disintegrate after 1945.) I do not mean that unanimity was realized, but the closest approach to it took place during this era. These were ten years when dedicated citizens of the United States hoped to achieve a broad and harmonious gathering-together of composers, performers, and audiences. If they could accommodate each other, classical music would be able to flourish more than it had in the past. However, this trend was short-lived. After World War II cultural fragmentation would characterize musical styles, genres, interest groups, and attitudes toward art. Exclusiveness, the clash of incompatible cultural interests, would come to compete with inclusiveness. The notion of drawing all Americans together into one cultural embrace would disappear.

Composers could not help but feel an incentive for writing to express not only themselves but the concerns of the American public during the ten years beginning around 1935. At the beginning of this period, they worried about their relatively unsophisticated country, whose cultural life nonetheless retained the vigor of a society in youthful though shaky evolution. An affinity with the American public and its concerns was growing within them. The Great Depression and World War II encouraged a move toward accessibility in melody and harmony. Contemporary classical music became easier to assimilate. A trend toward more comfortable communication helped audiences remain comparatively receptive to new compositions.

Performing groups, federal government policies, and radio worked together to present contemporary American works to any man or woman who cared to listen. One could detect the emergence of a common musical style with a kinship to American hymns, spirituals, jazz, popular music, and traditional song and dance. A shared approach to the handling of rhythm and a partiality for open sounds also prevailed. The adherence to tonal systems and the careful employment of dissonance aided understanding. In short, all the elements were in place to create works constituting a consonant whole and producing a unifying effect.

Finally and most importantly, among the highest achievements of American composers during this period were several symphonies of which any nation could and should be proud. Accomplished artists who had assimilated the Zeitgeist of the Depression and World War II years composed these symphonies. They expressed the spirit of the times in music suffused with personal and communal meaning. The music public was drawn to the sound and message. Even though these compositions deserve to belong to the standard symphonic repertoire, neglect quickly became their lot after 1950.

ATTITUDES

Historically, the United States has had the reputation of a pragmatic nation. Its citizens believed in hard work, a no-nonsense approach to accumulating wealth, and leisure activities that provided fleeting enjoyment. The "American dream," a commonly held ideal, stressed social equality and material prosperity. The "dream" was less concerned with cultural enrichment. James Truslow Adams was the first to use the term, in his book *The Epic of America,* published in 1931. He writes that the American dream is

> that dream of a land in which life should be better and richer and
> fuller for everyone, with opportunity for each according to ability or
> achievement. It is a difficult dream for the European upper classes
> to interpret adequately, and too many of us ourselves have grown
> weary and mistrustful of it. It is not a dream of motor cars and high
> wages merely, but a dream of social order in which each man and
> each woman shall be able to attain to the fullest stature of which they
> are innately capable, and be recognized by others for what they are,
> regardless of the fortuitous circumstances of birth or position.[2]

Later, a few commentators would claim that the American dream was mostly the quest for financial betterment and the accumulation of bigger and better material goods. Others would adhere to a thirties concept of the American dream, with less stress placed on monetary prosperity and more weight given to leading a spiritually rich and fulfilling life.[3]

Without doubt, most Americans gave an allegiance to athletic events, movies, ballroom dancing, and other popular entertainments that was rarely extended to the arts. Classical music inhabited a less important territory.

As early as 1831, when on a visit to America, Alexis de Tocqueville was commenting that "in America everyone finds facilities . . . for making or increasing his fortune. The spirit of gain is always eager, and the human mind, constantly diverted from the pleasures of the imagination and the labors of the intellect, is there swayed by no impulses but the pursuit of wealth." Affected by this condition, Americans, he concluded, "cultivate the arts that serve to render life easy," not those that require thought and effort.[4] The nurturing of classical music was a hit-or-miss affair, he thought. Little of what was created was of the highest quality.

For the most part, his observation seems true, although applicable to other nations as well as the United States. The more Americans led a hardscrabble existence, the less time they gave to education, and the more highly they valued the useful, the more they turned mostly to trifling amusements. Cultural historians have consistently noted a correlation between the cultivation of the arts and an older, more educated, and more affluent American populace. Yet exceptions have existed, particularly during the Roosevelt administration. During these years men and women from the lower to the higher walks of life turned to classical music, more often than before, in order to experience what was to them a rewarding enrichment of their everyday lives. To be sure, many people went to concerts for nothing but entertainment. Some may have gone to demonstrate their modishness or exercise their intellect. Yet a number of men and women attended because they genuinely loved music and its emotional expressiveness, not because they wanted to attain social superiority or quicken their minds.[5] Listening to classical music, they said, carried them swiftly to a different world and deepened their lives. They were able to join others in the audience in common appreciation of art at the finest expressive level. In a world as drab and incoherent as theirs had become, this sort of experience was prized.

A large minority of the populace during the Roosevelt presidency did subscribe to "uplift" and hoped to expand their cultural horizons. Elitism was not yet a bad word for them. They accepted the idea that leadership in the arts was worthwhile. The general public did not believe that the more cultivated higher-ups plotted against the ordinary citizenry. At the same time, the public did not hesitate to lampoon the pretensions of cultural snobs in movies, radio comedies, cartoons, and popular literature. I should add that the distinction between so-called refined patrician and vulgar plebeian taste—a distinction that extended back to Greek and Roman times—was not insisted upon as much here as in Europe.

Normally, men and women enjoyed the excellent dance music of swing bands and the moving and catchy melodies of songs by Irving Berlin, Jerome Kern, George Gershwin, Cole Porter, Harold Arlen, and others. People also found diversion in Shirley Temple singing "On the Good Ship Lollipop," Gene Autry singing "Back in the Saddle Again," and the Andrews Sisters singing "Boogie Woogie Bugle Boy." Such communication was direct, uncomplicated, and understood without a second thought. It provided a cheery antidote to the bleakness of the times. Music like this was plentiful and readily available, and it occupied a valued place in American culture.

It represented, however, a different kind of expressiveness than did art works such as Bach's *St. Matthew Passion,* Beethoven's Ninth Symphony, and Verdi's *Otello.* American symphonies of the Roosevelt years shared a tradition with these works, however much some of them alluded to popular and folk milieus. Classical compositions such as these symphonies were subtle, fairly complex, and profoundly probing. One could not listen idly to them and hope to absorb their meaning immediately. The music normally steered clear of references to detailed programs, written material, and visuals. Composers aimed at evoking a host of feelings that required some discernment and mental acuteness.

Out-and-out hostility to most new classical music from a majority of the music public was still in the future. The announcement of the premiere of a major American symphony, though it might fail to elicit an earth-shaking response, did excite curiosity in a number of listeners, anticipation in others, and real enthusiasm in a few. Most audiences tolerated even some extreme modern works. Furthermore, as Jacques Barzun explains, audiences like these were essential for new music. "Art does not disseminate itself unaided," he writes. "Artists need heralds, go-betweens, not to say procurers. The worst environment for an artist in a high civilization is dead silence."[6]

Fortunately, several prominent conductors came on the American scene in the thirties and forties to promote American composers and their music to audiences. The interest in and appreciation of the new American music flowed from baton to players to listeners. For example, Howard Hanson and the Eastman-Rochester Philharmonic Orchestra presented an annual Festival of American Music that featured compositions by living composers including John Alden Carpenter, Walter Piston, Samuel Barber, Douglas Moore, William Schuman, Peter Mennin, and Hanson himself. Because he was born and grew up in America, Hanson identified with native idioms, and his interpretations were one with the intentions of the composers. This went a long way, says Virgil Thomson, toward promoting listeners' sympathetic understanding.[7]

In 1943, Lawrence Morton was hailing the American-born Alfred Wallenstein's takeover of the Los Angeles Philharmonic and his announced commitment to an American program and a "fair representation to American Composers. These works will get Philharmonic premieres: Paul Creston's *First Symphony*, Roy Harris's *Third Symphony*, Copland's *A Lincoln Portrait* and *Billy the Kid* . . . Schuman's *A Free Song*, Barber's *Second Essay*, excerpts from *Porgy and Bess*, and an overture by Morton Gould."[8] Other, lesser-known conductors who directed the many orchestras midwifed by the WPA also aired native works, especially if the composers resided in their regions.

As far as the promotion of American symphonies is concerned, the most important conductor was Serge Koussevitzky. This musical head of the Boston Symphony Orchestra, though Russian-born, saw it as his duty to champion the compositions of American composers. He found especially congenial those styles that were tonal and not excessively chromatic. He devoted himself to promoting the cause of native music by means of commissioning new works, conducting premieres, and scheduling repeated performances. Among the works presented to the Boston audience were symphonies by Samuel Barber, David Diamond, Aaron Copland, Howard Hanson, Roy Harris, and William Schuman. Winthrop Tryon wrote, in 1943, "Speaking of the regular Friday afternoon and Saturday evening pairs in Symphony Hall, his [Koussevitzky's] audiences will take more unknown and lately-written works than he himself can prepare for them." Fortunately the concertmaster, Richard Burgin, was able to come to his assistance by rehearsing and conducting some of the new works.[9]

It is worth dwelling on Serge Koussevitzky for a while since his actions had a direct impact on composers. To cite one such action, he encountered Walter Piston soon after he took over the conductorship of the Boston Symphony Orchestra. Piston had just returned from Paris and begun teaching at Harvard. Immediately, Koussevitzky asked, "Why you no write a symphony? You write; I play."[10] For an orchestral conductor to ask an American composer to write a symphony was astonishing at that time. A surprised Piston complied with his *Symphonic Piece,* premiered in 1928. It was a significant start for a long association between conductor and composer. A genuine Symphony No. 1 came along a decade after, and seven more symphonies over the next three decades.

Another American composer with whom he worked closely was Aaron Copland. In his very first season with the Boston Symphony Orchestra, Koussevitzky began to promote Copland's music, performing the *Symphony for Organ and Orchestra* of the young composer, whom he had met in Paris in 1923. In a 1944 article in the *Musical Quarterly,* the composer wrote about his first meeting with Koussevitzky, which his teacher, Nadia Boulanger, had set up:

> Mademoiselle Boulanger, knowing the Russian conductor's interest in new creative talents of all countries, took it for granted that he would want to meet a young composer from the country he was about to visit for the first time. That she was entirely correct in her assumption was immediately evident from the interest he showed in the orchestral score under my arm. It was a *Cortège Macabre,* an excerpt from a ballet [*Grohg*] I had been working on under the guidance of Mademoiselle Boulanger. With all the assurance of youth— I was twenty-two years old at the time—I played it for him. Without hesitation he promised to perform the piece during his first season at Boston.[11]

Later, when Copland mentioned that the conductor might find the works of the neophyte composer William Schuman interesting, Koussevitzky programmed Schuman's music without delay. Furthermore, when the twenty-fifth anniversary of ASCAP arrived in 1939, Koussevitzky scheduled a festival of American music, presenting works by Arthur Foote, Deems Taylor, Henry Hadley, Howard Hanson, William Schuman, George Gershwin, Roy Harris, John Alden Carpenter, and Randall Thompson.

He made it less troublesome for composers to write new works and gain them a hearing. He performed scores that might have lain unnoticed or little-heard. He also established the Berkshire Symphonic Festivals and the Berkshire Music Center. The Festivals' purpose was to secure a new and larger public for symphonic performances. The Center's purpose was to train young composers and promising musicians.

Koussevitzky and his wife became American citizens in February 1941. He said to reporters, "This is where I have carved out my career in life. This is where my friends are, and this is where I want to spend the rest of my days, in an atmosphere of freedom and achievement. The United States is the only country in the world today in which artistic and musical ability can find free expression. I have great hope for the future of America and am proud to be adopted and accepted as one of its citizens."[12]

Finally, after his wife died, Koussevitzky founded the Koussevitzky Music Foundation in 1943 as a memorial to her. The fund has commissioned many European and American composers and has thus kept Koussevitzky's legacy going, even after his death in 1951. David Diamond's Fourth Symphony, Walter Piston's Fourth Symphony, and Aaron Copland's Third Symphony were three of the commissions.

By 1937, at least ninety-six symphony orchestras were active in the United States, with 57 percent of that total having been established after 1929. The growth had taken place despite the severe economic constraints of the Great Depression. Also by 1937, CBS radio alone was transmitting 1,231 broadcasts of classical music annually. At the same time, NBC was abetting the unprecedented classical music expansion by establishing a symphony orchestra for Arturo Toscanini. This internationally renowned conductor had returned to the United States in 1936 because of his disenchantment with Mussolini. His radio broadcasts were soon reaching a huge and loyal radio audience. *Life* magazine, on 12 December 1938, expressed amazement at the swift increase of attention given music at all levels, in particular classical music, and attributed it in large part to the influence of radio. It also noted that this increase had come together with a large growth in amateur orchestras.[13]

A fresh and growing group of listeners were coming on the scene, most of them having little or no previous experience with classical music but ready to learn. Their support had strengthened the 25,000 orchestras and bands established in the nation's schools and colleges. By 1940, nearly 300 professional and semi-professional symphony orchestras existed, and all were "recognizable instruments of public service." Their "appeal and the burden of expense [were] clearly being shifted from the classes to the masses."[14] Although they featured mostly tried-and-true older works, orchestras scheduled contemporary American compositions more frequently than they had before 1935 or would after 1950. Contemporary composers could expect, at last, that somewhere some ensemble was ready to play and an audience ready to listen to an American symphonic offering. They came increasingly to consider music, including the symphonic genre, to exist within a social context. Music was to be enjoyed by more than a select few. Some believed that the absorption of an inspirational musical message guided people toward pursuing a fuller life. Several of them felt that they could contribute to their society by addressing people's inner lives in meaningful ways and by seeking easier means for communicating musically with audiences.

The broader audience for classical music that emerged in the thirties and forties included a large unseen component—the huge numbers of men and women who attended next to no concerts but did listen to phonograph records and radio broadcasts. Disappointingly, only a limited number of the recordings that were made bore the titles of American works, and the distribution of these few was restricted. Then, from August 1942 to the end of 1944, the American Federation of Musicians, led by James C. Petrillo, went on strike and banned members from making any recordings. Bringing whatever was available of the new music to listeners was left, by and large, to radio. The broadcast of live concerts increased. NBC and CBS continued to sponsor their own symphony orchestras, whose performances were constantly put on the air.

Although invisible, the thousands who depended on radio and recordings for their music could not help but preoccupy and influence contemporary composers. A twist of the dial could end any reception of the new art. In 1938, Hans Heinsheimer spoke of the composer's need to deal with this vast audience.[15] Five years later, the influential Copland warned that

> The radio and phonograph have given us listeners whose sheer numbers in themselves create a special problem. They can't be ignored if musical creation is to flourish. More and more we shall have to find a musical style and language which satisfies both us and them. That is the job of the forties. . . . I do not advocate "writing down" to the

public. . . . Composers, too, sometimes talk as if they really were convinced that nothing but pure inspiration goes into the makings of a work. The truth is of course, that it is far from easy to throw off old composing habits, to think afresh on the subject of the purpose and functions of music in relation to the musical idiom used and the audience one is trying to reach.

Nobody, he said, "wants to write 'modern music' any more."[16]

By "modern music" Copland meant the convoluted, highly dissonant, tonally unanchored, and melodically unsympathetic sounds of the twenties and early thirties espoused by the "art for art's sake" coterie. He had come to the realization that his advanced compositions, with their deliberate break with the past and exploration of novel forms and sounds, were attracting next to no listeners. Though they were works of genius, his Organ Symphony (1924), Symphonic Ode (1929), and Short Symphony (1933) had failed to win the favor of more than a handful of concert attendees. From the point of view of a composer who desired some sort of audience, the situation was discouraging and change was needed.

Copland insisted that individuality and integrity could still be maintained even as a composer traveled the road to popularity. The artist, he thought, should not disdain pleasing melodies and attention-grabbing rhythms. He maintained that musicians capable of the most advanced musical writing were not compromising their finest impulses if they tried to win large followings.

He realized that, by 1935, the avant-garde audience had become too tiny in size and too fickle in taste to sustain contemporary American composers of ultra-modernist persuasion. An advanced contemporary style was in fashion for a couple of seasons and then abandoned for the next new thing. All that seemed solid melted into air. Nothing really lasted. On the positive side, he and other well-known composers were arriving at a more or less united approach toward reaching a substantial audience. It helped that, after World War I, some of the more prominent American composers had studied with Nadia Boulanger in France and held elements of style in common. The symphonies of several of them will be examined in the pages that follow—among them, compositions of Walter Piston, Aaron Copland, Roy Harris, David Diamond, and Douglas Moore. From Boulanger they learned self-discipline, avoidance of bombast, and taking pains with melodic lines. She taught them to employ modernisms based on a neoclassic Franco-Stravinskian model, and to provide judicious relief of highly rhythmic passages with contrapuntal activity. Within these parameters, all five Americans had received encouragement to develop their own styles. That they did learn to go their own way was established when by the mid-thirties most of them were writing symphonies (which Boulanger had not particularly encouraged) and regarding these compositions as the supreme demonstration of their art.

They modified the severity of the neoclassic idiom for these symphonies in order to allow greater warmth and dramatic expression. They introduced a tonal directness that abstained from the aggressive clangs and clashes of militant modernism. Creating alongside these five were two musicians, Howard Hanson and Samuel Barber, who held fast to the earlier Romantic tradition and wrote conservative but eloquent music. Another, Randall Thompson, believed in winning over the public with plainly stated compositions that smacked of the American soil. He felt that without a sizable audience behind him, a composer was nothing and his music meaningless. Finally, one maverick, Roger Sessions, would go his own uncompromising way, writing music of breathtaking complexity and unwavering harshness of tone.

Non-musical political factors also impacted on American composers during the thirties. Most of them had little money. Some joined or sympathized with radical organizations that urged making contact with or offering succor to the masses. At the same time, the Roosevelt administration advanced WPA projects that would allow artists to get economic relief and continue to create, writes the composer Arthur Berger. Publicly funded orchestras, often led by eminent conductors, catered to large audiences. Most of the concertgoers were recent converts to classical music, yet they remained receptive to listenable compositions of recent vintage. This was not a time for artists to engage in "esoterica or abstraction, and they developed a fairly recognizable and simplistic style."[17]

After hearing the new works of the late thirties, the music public began to develop some empathy for them. Before long, they started to have faith in and give support to American music and what its composers represented even though they failed to comprehend many of the sounds. Audiences recognized that these compositions had links to what they approved, took in, and identified with. Such music the public might come to need, even hunger after. It contributed to people's happiness, and, many thought, worked for their inner good.

By trying not to compromise quality and by employing an understandable language, composers of the new music, especially the symphonies, won respect among music-lovers, sophisticated and unsophisticated. Composers appeared to be laying the groundwork for a partnership with the public. They had grown sensitive to its needs and wished to gain its acceptance. The driving force and social aims behind recent classical compositions had thus changed. Isolation and hermetic thinking was out. Music was confidently stating an agenda the public could subscribe to. Whether the public would subscribe permanently was another matter.

THE TIMES

Creative artists cannot help but be affected by their times. Every composition they create does have its musical antecedents, but it also takes a direct or indirect cue from the goings-on in its surroundings. So it was with Bach and the German religiosity of the early eighteenth century, with Mozart and the rational classical thinking of the later eighteenth century, and with Beethoven and the revolutionary rhetoric and political drama thundering around him.

One should note that other factors besides economic conditions contributed to the unease prevalent in the thirties. These would affect artistic creation and the dominant moods and emotional tone of contemporary musical works, whether obviously or subtly. The artistic community was quite aware of negative aspects of the current scene. Open-minded liberals, among them composers, voiced alarm over support for Nazism, which promoted violent racism and hatred of "non-Aryans"; Italian Blackshirts, in favor of fascistic totalitarianism; Father Coughlin's bigoted radio addresses and admiration of Hitler and Mussolini; and the rampant anti-Semitism and racism that were a part of all these "isms" and that flew out of Coughlin's mouth. Artists puzzled over the ultraconservative members of the electorate scattered throughout the country—those Middle Americans whose fear of socialism caused them to act against their best interests. Southern Americans practiced rampant discrimination against

African Americans and by so doing ensured their own social and economic backwardness. Western Americans' biases meant that Japanese and Chinese residents who contributed vitally to the region's economic well-being were treated as second-class citizens. Northeasterners' suspicion of immigrants from Eastern Europe and the Mediterranean area had culminated earlier with the Sacco-Vanzetti execution. In no way could composers see themselves as living in the best of all possible worlds and in the best of all times.

However, they recognized also that while the American populace harbored a large minority of antidemocratic advocates and their gullible followers, it also included an immense number of well-meaning people. They were found among factory workers, farmers, miners, and public servants. These good citizens played a valued role in society and tried as best they could to provide for their families. They were the decent and temperate people that most composers wished to reach with their music. By so doing, American artists also hoped to gain fresh confidence in themselves and greater certainty of their place in the scheme of things. In 1967, Aaron Copland looked back at the thirties and concluded, "In all the arts the Depression had aroused a wave of sympathy for and identification with the plight of the common man. In music this was combined with the heady wine of suddenly feeling ourselves—the composers, that is— needed as never before. . . . No wonder we were pleased to find ourselves sought after and were ready to compose in a manner that would satisfy both our collaborators and ourselves."[18]

In addition, Copland and his colleagues saw their European counterparts moving in a similar direction. Hindemith and Weill had already engaged in writing *Gebrauchsmusik,* compositions for use by a musically knowledgeable public. Noted composers including Bartók, Stravinsky, Prokofiev, and even Schoenberg were writing softer-edged music. Shostakovich's works were transparent in their content and telling in their emotional impact. Most American composers envied this Russian composer's ability to win an international audience. His Fifth and Seventh (*Leningrad*) symphonies, in particular, were gaining immense followings.

The Roosevelt administration was instrumental in giving encouragement to native composers. It was committed to the financial aid of all members of the American society. It offered composers employment and made them feel "needed as never before." In 1935, as part of its economic relief effort, the Work Progress Administration established the Federal Project Number One, which had five divisions—art, music, theater, writers, and research into historical records. The Project was the first consequential venture into cultural advancement that the United States had ever undertaken. Under the direction of Nikolai Sokoloff, the music section, denominated the Federal Music Project, aimed at exploring fresh territory rather than aiding existing private establishments. Whatever the cultural programs the Project sponsored, whether groundbreaking or traditional, they aimed to minister to the unemployed musician economically and the public socially and educationally. Though under centralized management, the music division was sensitive to regional differences and attempted to respond to the specific needs of municipalities the nation over. Vocal and instrumental instruction and classes in theory, history, and music appreciation proliferated. New orchestras, chamber groups, opera and musical theater companies, and dance bands came into being through the Federal Music Project's auspices. Ensembles were formed in towns where none had previously existed. Through the offices of the Project, thirty-four symphony orchestras were added to the eleven that already existed. Part of the mandate to these orchestras involved the performance of works by Americans. Trifling admission charges ensured that concerts would often be played to full houses, despite scarce money and audiences not exactly clamoring for new compositions. Originating in New York City, Composers Forum-Laboratories, as subdivisions of the Federal Music Project, were set up in several large cities, among them Boston, Chicago, Philadelphia, San Francisco, Detroit, Cleveland, Milwaukee, Minneapolis, Tulsa, and Jacksonville. Project managers requested that contemporary composers submit compositions to regional committees of their peers. They told no composer what or how to write. The committees selected promising works to be rehearsed and performed before audiences. The attendees, in turn, were free to comment on what they heard and ask questions of the composers. The after-concert give-and-take promoted understanding in the audience and provided valuable feedback to composers.[19] One or two composers were uncomfortable about discussing their music with an audience and answering its criticism—especially if they were still proponents of one of the more severe styles. The majority of composers welcomed and learned from the exchange of talk.

In 1936, Nikolai Sokoloff issued a report on the Federal Music Project, "covering its scope and activities during its first nine months."[20] Its achievements were amazing. In an introductory note to his report, Sokoloff stated, "Music has no social value unless it is heard." To this declaration, most composers were now saying "amen." The 32 million people who attended concerts during these nine months "show that it [music] has not only been heard but that it has reached a greater number of our people than in any other period in the history of the United States." Moreover, "emphasis in all of these concerts [was] placed on the presentation of American compositions."[21] The project had discovered an enormous and unforeseen craving for music, old and new, among large numbers of Americans from all walks of life. Works by 622 composers had been performed. Among them were 27 symphonies, by 24 composers, presented in more than 60 programs. Pre-concert lectures explained the new music to be played. Repeated performances acquainted audiences with unfamiliar scores. Project leaders saw to it that units scattered throughout the country played those pieces that proved outstanding.

Most composers appreciated what the Federal Music Project was doing for them and American culture. Although its mandate was not to commission new works, it provided financial support to artists, allowed them to continue writing, and gave them exposure by having its ensembles perform their works. Otto Luening said, "The WPA focused national attention on the arts on a broad scale and as a part of our national life." Furthermore,

> in 1935, Carl Miller, music director of the New York City Federal Music Project, had written me that my *Serenade for Three Horns and Strings* had been performed numerous times before enthusiastic audiences. Subsequently, Franco Autori . . . wanted more of my works to perform with the Bronx Symphony Orchestra and the Greenwich Symphonietta. Such neighborhood concerts interested me greatly, because they were reaching new audiences and government-supported music and art was one of my fondest hopes.

Luening soon secured performances of his music with the Brooklyn Symphony, Buffalo Philharmonic, and Providence Symphony. "The WPA even paid me fifty dollars as rental and royalty fee for a week of performances."[22]

In January 1940, Samuel Barber wrote excitedly to Sidney Homer about the WPA-subsidized performance of his music and the audience's warm reception of it. Homer wrote back,

> Your description of the audience was great. I know those people, hungry for anything that will do them artistic good; used to being barred out of anything that costs money. We have done everything we could to put music beyond their reach.... When all people demand it, they'll get it, just as they got cathedrals, art galleries, pure water and cheap subways. The music will *count!* You may see the day and had better prepare some music on big lines just in case.[23]

However noble the WPA experiment to bring classical music to the general public, it was drawing to a close even as Barber and Homer wrote to each other, owing to the indifference of private music establishments and the attacks of conservative politicians who considered spending on painting and music to be wasteful and all artists to be subversives. Powerful congressional figures, among them J. Parnell Thomas and Martin Dies and the House Un-American Activities Committee, relentlessly fought to do away with the Federal Arts Project, using as their principal weapon the accusation of left-wing infiltration of the arts. There was no letup in their hostility. To give an example of Thomas's narrow frame of mind, he claimed that "Practically every play presented under the auspices of the Project is sheer propaganda for Communism or the New Deal."

The onset of World War II administered the final blow. Sokoloff left his post in May 1939, and the project soon ground to a halt. Before long the hostilities effort commandeered all of the nation's resources. Money went into war production; men went into the armed forces. The economy was stimulated; unemployment was a thing of the past. The Federal Music Project also became a thing of the past. However, the increased public taste for symphonic music remained. A number of orchestras that had started with WPA sponsorship continued to function, making do without federal funding. In many instances local citizen groups raised the funds to keep their community orchestras going. American composers, whether in or out of the armed forces, would continue to write symphonies. Regrettably, the composition of new symphonies and the frequency of their performances would lessen considerably after 1950. The Federal Music

Project's push to air native works and the huge amount of fellow feeling generated by the war would be a thing of the past.

SYMPHONISM ASCENDANT

"Symphonism" indicates orchestral music of large scope in both length and ambition. Usually involving a full-sized ensemble, the music of a symphony is normally serious in nature, and it unfolds in several movements or sections. This was the commonly accepted understanding of the term "symphony" until 1950. After World War II, this general agreement vanished. The notion grew among the more advanced composers that a symphony is anything its creator says it is. If the composer designates a two-minute work for a set of drums and a kazoo as a "symphony," then so be it. Consequently, the name began to have no meaning in itself. It became a vague label, so vague that many composers dispensed with it altogether.

At the same time, numerous composers have attacked even the notion of writing a symphony, insisting that such an effort is outmoded. Still others have decided that the audience for symphonies is entrenched in the compositions written before the twentieth century. They have claimed that the music public displays a marked lack of interest in any new classical compositions, symphonies in particular, so why write them? After World War II, a symphony that evoked national sentiments would be associated with jingoism, an excessive patriotism that did not deserve expression. Composers wished to stay clear of the association. When serial and indeterminate music came into fashion, many composers turned away from tonality. The symphony was at the bottom of the totem pole. More than a few musicians thought after 1950 that only reactionaries would write a work called a symphony.

Nevertheless, symphonies continued to be written. The pace even increased, especially in the years after 1980, when tonality made a comeback. Not far behind the return of tonality have come a number of new symphonies by composers including John Harbison, Philip Glass, John Corigliano, Aaron Jay Kernis, Christopher Rouse, and Ellen Taaffe Zwilich. At the same time has come an increased interest in the symphonies written in the 1930s and 1940s that the avant-garde had tried to relegate to the dustbins. The composers of these symphonies have also come in for new respect, and their music for sympathetic study.

Contrary to the sentiments that would prevail after 1950, major American composers active before World War II favored the writing of symphonies. The term "symphony" still retained its traditional meaning for nearly all musicians. They had not given up on the genre or the audiences that would hear the music. Artists wished to create compositions beyond ordinary expressive expectations. They wanted to give their music ample space for it to have its say and to allow for wide-ranging thought and vision. They wanted to write works for sizable instrumental ensembles, occasionally with voices added, and in an idiom sufficiently flexible to allow a fair amount of leeway in expression. Such compositions were called "symphonies."

The symphony genre by then was already almost two hundred years old. In the last third of the eighteenth century, Joseph Haydn and Wolfgang Amadeus Mozart had defined its structure: a first sonata-allegro movement; a slow movement, more often than not in A B A form; an optional minuet movement; and a very brisk finale, most often in rondo form, or sometimes in sonata or variation form. At the beginning of the nineteenth century, Ludwig van Beethoven had poured a new content into the symphony, one that promoted freedom of treatment, gave free rein to the imagination, encouraged introspection and emotional expression, and paid homage to nature or the liberation of the spirit. He substituted a fast scherzo for the minuet, made all movements longer, and enlarged the orchestra. His Third Symphony pursued the idea of heroism. In his Sixth Symphony he tried depicting aspects of the countryside. He added solo voices and a chorus to the Ninth Symphony. Later composers built on the precedents set by Beethoven—enlarging the orchestra still further, increasing harmonic complexity, and indulging in a great deal of chromaticism.

From the middle of the nineteenth century, composers of the New World wrote symphonies—starting with those of William Henry Fry, George Bristow, John Knowles Paine, George Chadwick, and Amy Beach. They would continue doing so. The symphonies of Fry and Bristow were rickety and overly derivative affairs. However, Paine's two symphonies showed polished craftsmanship and well-thought-out ideas. Chadwick added a decidedly Yankee flavor to his works. And Amy Beach planted the banner for women symphonists with her "Gaelic" Symphony of 1894. True, they were trying to follow European, mainly German, precedents. Nevertheless, the symphonies they wrote exhibited high competency and continue to be enjoyable.

In the earliest years of the twentieth century came Frederick Shepherd Converse, Henry Hadley, Daniel Gregory Mason, Arthur Shepherd, and Edward Burlingame Hill with their symphonies.[24] Several of these works were quite respectable. Almost all of them honored traditional guidelines. Most symphonic styles were still erected on conservative Central European foundations. The composers had either studied in Germany or received an American education from German-trained teachers. However, from Paine to Hill the tendency was to slowly loosen the Germanic ties. Composers were opening themselves to French and occasionally to Russian and Bohemian (read, Dvořák) influences. The anti-Germanism of World War I would reinforce this fresh direction.

At the same time, several European composers of the early twentieth century were responsible for a considerable degree of variety in the structure and subject matter of compositions that they identified as symphonies. Gustav Mahler built protracted works requiring huge orchestras, solo voices, and choruses. For example, his Third Symphony spreads out over ninety-five minutes and calls for not only a substantial symphony orchestra but also a chorus, boys' choir, and mezzo-soprano. At the opposite end, Anton Webern exercised extreme brevity in his nine-minute symphony. Jean Sibelius tried out a concise, one-movement approach in his Seventh Symphony, which lasts thirty-eight minutes. Igor Stravinsky's *Symphony of Psalms* dispenses with the usual orchestra and is a setting of psalms for timpani, bass drum, harp, two pianos, cellos, basses, and chorus. Bela Bartók composed his admired *Concerto for Orchestra,* which is a symphony in everything but name.

In America, too, there were one or two attempts at non-traditional symphonies. Virgil Thomson's *Symphony on a Hymn Tune* (1928), with its atypical instrumentation, reveled in an incongruous juxtaposition of popular ditties, hymn tunes, and ballroom dance rhythms. Aaron Copland offered a cryptic *Short Symphony* (1933) that tested the abilities of conductor and orchestra to perform the music, and the capacity of the audience to comprehend the complex rhythms and brittle dissonances.

A couple of the symphonies from the middle thirties through the forties would be in one movement, although sectionalized in a way that suggests the usual symphonic movements. One or two compositions would feature solo voices and/or a chorus. However, American composers would choose mainly to stay within the more conventional boundaries as inherited from Beethoven when they wrote their symphonies. They felt that by doing so, they would undergo the utmost test of their craftsmanship and demonstrate that they had to be taken seriously as artists. Moreover, they felt so attuned to their society in general and so comfortable using the traditional symphonic rhetoric that they considered it unnecessary to obliterate the symphonic forms and abandon symphonic procedures. In addition, experimentation in challenging post-tonal styles was not in the cards, owing to the prevalent economic, social, and political problems and resultant public attitudes.

Some artists also wished to convince instrumentalists and conductors of their skill and dexterity in handling instruments and of their music's playability. Additionally, they wanted to reach a general public as efficaciously as possible—a public they believed that they had a good chance of reaching. Trying out new procedures would only get in the way of realizing this goal. They sought to make the term "symphony" indicate a recognizable form that respected its own conventions and norms and proved welcoming to audiences. As for content, they most often chose to adhere to an elevated subject—one that symbolized their ideals and those of a free people. They did not use "symphony" as a label that anyone could apply to works of any instrumentation, featuring any caprice that entered the mind.

By naming a work a "symphony," they signified music given a measure of heft. They did not mean a work that would be overly brief or overly light and superficial. Weightiness was the rule. If the composer wanted to write a pithy or perky piece, better to call it a sinfonietta or suite, as in Morton Gould's *Latin-American Symphonette*, Ferde Grofé's *Grand Canyon Suite*, or Walter Piston's suite *The Incredible Flutist*.

With precedents going back to the nineteenth-century Romanticists, several American musicians believed that music, through the symphony, possessed the ability to achieve the highest and most comprehensive form of human communication. That is to say, through an individual and intense artistic "seeing," composers could offer insights into major areas of human feeling and communicate these perceptions to listeners. They might not change behavior, but they could try to reinforce the best in people. Certainly during the Roosevelt years the belief that music could and should convey sentiment was accepted as a civilizing device, thus diverging from the attitudes of important up-to-date composers from the 1920s and early 1930s, who practiced emotional restraint, avoided rich resonances, and introduced much dissonance and rhythmic complexity.

Ideally, the symphonic experience cranked a composer's creative ability up to its maximum. The result, he or she trusted, would be a work exhibiting technical competence and also having the power to grab the intellect and emotions. However, a lot of the more revolutionary composers (such as Edgard Varèse and Carl Ruggles) would have questioned such thinking. They rejected customarily accepted or sanctioned forms and emphasized individual experimentation with new, even radical, techniques. To them, the nineteenth century was dead, its criteria antiquated; only backward-lookers wished to have a regard for an old and, to them, outworn order and write symphonies.

Not so, said Barber, Hanson, and others. Symphonies were not obsolete. Although subject to time and place, composers including Barber and Hanson made an effort to go beyond this conditioning and to register meanings affecting all humanity. The aim of such symphonic composers was to create works breathing the youthful spirit of the nation. Their compositions had to remain direct in expression and, at the same time, offer an opening to the imagination. Their contents were meant to sound freshly minted. If all elements came together successfully the result would earn recognition as a great work of art.

Much discussed in the thirties and forties was the realization of what was denominated "the great American symphony." Who would achieve it? When? Where? How? Perhaps aiming for music that is *great* and *American* seems a bit pretentious and chauvinistic, but it was then the subject of lively debate. Music students, academics, critics, and composers discussed the question. No one agreed upon what was meant by greatness in a symphony. Who decided what superiority of accomplishment was? Was it the judgment of the composer's peers or a consensus reached by the music public over time? In addition, the American musical world of that time yearned for the American symphony that would cause Europeans to sit up and listen. The "great American symphony" was one that also required the imprimatur of the international community. However greatness was conferred, composers of these decades did aspire to achieve symphonic masterpieces, works perceived by all concerned—colleague, connoisseurs, general music public, Americans as well as people outside the national borders—as having unusual merit and loftiness of character. By the end of the forties, they had a certainty that an American musical identity had clearly established itself high up in the cultural hierarchy.

The term "masterpiece" means any superlatively carried out work. However, the worth of a masterly symphony may be located not just in the composition itself but in the set of circumstances surrounding it— in its understanding of human existence and grasp of the times in which it is written, and in the way it musters sponsorship from listeners. This brings to mind Kenneth Clark's comment on two further characteristics of a master work: "A confluence of memories and emotions forming a single idea, and a power of recreating traditional forms so that they become expressive of the artist's own epoch and yet keep a relationship with the past."[25] Although his description refers mainly to paintings, it can certainly apply to musical compositions.

Traditional forms, the patterns continuing from the past, were to be mastered and then reconstituted. They were to be given a unique American twist, even as they supplied structures such as sonata-form, rondo, canon, fugue, and variation-form that composers thought to be still viable. Tradition provided models of content management including thematic repetition, development, metamorphosis, and contrapuntal or block-harmony treatment. Tradition also mandated a reappraisal of native songs, dances, and hymn tunes dear to the American public. These could be reformulated to suit contemporary needs. More specifically, "tradition" referred to the ethnic heritage of Hanson, the Romantic expressiveness of Barber, the fluent classicism of Piston, the no-nonsense athleticism of Schuman, the cerebral patterns *à la* Bach, Brahms, and Schoenberg found in Sessions, and the various ways a native ambience was injected into the music of Copland, Harris, Thompson, and Moore.

However disparate their manner, these composers were together promulgating a contemporary concept of an American sound that mirrored their shared experience of the past and present and their hopes for the future. Roy Harris underlined his and his colleagues' rediscovery of tradition by saying that a composer was "supremely egotistical" if he believed that he as an individual could alone corral all wisdom. Harris added, "One generation is not long enough for man to become wise; and so we have suffered greatly in losing the wisdom of tradition. And so the romantic composer who thinks that he can in one lifetime offset the sum total of all the highest and best that all other composers in all times and periods preceding him have sifted out through experience, is condemned to produce an unbalanced and immature expression."[26]

To sustain itself, the American music that Harris spoke about had to seek a balance between deference to tradition and freedom to employ those traditions so that the artist could create works capable of standing up in their own time. For the most part, the symphonies of mid-century do communicate a spanking-new forcefulness, urgency, and sometimes brashness. They show impressive breadth and capacity to connect effectively with an American audience. In most of them, tonality is present, pliable, and equally responsive to expressive needs and structural design. Rapid scale passages may flash out to surprise the listener; singable melodies can make unabashed appearances; chords murmur insouciantly or pound forth powerfully; rhythmic devices may dominate the melody and harmony. Harmonies can be smooth, sonorous, or astringent. Rhythms, often uneven or syncopated, pulsate in the background or drive forward to an American beat. The American symphony's forte is found in the integration of this absorbingly dramatic give-and-take.

Peter Jona Korn, German-born composer, teacher, and writer on music, observed some forty years ago that the symphony had a particular appeal for American composers, and that a resurgence of symphonic writing had taken place in America "precisely at the moment when a generation of European composers had rejected it, at least temporarily." He tried to find a basis for the resurgence, saying, "A reason for this lies in the American character, which is marked by generosity, often to a fault, by a decided flair for the dramatic, by a preference for sharp contrasts and by a leaning to over-statement. The *al fresco* character of a true symphonic style is better suited to these attitudes, which in turn are a reflection of the wide, spacious character of a typical American landscape, than, for instance, chamber music, which tends to place greater emphasis on detail."[27] The symphony, of course, was a vehicle for demonstrating that American composers had to be taken seriously by their European peers and by America's musical establishment.

The Roosevelt administration and its Federal Music Project encouraged the articulation of a native musical viewpoint in symphonies. The resurgence of Americanism among academics and artists during the decade of Depression and, later, in the years of World War II abetted this movement. It was a national bent that was interpreted as untainted by "my country, right or wrong." Composers were aware of the warnings that Roger Sessions, for one, gave again and again in his talks and writings—"Music and Nationalism" (1933), "Vienna—Vale, Ave" (1938), "On the American Future" (1940), etc.[28] He cautioned them about a cultural nationalism that could lead to jingoism, narrow-mindedness, and imaginative sterility. He repeatedly observed that a viable American musical tradition would come "not through cultural isolationism or consciously nurtured 'Americanism' but through men who, having listened to the music which sings within them, are willing to let themselves be guided by it, wherever it may lead them. Such music, and only such music, will be truly and profoundly American."[29] Composers took note of his warnings but rejected Sessions's going-it-alone in music, without a single bow in the direction of an "American" sound, and his small regard for the capacities and inclinations of ordinary listeners.

Not for native artists was the blind devotion to a charismatic figure who might turn into a Hitler or Mussolini. The dedication of their art was not to nationalist bigotry and military oppression but to humanity in its entirety. As the composer Arthur Berger said, "The quest for a national character is not to be confused with breast-beating patriotism, 'my country right or wrong,' which is something many of us involved in the tendency would vehemently disavow."[30] He and his colleagues hoped to diminish the possible conflict between this quest and the achievement of a more universal appeal. They recommended giving attention to those musical associations that would connect with people beyond the national boundaries.

All the same, the urge existed to create outside the box, outside of an identity solely linked to established and contemporary European musical practices. Several American composers desired to convey sounds extrapolated from music of our cultural past or more closely evocative of the American nation—its landscape, history, people, and myths—through symphonic means. Here, a comment of William Schuman is pertinent: "When a composer writes music that is regarded as native or national, it follows that he has struck a responsive chord in his listeners, and that they recognize qualities that go back to their own sense of identification with their own land or culture." Furthermore, he claimed, "This has been achieved in American music despite the fact that the Americanisms really are very difficult to analyze or codify."[31]

Answering questions at a 1938 session of a Composers Forum-Laboratory, the conductor Lazare Saminsky made an attempt at an analysis of the "American" in American music. He said American music had gone beyond jazz, or sounding "Negro and Indian." Its characteristics were clearly the same as those of the whole American people, displaying "a certain snappiness, a certain clear-cut quality of speed and the direct grappling with any problem, with every fact of life, a peculiar sense of humor, a certain dash, vivacity, and verve, a certain snap, something which is carefree . . . and attractive showmanship." It was the Americanism of Mark Twain and Walt Whitman. Even Sessions's music showed "all the qualities, the broadness and starkness, the single-mindedness of the New England mind."[32]

However much it lacked an actual story or program, a symphony could help the citizenry rediscover America's social ideals and feel again what it was that united Americans. These ideals were usually expressed as social principles emphasizing egalitarianism and particularly material prosperity. Yet they could also point in a cultural direction through works capturing the spirit of the nation.

American composers including Schuman ardently believed this. Moreover, Schuman numbered among those composers who believed the symphony could be the voice of democracy to the world, calling attention to our standards of beauty. Highly fanciful as this might seem, it was a point that the composer Elie Siegmeister, for one, used to make over and over again to me about the music of the thirties and forties.

THE SYMPHONY'S PUBLIC ROLE

Thinking about the preferences of the music public, in 1942, the conductor Eugene Goossens concluded that concertgoers wanted diversion first. Whatever cultural enrichment they absorbed was usually "subconscious and incidental." Listeners to symphonic works, he said, could be "deeply moved and likewise entertained by music." They did not want "long, sententious symphonic works filled with morbid self-contemplation" and incapable of giving pleasure. They were happiest when given a tune they could remember.[33]

Several commentators wrote in the late thirties and forties that the ultimate worth of a symphony resided not in its arrangement of notes and rhythms, nor in its overall organization, but rather in the impression it made on listeners. The real test for a symphony was the way it provided for people's wants. The music public expected symphonies to give pleasure, even though they were abstract and more knotty than other kinds of orchestral composition. Some people who valued symphonies hoped the music might give expression to their otherwise inexpressible human feelings, reflect their very human concerns, and confirm their American identity. Listening would not make them better people but it could influence the way they perceived the world around them. To a few in the audience, such listening was a necessity for civilized existence.

It is true that orchestras playing symphonies and people attending concerts were found mainly in the larger American cities. Also true is that no symphony could fully accomplish all that the advocates for classical music had promised the public it could provide. On the other hand, a ripple effect did seem to be taking place. A greater familiarity with and respect for classical music was growing not only in the cities but also in less populated areas via radio, recordings, and touring orchestras. Admittedly, the growth outside the cities was sluggish. Yet it was taking place. John Mueller acknowledged this in 1950. In addition, he asserted, with a bit of overstatement, that symphonic music and its orchestras were "more peculiarly typical of America than is any other phase of serious music; and similarly, there is no country in the world in which the symphony orchestra carries more prestige than in the United States."[34]

It should be recalled that the democratization of music, encouraged by the Federal Music Project and attempted by composers, simply meant making all varieties of classical music available to a large portion of the populace and bringing artists and the public together. Seldom did the government or managers of the Project presume to tell composers what to write. The modification of music styles to make compositions accessible to the public (and possibly win it over) was up to the composer. Yet the idea was already in the air by the mid-thirties. Affordable music education, reasonably priced concerts, comprehensible compositions—these were evidences of the democratization of culture coming to the fore in the thirties.

Classical music does not normally appeal to as many people as does a commercially produced musical product. The symphony, in particular, is somewhat of an acquired taste. It can be boring on first experience and may be likable only after being experienced repeatedly. Its aficionados will always comprise a minority of the total population. Fortunately for the symphony, its musical language in the thirties and forties was not so complicated as to be hard to understand. Often it had links to folk and popular music. Novices to the genre were allowed the possibility of making the transition from popular to classical music. Speaking chiefly about the inexpert radio audience for classical music, Alfred Frankenstein wrote in 1943 that the less one said about the piece being "modern," the better the audience's receptivity. No ruffled feelings occurred at the sound of contemporary music that introduced some dissonance. Indeed, one-third of the total number of requests were for recently written music. Frankenstein concluded, "I do know that the broad public does take a lot of modern music in its stride when it hears it on the radio."[35]

As for the traditional-modern debate, the general music public did not see its role to include making judgments, except for deciding on future attendance at concerts. Giving authoritative opinions about new music was left to music critics and other musically educated individuals. On balance, listeners of mid-century willingly sampled any variety of new works. The music that engaged their attention was whatever seemed to speak directly to them, whether time-honored or contemporary.

From what has been said, it should be clear that the average listener, whether at a concert or at home via the radio or phonograph, heard music neither for the sake of education nor because he or she wished to partici- pate in the sounds and rhythms of their time. Listening to a symphony was without question for enjoyment of a sort unavailable through any other medium. In the second half of the thirties the federal government proved that a far greater number of people could get pleasure from classi- cal music than previously had been considered likely, and that enjoyment might occur without thorough understanding of the mechanics of music or its development. A listener could find attraction in an appealing tune, a catchy rhythm, a colorful sonority, or the way contrasts and returns of familiar material were handled. If a portion of the music stuck in one's memory and was recalled easily, so much the better.

Interesting in this regard is a letter that Virgil Thomson sent to Aaron Copland on 20 March 1939. Copland had sent Thomson his just-published book *What to Listen for in Music*. In it, Copland stressed the need for a music-lover to become an intelligent listener—that is to say, one who critically studied a music composition and understood the essential ele- ments of melody, harmony, rhythm, and form. The no-nonsense Thomson wrote that he found the book a bore and did not believe that analytic lis- tening of the sort Copland advocated was "advantageous for the musical layman." It still remained to be proved, he said, "that analytic listening is possible even. God knows professional musicians find it difficult enough. I suspect that persons of weak auditive memory do just as well to let them- selves follow the emotional line of a piece, which they can do easily, and which they certainly can't do very well while trying to analyze a piece tonally."[36]

The widespread mindset of Americans during the economic and po- litical troubles of the thirties and forties did not incline listeners to wel- come symphonies that offered no hope in their "emotional line" and that closed on a glum note. Men and women had their fill of despair and disil- lusionment in everyday living. They wanted sounds that were upbeat and confident for the future. Sharing this state of mind, composers consciously or unconsciously wrote symphonies that sounded confident, decisive, and emotionally strong. They avoided whatever might be interpreted as insipid and empty of inspiring qualities. Even when ostensibly "tragic," their symphonies attempted to convey strength, high-mindedness, and the courage to endure. Symphonies were intended to come across as special and uncontaminated with the commercialism associated with popular amusements. They were meant to be bulwarks against barbarism, and honest in the expression of personal emotion.

The idea that a symphony was merely organized sound cast in traditional molds and incapable of expressing emotion had been advanced from time to time by music critics and composers. Eduard Hanslick had promoted it in the nineteenth century, Igor Stravinsky in the 1920s. The notion was unacceptable, indeed inconceivable, to the music public of the years under examination. Symphony-goers did not theorize about the listening experience. They chose to hear emotion, and so they did! They chose to benefit from what melodies they could in a symphony, and why not? Those melodies that were the most vocal and the easiest to remember, they might call beautiful. Fluent and sonorous harmonic movement and catchy rhythms were welcome. Most listeners pushed no further than this.

However, some in the audience sought to experience more than a jag of emotion and the pleasure of a good tune as they listened. To borrow the words of Ellen Dissanayake, the most sensitive listeners defined the symphony as art with a "capital A," a vehicle for conveying genuine and deep feeling, if not "sacredness and spirituality in a profane world." The problem was to join the symphonic experience to the art of living—that is to say, to allow art to become "a way of imposing coherence (shape, integration) on selves and experiences that have fragmented."[37] The crossover was difficult and rarely realized. Indeed, many writers thought it was an impossibility. Yet it remained part of the symphonic ambiance. The artist was supposed to keep this crossover in mind as he composed. In an important way, the trying was all. If he did not quite succeed, at least he had tried.

In the chapters that follow, each composer is taken up in an order determined by the date of his principal symphonic contribution during the years under consideration. The reader should keep in mind the vast differences in age of these musicians. Carpenter (b. 1876), Moore (b. 1893), Piston (b. 1894), Hanson (b. 1896), and Sessions (b. 1896) were writing as mature artists; Barber (b. 1910), Schuman (b. 1910), Diamond (b. 1915), Bernstein (b. 1918), and Mennin (b. 1923) wrote at a younger age—a couple of them were still students. The rest were somewhere in between: Harris (b. 1898), Thompson (b. 1899), Antheil (b. 1900), Copland (b. 1900), Blitzstein (b. 1905), and Creston (b. 1906). Age cannot be taken as an indicator of an older or a more advanced style. Moore, one of the oldest composers, did compose in a conservative nineteenth-century manner. Yet Sessions, who was close to Moore in age, wrote in the most forward-thinking twentieth-century manner of all the composers. Other artists, including Antheil and Copland, started off as avant-gardists but changed over to more accommodating techniques by the mid-thirties.

2

SYMPHONIES OF THE
MID- TO LATE THIRTIES

The year 1935 found the United States in the midst of social and economic crisis. The nation was threatening to come apart. Swift action was needed. Newly elected president Franklin Delano Roosevelt and his federal administration immediately launched a wholesale attack on the country's problems, seeing them as involving not just jobs but also lifestyles. He begged citizens to see themselves as belonging to one extended community, united in seeking the common good. He stressed making a united effort. The twenties belief that only the interests of the individual himself (whether business person, worker, or artist) ought to be paramount in decisions about his activities should and had to be put aside.

Together, Roosevelt said, Americans could overcome the problems besetting the nation. In a radio address made to Young Democratic Clubs of America on 24 August 1935, the president spoke about the "higher obligation" to analyze and set forth the "national needs and ideals which transcend and cut across all lines." The recent depression, he continued, had taught Americans that no "social class in the community is so richly endowed and so independent of the general community" that it can go it alone: "It is my firm belief that the newer generation of America has a different dream. . . . Your advancement, you hope, is along a broad highway on which thousands of your fellow men and women are advancing with you. . . . The errors of unrestrained individualism" have been serious. If "each and every one of us were marching along a separate road . . . , if we insist on choosing different roads most of us will not reach our common destination."[1]

Fourteen months later, on 28 October 1936, Roosevelt traveled to Bedloe's Island, New York, to deliver an address on the occasion of the fiftieth anniversary of the Statue of Liberty. He insisted that Americans had "but a single language, the universal language of aspiration." The aspiration of America continued to be upward, toward a better life—economically, socially, and culturally. "Even in times as troubled and uncertain as these I still hold to the faith that a better civilization than any we have known is in store for America."[2] Two and a half years later, he would speak specifically about the arts: "Art in America has always belonged to the people and it has never been the property of an academy or a class. . . . While American artists have discovered a new obligation to the society in which they live, they have no compulsion to be limited in method or manner of expression."[3]

The thinking of many classical composers was now coinciding with that of their president. The lack of financial support, as jobs and monetary grants disappeared and the core of supporters shrank, forced recalcitrants to realize that artists are not so exceptional that they can "go it alone." The principle that the interests of the artist alone are to be paramount in determination of what constitutes art was abandoned. The philosophy of modernism, especially that encompassing a conscious and deliberate break with the past and a hunt for novel forms of expression, was put aside.

This large number of American composers became caught up in the notion of service and the optimistic spirit pervading the new administration. Those who had been modernists proceeded to reexamine the premises behind the music revolution of the twenties in which they had participated. A rapport began to develop between the arts and the national spirit and aspirations that Roosevelt was trying to foster. These musicians did not see their actions as surrender to the doctrine of mediocrity and abandonment of high artistic principles. Roosevelt's New Deal dream was admittedly a tactic to raise the morale of Americans and encourage them to pull together. Yet it was, at least in part, also a vision meant to stand as a beacon for all in its expectation of a better future. The artist's commitment was toward realizing this vision.

On the other hand, a minority of artists would take slight notice of the Roosevelt administration's desire for accessibility and would maintain the severity of their styles. They continued during the thirties to write in challenging modes that tested the ordinary listener's understanding. Most of them were older musicians, including Carl Ruggles (b. 1876), Wallingford Riegger (b. 1885), John Becker (b. 1886), Adolph Weiss (b. 1891), and Roger Sessions (b. 1896).

Still others, not obviously responding to Roosevelt's admonishments, would demonstrate continuity with the traditional tonal styles of the nineteenth century and offer compositions that were lyrical, harmonically rich, and often rhythmically complex. This they did out of personal preference mostly. Howard Hanson (b. 1896) and Samuel Barber (b. 1910), for example, had not subscribed to the revolutionary practices of the twenties and early thirties. Their works were already well matched to the music public's understanding. Audiences responded positively to them. The two musicians felt no imperative to ally themselves with the folk and popular idioms of the nation. The music they wrote arose from within them. It had a respect for and drew nourishment from tradition. Harmony and melody that the general public relished streamed through their measures. In their own way these two artists successfully reached out to Americans by filling responsive ears and inner selves with musical offerings that gave pleasure. The music public welcomed the works they created, and to this day finds reason to cherish them. If only because of this, these composers deserve credit for making durable contributions to the cultural life of the United States and to mankind.

These two composers are taken up first because their compositions could not help but serve as guides to other composers as to what sort of music would reach the general music public. They had not fallen into the "error of unrestrained individualism" nor marched "along a separate road." While not necessarily subscribers to Roosevelt's ideas and political stance, they did demonstrate the communicative warmth that could be generated through fresh aspects of a traditional approach. The road to popular esteem was made manifest. Other composers could not help but take notice.

Barber is the earliest considered because his First Symphony (1936) stands at the beginning of the long line of important symphonies generated during the Roosevelt years. Hanson, although Barber's senior by a decade and a half, comes next because his Third Symphony (1937) stands second in date of composition.

THE ROMANTIC SYMPHONY: BARBER

Samuel Barber was one of the most talented musical artists ever born in America. He occupies a position of preeminence among twentieth-century composers. From his earliest years, he knew that he would become a composer. He had declared his future profession in a message written to his mother when he was nine years of age: "I was meant to be a composer and will be I'm sure. . . . Don't ask me to try to forget this unpleasant thing and go play football—please." To ordinary American boys playing football would have been the preferred activity. Samuel Barber was not ordinary.

He had the good fortune to be born in West Chester, Pennsylvania, in 1910, to affluent parents who loved music and were sympathetic to his musical inclinations. He was additionally fortunate to have the noted contralto Louise Homer and song-composer Sidney Homer as aunt and uncle. They served as mentors and critics and smoothed the way for him so that he could pursue his musical calling. These circumstances and the support of influential family members and friends helped him along in his musical career. However, these would have come to nothing if the young Barber had not also possessed an immense talent and a drive to achieve the best in him.

He enrolled at the recently established Curtis Institute of Music, in Philadelphia, at age 14. While a student at Curtis he met future opera composer Gian Carlo Menotti, with whom he would establish a close and lasting personal relationship. At the Curtis Institute, Barber studied piano with George Boyle and Isabelle Vengerova, voice with Emilio de Gorgorza, and musical composition with the eminent Italian teacher Rosario

Scalero. Scalero disfavored revolutionary styles and insisted on a thorough knowledge of tonal techniques, including counterpoint. He taught Barber to take care in handling textures, especially those resulting from intertwining individual melodic lines. Undoubtedly, he also initiated an abiding love for sensuous Italianate lyricism in his young student. Add to this the young Barber's taking seriously the cultivation of his voice (witness his recorded baritone voice singing the early *Dover Beach* on a commercial disc), and we can understand why so often his melodic lines are so hummable and comfortable to the ear.

Barber's family and teachers approved of the creative flair in the boy and joined forces to foster it. The outside world was soon also taking notice. He was no more than twenty-three years of age when Alexander Smallens and the Philadelphia Orchestra gave the performance of his earliest composition for symphony orchestra, the Overture to *The School for Scandal*. This engaging composition, which is still in the repertoire of many American orchestras, demonstrated the musical precociousness of the youth.

When his father lost a great deal of his money in the stock market crash of 1929, Barber had to consider fending for himself. He learned, also, that the Curtis Institute's endowment had sunk to nothing, forcing the school to retrench. The school's composition department was closed temporarily. The young musician tried teaching but found he had no affinity for it. Fortunately, first a Pulitzer Traveling Fellowship and, next, the Prix de Rome allowed him time abroad to compose music. The money saw him through the writing of his First Symphony. While he was working on the composition, his parents sent him a letter asking if he was happy where he was, doing what he was doing. He replied, "Yes and no. In fact no different from any place else. My great satisfaction and consolation is that I am not a bother to anyone for two years, and this means *a great deal:* and that I am able to do the work which interests me to my heart's content (or discontent)."[4]

A few years later, he would achieve phenomenal success when Toscanini premiered his *Adagio for Strings* and *First Essay* for orchestra, in 1938. It was from then on that American audiences would take so much to his music that he could live comfortably off his royalties, commissions, awards, and performance fees. Teaching was mostly a thing of the past.

He was able to compose what he wished, as he wished, with no worries about scrounging for money to support himself. Fortunately his personal predilections and those of the music public coincided.

Barber worked circumspectly and fastidiously. He hewed to a traditional late-Romantic style, but avoided the extravagant gestures of that style. As the composer grew older, he gingerly tried out a few bolder approaches—nonfunctional dissonance, nontriadic harmonies, bitonality, muscular lines, and aggressive rhythms. They and the composer would usually make an uncomfortable fit. He was happiest when his music could sing freely and tonally. About his style, Walter Simmons wrote with sympathy and insight:

> Though Barber's musical language is thoroughly rooted in that of the late nineteenth-century European masters, his works display fewer overt reminiscences of his predecessors than do the other [traditional American] composers. . . . In his early works, he succeeded in forging an identity of his own without rupturing the Late Romantic lingua franca with which he was comfortable. His own sensibility was so cosmopolitan that he was able to distill the generalized attitudes and principles of his romantic predecessors without allowing individual accents to upset the subtle balance upon which his language was based. . . . Barber's impetuousness is far from Brahms's stern, German formalism. Although his gentle modality, urbanity, and surface immediacy have often been described as French, his emotionalism and textural clarity distinguish his music immediately. Barber's spontaneous lyricism has often been characterized as Italianate, but it is far more refined and elegant than typical Italian melody. The elegiac character of his music, constrained by a dignified reserve suggests . . . Elgar, but the Englishman's imperial grandeur was foreign to Barber's more modest nature.[5]

Toward the end of the twenties Barber traveled to Europe, financed by his parents and also through money awarded him for winning Columbia University's Bearns Prize. In Munich he heard Richard Wagner's *Parsifal,* which he disliked. He said, "I choked in a maddening mêlée of sickly chromaticism hiding under an ironical masque of religion."[6] Although he repudiated Wagnerisms, he did not turn to homey American scenes in order to fill out his pages; nor would he try to delineate, as Howard Hanson consciously tried to do, aspects of American spiritual life. No American folk or popular tunes invest his melodies; no jazz rhythms propel his measures; no radical "isms" infuse his procedures.

His is the realm of intuitive personal feeling. His compositions reveal, on the one hand, a persona gentle and responsive musically to inner feelings; on the other hand, someone with dramatic inclinations who is disposed to appeal to the senses. They show constructive skill of a high order. Nowhere do we find breaches of taste. Not least, they are works provided with means for wide appeal—warm, likable tunes bathed in sumptuous harmonies.

Barber employed an array of musical practices ranging from those of the Renaissance to the contemporary. He combined these elements to form an integrated whole. The result was an individual compositional style. He explained, "[When] I'm writing for words, then I immerse myself in those words, and I let the music flow out of them. When I write an abstract piano sonata or a concerto, I write what I feel. I'm not a self-conscious composer . . . It is said I have no style at all, but that doesn't matter. I just go on doing, as they say, my thing. I believe this takes a certain courage."[7]

Because he refused to compose in an original, forward-looking style, Barber baffled major critics and advanced composers. Their mantra was, try to sound unlike anyone else, even if to the point of idiosyncrasy; his was not. His music gave them no handle for understanding what made the composer tick—how to explain the music's appeal and Barber's motivations. Commentators heard him try out a variety of approaches, testing and discarding at will. On balance, he remained faithful to the methods of late-nineteenth-century Romanticism. Throughout his life he was reluctant to give details about himself or his compositional methods. Accusations arose that he was reactionary and a fuddy-duddy. He took these comments personally.

A loner, Barber brought no compositional school into being. Because he did little teaching, scarcely any future composers would have the benefits of his instruction and person-to-person example. In public, he seemed unruffled by the disputes between his more *au courant* colleagues. He would not engage in their disputes over whether music should be tonal or atonal, follow Stravinsky or Schoenberg, or profoundly change tradition or reject it completely. Most of his prominent contemporaries, including Roy Harris, Walter Piston, Aaron Copland, David Diamond, and Roger Sessions, had belonged at some point to one ideological group or another. Barber was happy to stand on the sidelines and just write music as he saw fit. Since most of his pieces realized widespread success, musicians with advanced tastes could not ignore him. It follows that Barber continued to be subject to controversy and his music something for the cognoscenti to damn or praise throughout his life. His nadir in reputation would come in the first three decades after the end of World War II, when the doctrines of atonalism and indeterminism battled to gain ascendancy in the contemporary music world. He would be restored to good repute in the late eighties.

What generated the most discussion was his insistence on tried-and-true lyricism, especially of a vocal kind, when such lyricism was coming to be out of fashion. Yet his talent did lie in writing superb and memorable tunes. Before the Roosevelt initiatives began, the still-unreconstructed modernists said that *Dover Beach, op. 3* (1931), Overture to *The School for Scandal,* op. 5 (1931), and *Music for a Scene from Shelley,* op. 7 (1933) made Barber out to be a backward-looker, a young fogy who catered to the Babbitts of America. He was conforming too readily to trite bourgeois standards, they claimed. The melancholic and moving *Dover Beach,* however affective the music and assured the writing, failed to win them over. The cheery overture fell on hostile ears. Though audiences found it enchanting, critics declared the Shelley music to be exceedingly trivial.

To the unbiased listener, the three works reveal how exceptionally early his development was, how quickly he attained artistic maturity, and how securely he realized his artistic goals, though still in his early twenties. One can scarcely believe that at twenty-one years of age, Barber could so completely realize Matthew Arnold's "Dover Beach" [1867] in his setting for baritone (or mezzo-soprano) and string quartet. This musical gem captures the poem's ominous threnody for a human race of little faith. A world-weary voice and subdued strings invoke an "eternal note of sadness." A weighted-down musical ending catches the desolation in

Ah, love, let us be true
To one another! for the world, which seems
To lie before us like a land of dreams,
So various, so beautiful, so new,
Hath really neither joy, nor love, nor light,

Nor certitude, nor peace, nor help for pain;
And we are here as on a darkling plain
Swept with confused alarms of struggle and flight,
Where ignorant armies clash by night.

This was the first truly significant work to come from Barber's pen. I dwell upon it because it illustrates from the beginning his outstanding traits—lyricism, sensitivity to mood, a keen exploration of feeling, and the talent to clothe measure after measure with meaning.

One can find touches of twentieth-century dissonance, bitonality, and orchestration in his works, especially the later ones. The impartial listener would note that even these early three compositions could not have been produced by anyone from the nineteenth century. Barber's is a twentieth-century mind. His sounds are fresh, not hackneyed. His harmonic structures are more adventurous than those of the nineteenth century. His voice leading is free and his formal structures are distinctive, though lengthy movements may show some weaknesses at times. Atmosphere and the projection of genuine feeling are his strong points. A convincing knitting-together of extended structures is sometimes his weakest. Nevertheless, the vibrancy and fertility of his musical ideas, linked to the impression of sincere emotionality, indicate that the course he followed was a winner.

Barber, who had turned twenty-six years old on 9 March 1936, completed his Symphony No. 1 in E minor, Opus 9, in the same year, during a stay at the American Academy in Rome as winner of the American Prix de Rome. He attended its premiere, given by Bernardino Molinari conducting the Augusteo Orchestra, in Rome on 13 December 1936. Arthur Rodzinski and the Cleveland Orchestra gave its American premiere on 22 January 1937. Five years later the composer would revise the symphony, especially its 6/8-time, *Allegro molto* second section.

He had come to love Italy and had visited it previously with his close companion Gian Carlo Menotti. If he was deeply conflicted by Mussolini and the Fascists, he did not say. Apparently, he would not allow the political scene to intrude directly on his creativity. Barber's biographer, Nathan Broder, explains:

> Shut off though he had been, by upbringing and inclination and fate, from the political and economic forces that swept the nations along into war, the cataclysm that engulfed the world could not fail to affect the life of Samuel Barber. Outwardly his life changed little in the next three years; he remained immersed in his private world of music, books, and art, and worked hard. . . . Inwardly, however, there was a deepening of character, a greater sense of responsibility to others—a new maturity nourished not only by the events of the outer world but by the onset of his father's lingering, grave, and eventually fatal illness. This growth . . . is clearly reflected in his music.[8]

The First Symphony would be an utterly personal expression. It asserted its humanity in the teeth of the political tensions burgeoning at the time—Hitler's start of German rearmament, Roosevelt's struggle to establish the New Deal, the persecution of German Jews, and Mussolini's invasion of Ethiopia. As he worked on the symphony in 1936, Hitler invaded the Rhineland and then the Spanish Civil War began. Nazi Germany, Fascist Italy, and militaristic Japan became allied as the Axis Powers. The threat to the rest of the world became palpable.

Barber lived through all of this, laboring over his music. Like all artists, he lived through and interpreted the world's events in his own way. Surely, at least unconsciously, Barber's symphony was in part a response to contemporary conditions. Whatever he had to say about the turmoil around him, he said through his music. At any rate audiences immediately took to the piece. They loved its sounds and its meditations on the nature of nostalgia, melancholy, and private anguish.

In Barber's composition, the traditional four-movement symphony is restructured into a well-integrated one-movement work in four sections. The composition lasts almost twenty minutes. (Roy Harris would compose a similarly structured symphony two years later.) The symphony is concise and dramatic. No note is wasted. Barber neither attached a descriptive title to the score, nor gave any other hint of a program. The drama remains nonspecific. The listener is taken fairly rapidly from event to event, to situations having intense, exciting, conflicting, and arresting effects.

The sections, corresponding to the movements of a symphony, are cast as a fast first, scherzo second, slow third, and passacaglia-based fourth.[9] Although the style looks back to the end of the nineteenth century, suggestions abound of Barber's own time period. The orchestra is large—woodwinds by threes, ten brasses, harp, timpani plus other percussion instruments, and strings. The orchestration is brilliantly colored. Harmonies are often nonfunctional, usually triadic and sporting chords of the seventh and ninth. They are obviously set down with an ear to their sonorities. These harmonies, added to kaleidoscopic key changes, give an overall impression of sumptuous richness. Harmonies are further thickened and enriched with dissonances resulting from unresolved escape notes, changing notes, and appoggiatura chords. Strong driving rhythms, especially in the second of the four sections, underline how contemporaneous is much of the composition despite its traditional façade. And surmounting everything else are the engrossing melodic lines that run through all sections. Given all of these, the listener cannot but remain engrossed.

The first section, in a modal E minor, is marked *Allegro ma non troppo*. An adamantly bold opening grips the listener's attention. Ominous brasses, underpinned with a loud timpani roll, intone a dissonant harmony. Massed strings and woodwinds enter to proclaim the three-measure principal theme of the entire work. The theme is repeated in augmentation. The effect is arresting. A powerful but brief discourse on the motif ensues, getting louder and more animated. Suddenly all is hushed. Low strings and harp murmur the same harmony as at the beginning. An English horn commences a second theme, engaging and achingly lyrical. A transitory passage reaches a crescendo, and at the climax, a third theme breaks out as the high woodwinds and strings sing excitedly and apprehensively. The effect is that of a codetta, a rounding-out of what has gone before and a move toward a provisional conclusion. The codetta is superseded by a development of the three themes (the opening in particular) that mounts to a grand climax.

The concise development is stimulating. After it, one anticipates a restatement of the three themes. However, instead of the expected and customary recapitulation, the first theme, in notes of shorter duration than those of the symphony's opening, reappears as the basis of an *Allegro molto* scherzo section, in 6/8 time. The action is sprightly; the mood, humorous. The section provides a welcome contrast to what had come before; the change is refreshing. The light and playful character of the traditional scherzo is frequently modified here by impositions of key instability and melodic jitteriness. Violins push forward restlessly. Their nervous sixteenth-note passages scurry over dissonant punctuations from the woodwinds. A clarinet enters with a new idea that lurches ahead over three measures. The rest of the section expands on these ideas, getting more and more rhythmically propelled. The expression comes across ultimately as comic-serious. A prolonged climax closes the section, followed by a few twitters from clarinets and bassoons and a moment of silence.

One wonders what surprise will come next. Will it be a trio, the usual subordinate middle part of a scherzo? Will it go on, as at the end of the first section, to something quite different? Barber elects to go the latter route. One now hears smoothness replacing jitteriness, quietude replacing restlessness, gentle motion replacing vivaciousness. Again, the listener finds the differences in procedure and expression welcome.

The third section, in short, is an *Andante tranquillo,* played slowly but not excessively so and evoking a deceptively calm atmosphere. It begins with muted strings divided into nine parts. They play softly undulating broken chords. An oboe, allotted a prolonged solo, sings a slow version of the second theme. The double reed's melody is fluent and eloquent but gives off twinges of suffering and regret. Here is a tune that listeners may have found deeply affecting, easy to remember, and worthy of humming on the way home.

A powerful crescendo launches us into the final section. Again, the contrast is enormous. A six-measure passacaglia, a ground bass in a moderately paced triple time, starts up and constantly repeats. It derives from the first theme. The initial presentation is made by the cellos and contrabasses. Over the theme, one hears snatches of all three themes (the first theme is heard in note values different from the ground bass). In effect Barber gives us a recapitulation for the entire opening segment of the symphony. This last section is beholden not only to the Baroque passacaglia but also the last movement of the Brahms Fourth Symphony. The mood is stern; the feeling, intense. The denouement closes with mighty authority.

This symphony unfolds, beginning to end, with the sureness of a remarkable artist. Barber does not linger longer than he should in any section. He says what he has to say as succinctly as possible and succeeds in realizing his expressive objective. The listener is carried away by the attractiveness of sound and authenticity of expression. In sum, the symphony is a worthy addition to any symphonic repertoire.

Some other admirable and well-received works that remain in the performance repertoire are Barber's witty Overture to *The School for Scandal* (1933) for orchestra, his grave *Adagio for Strings* (1936), the terse *First Essay* and *Second Essay* for orchestra (1937, 1942), and the constantly singing Violin Concerto (1939). *Knoxville, Summer of 1915* for high voice and orchestra (1947), a mediation on the past, is especially haunting and moving. Well received were *Medea's Meditation and Dance of Vengeance* (1953) for orchestra, and *Prayers of Kierkegaard* for chorus and orchestra (1954). Regrettably, his two excellent operas, *Vanessa* and *Anthony and Cleopatra*, though having many magical pages, failed to win a place in the standard opera repertoire. On balance, his compositions make a convincing case for declaring Samuel Barber to be one of the finest American composers of the twentieth century. The *Adagio for Strings,* especially, has made its way to the four corners of the world and won the affection of diverse peoples.

Still waiting to be discussed is Barber's Second Symphony, which will be taken up in the section on the symphonies of World War II. Perhaps my decision to do so is arbitrary, especially since I do not grant a like privilege to any other composer. However, I do believe it merits separate discussion because it came into existence during wartime and was influenced by war conditions, a rare instance of a Barber work linked to contemporary events. In addition, the composer's thinking and musical style would present significant departures from those affecting the First Symphony. Third, Barber himself remained ambivalent about the work, even trying to destroy it. And finally, to today, its merits and perceived failings are subject to debate.

THE SPIRITUAL SYMPHONY: HANSON

During 1937–38, the instances of cruelty and tragedy in the world increased as nations careened toward war. The dictator Joseph Stalin was purging thousands of Soviets considered threats to his regime. On 26 April 1937, warplanes of the German *Luftwaffe* destroyed the Spanish town of Guernica and its innocent inhabitants, prompting Pablo Picasso to paint his anguished protest, *Guernica*. In October, the Nazis invaded the Sudetenland and annexed it on 10 October, depriving Czechoslovakia of a huge chunk of its territory. World War II was imminent. An important and redeeming cultural event took place on 21 October—the premier of Dmitri Shostakovich's Fifth Symphony in Leningrad. The work's popularity would spread into Europe and America and have an influence on more than one American symphony.

Howard Hanson was very much aware of what was occurring, but felt that his response was best made through his art. His was the conviction that music could and should address what was best in mankind and provide sustenance to the spirit, particularly during times of darkness, such as his own. To promote fine American music among the people was his mission. To compose the finest music within him was his prayer. To advance the education of the young, he thought, was his personal responsibility.

He was born in 1896 in Wahoo, Nebraska, to Swedish parents. His music education began with his mother. He took lessons at Wahoo's Luther College, later at New York City's Institute of Musical Art (where he studied with Percy Goetschius), and finally at Northwestern University, where he earned his B.A. degree in 1916. His talent for teaching and school administration appeared early; witness his promotion to Dean of the Conservatory of Fine Arts at California's College of the Pacific in 1919. In 1921, Hanson won the Prix de Rome and began a three-year residence at the American Academy in Rome. Ottorino Respighi was briefly his teacher here.

He completed his First Symphony (*Nordic*) in May 1922 and conducted its premier with the Augusteo Orchestra of Rome in the same month. When heard, in March 1924, in Rochester, New York, it won strong audience support and critical praise. It also brought Hanson to the attention of George Eastman, the inventor of the Kodak camera and roll film and the endower of the Eastman School of Music in Rochester. It led to the engagement of Hanson in 1924 as music director and teacher at the school.

Shortly after he joined the faculty of the Eastman School of Music, Hanson became director of both the school orchestra and the Eastman-Rochester Symphony Orchestra. Otto Luening, who would also teach at Eastman, writes that "Hanson was a strong executive and completely devoted to the welfare of the school and the development of American composers. He was also among the first to establish high standards for music in primary and secondary schools."[10]

Soon after his appointment, Hanson started his American Composers Orchestral Concerts and the annual Festivals of American Music. These were meant to encourage the production of American compositions and give them proper and repeated hearings. Hanson stayed at his dual Rochester posts for forty years. He would later estimate that he had conducted the premieres of more than two thousand works by five hundred American composers during his residence at Rochester. Among his students were the future American composers Jack Beeson, William Bergsma, Peter Mennin, Vladimir Ussachevsky, and Dominick Argento.

In 1939, he would become a cofounder of the American Music Center, whose object was "to foster and encourage the composition of contemporary (American) music and to promote its production, publication, distribution and performance in every way possible throughout the Western Hemisphere." Over the years he wrote articles and made numerous appearances throughout the country. He spoke about the reform of music education in public schools and colleges, the importance of fostering American composers and recognizing the value of American music, the cultivation of new media such as radio and television on behalf of American music, and the importance of the arts to mankind in providing answers to life's questions. An example of his commitment to education was the 1960 publication of his instructive *Harmonic Materials of Modern Music: Resources of the Tempered Scale,* which goes beyond traditional practices and gives a compilation of contemporary methodologies in musical composition. In 1961–62, he and Frederick Fernell took the Eastman

School Philharmonia on a four-month tour of Europe, the Middle East, and the Soviet Union under the auspices of the State Department. The compositions played included those of Americans—Piston, Hovhaness, Barber, Schuman, and Hanson himself (his Symphony No. 2, captioned the *Romantic*). From what has just been said, it should be obvious that Hanson labored hard in the public sector, in contrast to Barber, who kept mostly to himself.

Hanson's Second Symphony (*Romantic*) had been given its premiere in Boston in 1930, with Koussevitzky conducting the Boston Symphony Orchestra. Its success was and continues to be extraordinary for an American composition. Seven symphonies altogether came from Hanson's pen before he died in 1981.

Hanson and Barber composed their First symphonies at about the same age. Both are fully imagined compositions worthy of their authors. Both hew to musical styles characteristic of the late nineteenth century, as indicated by their adherence to tonality, triadic harmonic constructions, unobtrusive dissonance, and unrestricted employment of imagination and emotion. The earlier *Nordic* is less internalized than Barber's First Symphony. It does, however, dispense one sumptuous tune after another. By "Nordic," Hanson was making reference to the Scandinavian people (Norway, Sweden, Denmark, Iceland, and Finland). He also admitted to the influence of two "Nordic" composers, Finland's Jean Sibelius and Norway's Edvard Grieg, in this and other works. The symphony's harmony is rich in seventh-, ninth-, and thirteenth-tone additions to the basic triads. Its orchestration is expert. This symphony and *The Lament for Beowulf* for chorus and orchestra (1925) set his feet along the road to public recognition and won critics' respect for his musical gifts.

Curiously, his later *Romantic* Symphony harbors some off-putting traits that were not found in the *Nordic*—more static motion, a greater reliance on repetition and sequence, and a disconcerting disjointedness in the formal structure. Yet this symphony became instantly popular, perhaps owing to its luxuriant chromaticism, sonorous harmonies, congenial melodies, and assured handling of the orchestra.

Hanson opposed the use of unrelieved dissonances and atonal procedures because, he said, they conflicted with the music public's willingness to accept what it heard. He believed that these techniques invited skepticism of, if not opposition to, all new works, and made impossible the communication of any spiritual value. As for the use of Americanisms, he insisted that true Americanism in a creative work was indefinable yet unmistakable when heard. It could not be consciously sought. One could detect it, he said, in the music of Roy Harris, George Gershwin, and Randall Thompson. A composer had to express himself with "a downright honesty," and for this reason was not duty-bound to use folk tunes or American Indian or African American melodies if they were not natural to him. His was a different heritage. Hanson urged a tolerance for different styles, whether traditional or more advanced, harmonious or discordant, lyrical or with angular melody.[11] All this said, he himself believed in and wished to carry forward the values and idioms that had prevailed at the end of the nineteenth century.

The early *Nordic* Symphony, for example, strikes me as spontaneous and polished and a good forecaster of things to come. It delineates freely some of the unique aspects that make his music attractive, especially in its delivery of a constant progression of agreeable and rhythmically well-organized lyric lines. Dull places are avoided, as are stagnant or unconnected sections. Pauses are rare. Surprising for a young composer, he succeeds in staying away from clumsy constructions and affectations (which is not always the case in some later works). From first to last, his symphonies, however freely they roam, will remain affixed to some underlying tonality, which allows the listener to hold fast to the music. Harsh harmonizations, in consequence, prove acceptable to the ear. The simultaneous occurrence of two tonalities set an augmented fourth apart sometimes appears in his measures. It adds piquancy to the sonorities. He vitalizes his proceedings further through the judicious management of irregular rhythms and compound time signatures. The grand arches of sound are immediately noticeable.

Like the Finnish composer Jean Sibelius, he was most comfortable when writing for instruments, and he composed chiefly for symphony orchestra. "Both [men] explore the inner spiritual world of man; both are universal in their appeal," says Nicolas Slonimsky.[12] Hanson and Sibelius have a penchant for the darker resonances of the orchestra. The two composers exploit the low instruments and the lower ranges of those instruments that are higher in register. However, Hanson does not project Sibelius's gloominess. He speaks in a contemplative manner, as if absorbed in thought, and not with Sibelius's sense of seclusion. Every symphony tries to reach for the sublime through an elevated language that Hanson has carved out for himself. Whatever the resemblances to Sibelius, they melt away as Hanson goes from symphony to symphony.

Slonimsky points out that Hanson's distinctiveness may be found in the generous contours of his melodies, the cyclic deployment of his themes, and his majestic symphonic structures.[13] Peculiar to him are the frequent ostinato passages for timpani and the easy, smooth, and uninterrupted flow of modal counterpoint through significant segments of a work. The captions prefacing several of his symphonies are not programmatic in intent. Rather, they are meant to indicate the main expressive content of each composition, what thoughts and feelings are preoccupying him.

The Columbia Broadcasting System commissioned Hanson's Symphony No. 3 in 1936. By writing the music, the composer intended to commemorate the 300th anniversary of the first Swedish settlement on Delaware's coast, in 1638. He explains that the symphony was inspired by "the composer's reverence for the spiritual contribution that has been made to America by that sturdy race of northern pioneers who were in later centuries also to constitute such a mighty force in the conquering of the West."[14] Thus, whatever "American" character is revealed in the score relates to his own American background, not to something acquired. He is comfortable with the Swedish-immigrant reference and reminds his fellow citizens that despite current troubles, all have descended from one or another "sturdy race of . . . pioneers," who have made a revered "spiritual contribution." This is the compelling undercurrent—the plea for pluck and staying power in confronting hard times—which runs through the movements. In this way, this engrossing composition attains the added quality of all-inclusiveness. The orchestra required to perform the symphonic score is large and similar to Barber's—woodwinds by threes, eleven brasses, timpani, and strings. The dedication is to Serge Koussevitzky.

The Columbia Symphony Orchestra performed the first three movements for a radio broadcast on 19 September 1937. The next year, the NBC Symphony Orchestra, with Hanson conducting, played the symphony in its entirety over the air. At the time of the 1937 radio performance,

Hanson was quoted by David Bruno Ussher as saying, "Like my second or 'Romantic' Symphony, the third one, too, stands as an avowal against a certain coldly abstract, would-be non-sentimental music professed by certain composers of high gifts."[15] He added that this symphony was more polyphonic, was harmonically purer, and had fewer superimposed intervals than his previous composition. The Boston Symphony Orchestra gave the first public performance on 3 November 1939.

This composition strikes me as the most outstanding of all Hanson's symphonies. It comes across as ruggedly built and sincerely felt. The composer paints with a broad brush and applies lavish coloration. The musical technique is sophisticated; the expression, thoughtful; the impulse, lyrical. Brief, figural patterns and longer melodies are sufficiently distinctive that they are readily remembered. Through their repetition and skilled elaboration, they enhance listeners' comprehension. The work is thirty-six minutes long.

In a review of its Boston Symphony performance in New York City, with Koussevitzky conducting, Elliott Carter states: "Howard Hanson's *Third Symphony* proved once again how skillful, fine and ambitious a composer he is. It rightly won acclaim for its clear, excellent writing and seriousness of mood. . . . It has many a place where the somber atmosphere reminds one of Sibelius. To me this work compares more than favorably with the best work of the Finnish composer (the *Fourth* and *Seventh Symphonies* and *Tapiola*); it has many more interesting musical events and more meaty material."[16]

The first movement starts in A minor as an *Andante Lamentando* (moderately slow and mournful), in 5/4 time. A one-measure, legato eighth-note figure glides upward again and again, above the throbbing beat of timpani on the tone A. It helps concentrate the listener's attention. The cellos and basses play the figure first. Then it is handed to the violas; next, to the second violins; next, to the first violins. Long-drawn two-note horn calls drop from a high tone to a tone an octave below. It is as if the composer is slowly drawing open the curtains on an ominously dark scene. The working-out of this material is prolonged, giving an impression that the composer is absorbed in thought. A *fortissimo* climax brings matters to a head. Soon the music quietens and introduces the tranquil second theme, in 4/4 time. The ear responds sympathetically to the three horns harmonizing in second-inversion and proceeding in parallel motion, as they croon a chorale-like melody. The passage conveys the expectation of better days to come, of light after darkness. Underneath, the timpani returns to supply a syncopated ostinato beat on the tone E. A lengthy stretch of development of the first theme, together with the downward octave plunge first heard in the horns, follows. The mood turns more somber. Suddenly a brisk, somewhat jaunty idea breaks out in the woodwinds, based on an inversion of the first theme. It introduces a surprising and welcome sense of relief. A grand climax is achieved. Again the music quiets down. The brasses return to sing the chorale theme for a final time. The movement closes with a sense of spaciousness and solitude.

The second movement, *Andante Tranquillo,* starts with repeated octave motion downward and upward in the woodwinds. They introduce and then accompany the main tune, played by a solo horn. The melody is a longer and more expressive variation of the second theme in the first movement. At least unconsciously, the listener senses the connection. The solo instrument intones its song tenderly. In some ways it sounds like a gentle ballad that Jerome Kern might author. The strings take up the tune in halved note values. The atmosphere remains peaceful. Soon, a free fantasy centered on the melody grows in intensity until it reaches a peak in volume. The volume decreases over nine measures. The music settles onto an E minor harmony while above, the clarinets execute a soft downward octave skip. This signifies the end of the movement.

The next movement begins. A solitary timpani commences an ostinato eight-note rhythmic motto, in 3/8 time. The speed is fast, a *Tempo Scherzando.* Expectation is built up. At last, by the 21st measure of drumming, woodwinds and brasses enter to add stretched-out harmonizations. The drumming continues. The listener waits expectantly. Next, a solo oboe flings out a new four-measure staccato phrase that sounds somewhat like it was derived from the third movement of the Dvořák *New World* Symphony. All in all, the effect is that of an energetic, playful scherzo. Hanson manipulates his rhythm-based material for a long stretch. After this display, a slower, smoother middle section interrupts the staccato proceedings and adds some fervor to the goings-on. Finally, the earlier four-measure phrase returns. Near the movement's end, this phrase is intermixed with references to the opening figure of the first movement.

The finale further emphasizes the cyclic nature of the music. It begins *Largamente e pesante*—broadly, with full sound and impressive weight. At the 14th measure, the time signature changes from 4/4 to 5/4. The one-measure legato eight-note figure, the repeated timpani beat, and the octave-dropping calls heard in the first movement reappear. The chorale second theme of the first movement enters next. It soon mixes with the slow-movement version of the melody. A powerful rapturous peroration, sounding like the climactic point of a formal ceremony, brings the symphony to a close. Audiences come away feeling that they have heard a composition of lofty concept and exalted thought.

The listener listens to the final notes aware that they conclude a musical poem of near-epic proportions. The subject has been grave. It has been dealt with in a lucid and unified manner. The composer has attempted to capture the ideals and traditions that he believes characterized his ancestors and the American people. These are important reminders given symphonic expression. They came at a time when Americans were burdened with domestic woes and unrest and with worry over the subversion of these ideals by the increasingly belligerent Nazis and Fascists. About the composition, Walter Simmons writes: "Overall the symphony seems to be a statement about courage and fortitude in the face of adversity, supported by a simple, straightforward reliance on faith, hope, and trust. . . . The symphony's power lies in the unabashed hyperbole of its gestures, the unstinting lavishness of its orchestration, and, most of all, in its youthful fervor and sincere conviction."[17]

Of the four symphonies that Hanson wrote after his Third, none equals the Third in interest, and only one was completed in the time period under consideration—Symphony No. 4 (*The Requiem*) of 1943. It was a winner of the 1944 Pulitzer Prize. Its premier came in Boston on 3 December 1944, with Hanson conducting. The dedication on the score reads, "In memory of my Beloved Father." (Possibly he was also thinking of the war dead.) The orchestration is the same as that of the Third Symphony but with an added xylophone.

The entire composition is a little more than half the length of the Third. Each of the four movements has a heading taken from the Catholic Requiem Mass. Hanson tries throughout to preserve a state of equilibrium between what is lyrical and what is dramatic. The integration of the whole is helped by the appearance of a motif based on two tones that appears in all movements. The build-up of emotion grows logically from movement to movement, although one hears more a repetition than an expansion of ideas. However, the brevity of the entire composition prevents the repetition from getting in the way of enjoyment.

The first movement, entitled "Kyrie," refers to the first section, "Lord have mercy," of the Ordinary to the Catholic Mass. Hanson wants it to be played as an *Andante inquieto*—that is to say, to be performed in a moderately slow tempo and perturbed manner.[18] A French horn begins with an octave leap upward to a held D, while lower strings begin a passage of triplets, executed pizzicato and then bowed. (Note that the octave leap, but downward, was prominent in the Third Symphony as well.) A bassoon line adds a clashing sound and creates unease. Four unison horns then begin the *Kyrie eleison*, the intonation begging God for mercy. Next, the cellos play a slower variation of the theme. The woodwinds follow with what resembles a rustic dance. Eventually, the strings lay out a lyrical line at the same time that trombones chant a chorale. The music gathers strength and increases in dissonance until the climactic point, indicated in the score with the caption *Christe eleison*, "Christ have mercy." The ending is brief. As in the opening, a horn leaps an octave to a loud accented note, echoed by a softer bassoon; then the movement ceases.

The second movement, entitled "Requiescat" (prayer for the repose of the soul of the dead), moves in a very slow *largo* tempo. Hanson means the music to be a broad and dignified entreaty for eternal rest. The octave leap reenters, coming from the horn. Low strings again play pizzicato and then supply a walking bass. At this point, the prayer is heard mainly in the form of a gentle melody, which is given first to a bassoon and then is circulated among the other instruments as it grows more elevated and garners increased breadth.

The "Dies Irae" (day of judgment) third movement is a vehement *presto*. The main idea derives from the principal theme of the first movement. One would expect awe and apprehension. Yet, paradoxically, the music comes across as cutting and bitter. The listener is struck with surprise at the suggestions of questioning and protest that run through the movement.

The finale, "Lux Aeterna" (eternal light), is a personal plea for everlasting peace after death. Labeled *largo pastorale,* it redeploys themes from the previous movements, but on the whole it translates into a hymn, mild but sometimes intense, loving but sometimes inconsolable. The last measures of the movement achieve serenity and offer solace. The sentiments are exactly right.

Writing about this symphony, Hugo Leichtentritt says, "This is not merely a solemn, ecclesiastic work of art. Opposing its religious emotions dealing with the mystery of death are the joys and sorrows, doubts and turmoil of human life. And the composition gains its peculiar individual character by this very mixture, this intertwining of the two fundamental conditions of the world of nature—life and death."[19]

Additional works that Americans can hold in high esteem are Hanson's opera *Merry Mount* (1934) and the Concerto for Organ, Harp, and Strings (1941). I also take pleasure in the *Cherubic Hymn* (1949), *Dies Natalis* (1968), and *A Sea Symphony* (1977). A couple of years before Hanson's death (1981), Otto Luening commented on how the proponents of modernism had been reinstated and had acted to push aside Hanson, Barber, and other conservative composers. Although Luening was at the forefront in the experimentation with electronic music, he stood up for Hanson: "I believe he is at present underrated, for he is a fine musician and was a force in educational circles throughout the United States. He is a composer of talent and real craftsmanship."[20]

THE ALL-AMERICAN SYMPHONY: HARRIS

Our next composer never underrated himself and for a while occupied a high position in the music world. He had plentiful talent but occasionally showed shaky craftsmanship. His ego was huge. Roy Harris regarded his compositions as the musical personification of the people of the United States and himself as an artistic Uncle Sam. To say the least, his was an outsized personality. "Each bird loves to hear itself sing," but Harris more than most. Fortunately for him, his music now and again came close to authenticating his image of himself. He did have a genius for composition. So it was with his Symphony No. 3, whose merits critics and audiences acclaimed. It made him one of the most celebrated composers in America during the forties.

As we progress from the symphonies of Barber to Hanson, to Harris, and beyond, we discover how distinctive each work is. Every composer put an individual stamp on his music. It is not easy to confuse, say, the warm, romantic First Symphony of Barber with the glowing, spiritual Third of Hanson or with the preoccupied, Americanistic Third of Harris, which we will come to shortly.

Harris took pleasure, even took excessive pride, in the fact that he was born in Lincoln County near Chandler, Oklahoma, on 12 February 1898, Abraham Lincoln's birthday, and under straitened conditions. His father was then making a meager living on a hardscrabble farm. Ten years later, his father traveled westward with the family in order to try farming in the San Gabriel Valley, California. California became the locale of Roy Harris's boyhood and youth.

Like Barber and Hanson, he had his mother, a pianist, to thank for introducing him to music and giving him his first lessons. For a while he remained uncertain of his future direction. The young Roy tried farming and then truck-driving. He remained basically untaught in music until twenty-four years of age. However, by this age he had discovered that his real bent was for music. He attended the University of California, Berkeley, for a while and next left for Paris in 1926, after receiving a Guggenheim Fellowship, in order to study with Nadia Boulanger.

Under Boulanger's tutelage, he embarked on a trip of discovery, exploring an extensive span of past musical traditions. The investigation led to an admiration for many former musical practices, particularly an abiding esteem for the symphony as a vehicle for large statements. He would compose thirteen numbered symphonies. An older Harris would claim that he had rejected Boulanger's teaching. Nevertheless, her teaching did make a lasting impact on him. He would honor the composer Arthur Farwell, his teacher in California, who had made use of Amerindian melodies and championed American music independent of European influences. Farwell initiated Harris into the poetry of Walt Whitman and urged his student to develop a style all his own.

Harris came forward as a composer to be noticed in the spring of 1927, with the performance of his Concerto for Piano, Clarinet, and String Quartet. It was then that a debilitating accident cut short his stay in France. He had to return to the United States for surgery and soon after recovery taught summers at New York's Juilliard School of Music.

Responding to a request from Serge Koussevitzky, Harris composed his Symphony No. 1 (*Symphony 1933*), whose Boston premiere under Koussevitzky, in 1934, received an enthusiastic reception. It has not weathered well, despite many fine moments. His style was still coming together, empty rhetoric occasionally intrudes, and the structure remains wobbly. His Symphony No. 2, heard in Boston in 1935, was a failure. Harris himself owned up to its inferiority and renounced the composition. Hearing it today, one finds it uneven in quality. The ideas are feeble. Each movement is chopped up into poorly integrated sections. Its ultimate sin is the boredom that listeners claimed they experienced.

Meanwhile, throughout the thirties, Harris was assimilating a style that would hold him in good stead in the future. He consciously sought to establish a distinctive national mode of expression, one representative of his native land yet individual to him. Paradoxically, he borrowed from plainchant, Renaissance harmony, and Baroque counterpoint, as well as from American traditional music. Into the mix he inserted passages using more than one key at a time, rhythms that quarreled with each other, and hints of jazz. Harmonies built on fourths and fifths or piled-up thirds turned more or less dissonant depending on the emotional context he wished to bring out. A motif seeds a longer phrase; the phrase, a melody; the melody, a longer spinning out over quite a few measures. His biographer, Dan Stehman, observes: "On occasion, as in a large portion of the Third Symphony," Harris makes a "historic concept explicit by starting with a texture built on the unison and the octave and gradually expanding it to organum harmonies, then simple triads, and finally polychords."[21]

He meant his formal structures to evolve from the essential character of the musical materials; his materials, from the overall expressive arch binding beginning to end. In his symphonies he would attempt to take more care in the selection of his materials and in the manner of their expansion, including a cyclical revisiting of previously heard matter. Orchestration would often involve instrumental choirs that talk to each other antiphonally. The sound, as usual, is frequently rough-hewn, sometimes winsome, sometimes brusque, but constantly demonstrating what he thought he stood for. At moments his writing is so competent as to be amazing.

On other occasions, he seems to engage in automatic writing. Now and then, as in the regulation of a finale's coda, he blunders to a close, unsure of how to round off a movement. His ideas are not continually top-quality, more often than not because he was deficient in self-criticism. Moreover, it is usually in the cumulative effect of a movement or symphony that his virtue shines, not in the invention of memorable tunes.

The wellspring of his musical output, according to Harris, was the rural West. He was especially filled with nostalgia for its past and concern over the contemporary dynamics changing it. Additionally, the words of Abraham Lincoln and Walt Whitman resonated in his mind. He composed *Abraham Lincoln Walks at Midnight,* for solo voice and chamber ensemble. His Symphony No. 6 was entitled *Gettysburg;* his Symphony No. 10, for speaker, chorus, brass instruments, pianos, and percussion, was named *Abraham Lincoln.* As for Whitman, there was the *Walt Whitman Suite* for chorus and orchestra ensemble and the *Whitman Triptych* for chorus.

Arthur Berger says that for Harris to achieve a "national character" in his music, it was not enough just to quote a folk tune (although he quoted plenty of them in his *Folksong* Symphony of 1940). Berger states:

> Most of the time Harris did not literally quote folk sources (though there are examples such as . . . *When Johnny Comes Marching Home*). What he did, rather, was skillfully shape melodic lines with the contours of American hymns as well as folk and patriotic songs. These certainly helped to yield an American character, but made curious bedfellows with the European symphonic aspects of the music. The quite impressive long unison line of the cello section at the opening of the Harris Third Symphony is almost a folkish pentatonic, the few B-flats and Cs being the exceptions. In other instances of his music such writing was likely to be embedded in a fabric of orchestral counterpoint (with the inevitable fugue and its Baroque evocation), as well as an ample orchestral sonority and a fairly agreeable harmonic pallet.[22]

Hans Kindler and the National Symphony Orchestra gave Harris the commission for a new work, which turned out to be Symphony No. 3. However, when Harris completed it, either Kindler was unable to schedule it right away, or Harris desired greater public exposure than Kindler and the National Symphony offered, or both. He handed it to Koussevitzky and the Boston Symphony Orchestra, who were the ones to give it a first performance on 24 February 1939. Some revision took place in the days immediately following this presentation. After winning a moderate success in Boston, the symphony rapidly became a hit and received performances throughout the United States, in Mexico, and in England. So much enthusiasm was generated among musicians, music commentators, and the public that many writers of the time claimed that "the great American symphony" had at last been created.

The year that he began the symphony was the disastrous year 1938, full of conflict and tragedy. December would lead directly into the terrible year 1939, when the work received its first performance.[23] That year began with Hitler decreeing the extermination of all Jews. German troops were sent to occupy Czechoslovakia. The Spanish Civil War ended with Franco the victor in March. Mussolini ordered the invasion of Albania in April. The next month the Soviet Union engaged in an undeclared war with Japan that lasted until September. In September, Germany invaded Poland, and Great Britain and France declared war on Germany. World War II had begun. Russia took its own bite out of Poland before the Polish surrender to the Germans, and then began its own war with Finland. The United State declared its neutrality but allowed "cash and carry" aid to the Allies—a move portentous for the future.

Harris has admitted that the world events just described were on his mind when he composed the music and subtitled the five sections of his one-movement work "Tragic," "Lyric," "Pastoral," "Fugue—Dramatic," and "Dramatic—Tragic."[24] At the least, it is an undoubtedly American-flavored symphony that closely captures an edgy, assertive populace, apprehensive about what the future might bring. At the same time, it represents the uneasiness affecting all people of goodwill in 1938–39. Its picture of life is at once pathetic and confident of man's capacity to endure.

The orchestra is the usual large symphony ensemble—woodwinds mostly by threes, twelve brasses, a large percussion section, and strings. Each instrumental choir is given a distinctively differentiating treatment.

Harris's own outline is:

Section I: Tragic—low string sonorities.
Section II: Lyric—strings, horn, woodwinds.
Section III: Pastoral—woodwinds, with a polytonal string background.
Section IV: Fugue—dramatic.
    A. Brass and percussion predominating.

B. Canonic development of materials from
Section II constituting a background for
further development of the fugue.
C. Brass climax, rhythmic motif derived from the fugue subject.
Section V: Dramatic—tragic.
A. Restatement of the violin theme of Section I; *tutti* strings
in canon, with woodwinds against brass and percussion
developing rhythmic ideas from the climax of Section IV.
B. Coda—development of materials from Section I
and II over pedal timpani.[25]

The intelligibility of the structure is welcome. The symphony is best understood as a succession of expressive situations. The music opens on low mysterious sounds portending calamity. These initial measures could only have come from someone comfortable in manipulating a large ensemble. They reveal that Harris's creative ability has grown to be both spontaneous and irresistible, at least here. The listener senses that the composer has important things to say and now has the means for saying them. Long phrases flow one into the other. The dark coloring of the bottommost strings, bass clarinet, and bassoon predominates. The feeling is that of old American hymns. Soon the music grows into a full chorale for the entire orchestra. Intervals of the fourth and fifth generate spacious resonances (so typical of a majority of symphonies from this era). Later, triadic formations (built on the interval of a third) appear. Eventually, the piece progresses out of darkness to become brighter, as it proceeds through its lyrical and pastoral sections.

The lyric portion of the symphony moves faster and in a continuous stream, and occasionally with great force. Eventually, the mood turns lighter. A solo flute moves downward to signal the start-up of a fresh theme heard in strings, horns, and woodwinds. For a short while the composer allows the orchestra to sing. We are brought to the pastoral section, which, Stehman writes, is Harris's first fully realized example of the sound and texture he will use henceforth to simulate an open-air atmosphere.[26] Solo woodwinds bandy melodic phrases about in continual profusion, while undulating string arpeggios provide an attractive backdrop. Polytriadic harmonies (two or more triads erected on different fundamental tones that sound simultaneously) add richness to the resonance. Here and elsewhere, the cumulative effect, not any individual melody, is the most significant factor of the listener's experience.

This section, in turn, leads to the passion and forward thrust of the striking fugue. Its initial sounding is impossible to forget. This fugue's subject is terse, strong, and impressive and is presented by the brasses. Its curtness and the heavy percussion blows that go with it compensate for the more sinuous themes of the previous sections. Next, the music re-asserts its tragic nature by means of an eloquent dirge in violins and brass. Finally, the fugue subject returns to urge the music on to a brief Coda. One reservation about the work is that the last measures move along too hastily, and the abrupt ending is not entirely convincing. Even so, the Third Symphony is a work of stunning originality. What is more, it communicates without problems for the music public.

Stehman insists that the last section was daring for its time, because "it and the Romantic intensity of expression of the symphony as a whole ... seemed to go against the aesthetic grain of a period in which acidic satire and brittle smartness were cultivated with some success as part of a reaction against this same late 19th century expressiveness. The great melody [in the last section], more clearly diatonic than usual for Harris, is a perfect example of the descending spiral which generally forms the final segment of his mature arch designs."[27]

One does conclude that this sturdy, sometimes rough composition evokes the rustic American landscape without any direct allusions to folk material or any patronizing of country people. It helps that the melodies and rhythms are outgrowths of American psalmody and traditional songs that are filtered through the composer's sensibilities. Consequently, the symphony exhibits a national quality that resists definition. Whatever nobility it displays is that of plain, hard-working men and women of the American plains and mountains.

Harris was constantly moving his residence. Around the time he wrote the Third Symphony, he had sojourned in New Jersey and then come to New York City. In 1940 he joined the faculty at Cornell University in Ithaca, New York. Further, in 1940 he would finish his Fourth Symphony, the *Folksong Symphony* for chorus and orchestra. Its premiere took place on 25 April 1940 at the Annual Festival of American Music, sponsored by the Eastman School of Music. Howard Hanson conducted the

Eastman-Rochester Symphony Orchestra. The symphony was a success but less so than the Third. He would revise the work, producing a final version in 1942. Interestingly, it was broadcast to the American soldiers in North Africa.

During the first half of the twentieth century, collectors had made extensive compilations of folk and traditional song from every part of the country. During the two or three years when Harris's Third and Fourth Symphonies were being written, several important collections had come out: John Jacob Niles's *Ballads, Carols, and Tragic Legends from the Southern Appalachian Mountains,* Helen Harness Flanders' *Country Songs of Vermont,* Josiah Henry Combs's *Folk-Songs from the Kentucky Highlands,* and John Harrington Cox's *Folk Songs Mainly from West Virginia and Traditional Ballads Mainly from West Virginia,* to name a few. The invitation to examine and use folk song was in the air. Surely, Harris knew his teacher Arthur Farwell's 1905 publication, *Folk-Songs of the West and South: Negro, Cowboy and Spanish-Californian.* And he would definitely borrow tunes from John and Alan Lomax's *Cowboy Songs and Other Frontier Ballads* and from Carl Sandburg's *American Songbag* for use in the *Folksong Symphony.*

The symphony succeeded in defining him most definitely as an *American* composer taking pride in his nationality in the face of international conflict and taking strength from his country's musical traditions. Its pages gave concrete form to his love for traditional song. The tonal treatment admits a great deal more consonance and triadic construction than heretofore had been the case with him. Each movement obtains an uncomplicated form dictated by the needs of the featured song. A calculated naivety is the result. It is music originally from the lips of ordinary people, reinterpreted for ordinary people.

In the symphony's final version, movement I employs the tunes "The Girl I Left Behind Me" and "Good Night Ladies." Movement II, subtitled "The Western Cowboy," has "Bury Me Not on the Lone Prairie," "Streets of Laredo," and "The Old Chisholm Trail." Movement III, "Interlude—Dance Tunes for Strings and Percussion," dwells mainly on "The Irish Washerwoman." Movement IV, "Mountaineer Love Song," features "He's Gone Away." Movement V, "Interlude—Dance Tunes for Full Orchestra," gives out "The Blackbird and the Crow" and "Jump Up, My

Ladies." Movement VI is a "Negro Fantasy" on "De Trumpet Sounds It in My Soul" and "Li'l Boy Named David." Movement VII concentrates on Pat Gilmore's "When Johnny Comes Marching Home." The focus of the entire composition is movement IV, where Harris composes variations filled with deep sentiment on "He's Gone Away." The composer wrote the symphony, in part, to encourage cultural cooperation between the high-school, college, and community choruses of the American cities and their symphony orchestras. Not a symphony in the ordinary sense, it should be enjoyed for what it is—a delightful setting of time-honored and much-loved music given pleasing treatment.

According to Herbert Elwell, the writing of the symphony required "a subjective approach, an identification of self with the material, such as few composers have ever mastered. It almost involves nourishing the exalted conviction, *le peuple, c'est moi.* Yet I find nothing presumptuous about such an attitude in Harris, because his expression of it shows too deep a reverence for emotional realities to bear only symptoms of mega-lomania."[28]

Harris's Fifth Symphony was completed in 1942 (and revised in 1946). Koussevitzky and the Boston Symphony Orchestra commissioned the composition and played it on 26 February 1942. By this date, the United States had already been embroiled in World War II for a little over two months. In his dedication, printed in the concert program, Harris cites Vice President Henry Wallace on the wartime sacrifices of the Russian people and the expectation that they and the American people would build a new "democracy" in the world. The composer then states, "As an American citizen I am proud to dedicate my Fifth Symphony to the heroic and freedom-loving people of our great Ally, the Union of Soviet Social-ist Republics, as a tribute to their strength in war, their staunch idealism for World peace, their ability to cope with stark materialistic problems of world order without losing a passionate belief in the fundamental impor-tance of the arts."[29]

The composer's statement about the Soviet Union romanticizes the nation excessively, but America's entry into the war was a time of excited feelings. Harris presents himself as almost a superpatriot. In 1940, he pro-voked the comment from Virgil Thomson, "No composer in the world, not even in Italy or Germany, makes such shameless use of patriotic feelings to advertise his product. One would think, to read his prefaces, that he had been awarded by God or at least by popular vote, a monopolistic privilege of expressing our nation's deepest ideals and highest aspirations."[30] I would temper Thomson's criticism with the observation that the Harris sort of temperament was a means for his carrying on and persevering as a classical composer in America.

Fortunately, fine music abounds in the symphony. The music is more dissonant than that in the previous symphony; the expression is more succinct. The first movement, at first subtitled "Martial" and later "Prelude," is in two subdivisions and includes a theme that lends itself to free variations. It is brief and lacks development. But then, few of the ideas are particularly distinguished or warrant development. The music begins jerkily, takes on force, and makes an excellent close. Energy, a diversity of rhythms, and forward-driving power are its main characteristics. The second movement, "Rhapsodic" or "Chorale," is characteristic of Harris; a slow movement with long, breathing melodies, each new idea evolving from what preceded it, is cast in ternary form. The last movement, "Triple Fugue," consists of three themes presented fugally and subjected to change until assuming a final form. Excessive use of loud volumes and of brass and percussion detract from the total effect. The symphony's strength is in the expert orchestration and in the lyricism of the second movement.

Harris moved to Colorado Springs in 1943 to become composer-in-residence at Colorado College. Here he finished his Sixth Symphony (*Gettysburg*), which was also premiered by Koussevitzky and the Boston Symphony Orchestra, on 14 April 1944. It consists of four movements. Movement I, "Awakening," based on the words of the Gettysburg Address beginning with "Fourscore and seven years ago," is bathed in light and moves unhurriedly. It develops short melodic phrases, knitting them together so as to form a unity. The sonority is rich. The expression is rapt. The ending on a high-flying melody is moving.

Movement II, "Conflict," refers to the line "Now we are engaged in a great civil war," and begins with a musical anticipation of the unavoidable tragedy. A slow march expands with the deep and full resonances of organum. Then the clash of arms, a faster march-like section, represents Harris in his most dissonant mode—quite appropriate for letting loose the barbarity of battle. Movement III, "Dedication," is on the line beginning "But, in a larger sense, we cannot dedicate." Now the music turns melancholic and thoughtful; harmonies cease their aggressiveness; strings and woodwinds predominate. They set forth their subject with eloquence. Movement IV, "Affirmation," declares "that we here highly resolve that these dead shall not have died in vain." As in the previous symphony, a triple fugue is introduced, with the music accelerating and increasing in volume to symbolize the spirit of human endurance. As is frequently the case with Harris's finales, the intended effect falls flat for many listeners, owing to a sense of haste and clumsiness.

Seven more symphonies would follow in the postwar years. All of them, with the exception of the Seventh, have lengthy passages that are not out of the top drawer. Beginning in the 1950s, Harris was under frequent censure for writing too much, too hurriedly, and for being too welcoming of weak ideas. Self-criticism was not his forte. His self-admiration never abated. He died in 1979.

On balance, Harris's accomplishments were indisputable and added fresh and singular works to the symphonic literature. When at his best, as in the Third Symphony, Harris gives us music of extensive scope. One finds strength and emotional vigor. His rhythms, however bumpy at times, take the pulse of America. His melodies sing with an American voice, though occasionally with awkwardness. His sectionalized blocks of sound are impressive, but now and again Harris has problems realizing their shape and linking one to another smoothly. Aaron Copland summarizes the music by saying, "It is crude and unabashed at times, with occasional blobs and yawps of sound that Whitman would have approved of. And always it is music that addresses itself to a big public, sure sign of the composer of a big country."[31]

THE MUSCULAR SYMPHONY: SCHUMAN

William Schuman was a student and direct musical descendant of Roy Harris. The image that first comes to mind when thinking about Schuman is that of Casey in Schuman's eighty-minute *The Mighty Casey* (baseball opera in three scenes, 1953) and the forty-minute *Casey at the Bat* (baseball cantata, 1976). Schuman often resembles a batter who comes to the plate ready to swing, tries to wham the ball away, and then rushes around the bases to score a home run. Or he has his music leap up and down, twist about, and roll end over end as if an athlete is busy exercising. His scores appear sturdily built; his measures sound sinewy.

Schuman's background looks little like those of the previous three composers. For one, he was a big-city boy, born in New York City in 1910. He played the violin and banjo but was far more enthusiastic about baseball (note the contrast to Barber's preferences). Informal family songfests in the shape of spontaneous evening gatherings kept him aware of music. During these get-togethers, he and his family sang impromptu ballads from operettas and Broadway musicals. While in high school, he organized a dance band and tried his hand at composing a piece or two. Yet baseball continued to be his strongest passion.

At eighteen years of age, he entered New York University's School of Commerce in order to earn a business degree. At the same time he found employment at an advertising agency. Popular-song writing continued to interest him, and he wrote over three dozen of them in collaboration with his friends E. B. Marks Jr. and Frank Loesser. Loesser would win fame later as a popular-song lyricist and writer of the Broadway musical *Guys and Dolls*. No songs set to music by the young Schuman broke into the big time.

In 1930 Schuman was coaxed into attending a symphony performance and was so captivated by the music that he make up his mind to become a classical-music composer. He had watched Arturo Toscanini conduct the New York Philharmonic in a program consisting of Robert Schumann's Symphony No. 3, Richard Wagner's "Funeral Music" from *Götterdämmerung*, and Zoltan Kodály's *Summer Evening*.

While baseball and popular song continued to engage his attention, they became subordinate to his new interest. He left New York University, took lessons in musical theory and composition, and attended symphony concerts regularly. In 1935 he graduated with a B.A. in music education from the Teachers College of Columbia University. Despite the depressed economic conditions, he managed to find a teaching job at Sarah Lawrence College while earning a master's degree from Columbia University.

He heard and became excited by Roy Harris's Symphony No. 1 (*Sym-*

phony 1933) and wished to study with its composer, which he did at the Juilliard School of Music. Michael Steinberg says, "Harris's declamatory, tough, broad-spanned, extroverted style affected Schuman powerfully. His own leaning was in just those directions, and he came away from his lessons with a vocabulary, the beginnings of a technique, and a validation of his own expressive stance."[32] Roy Harris found his young student so promising that he recommended him to conductor Serge Koussevitzky. Koussevitzky and the Boston Symphony Orchestra would give the premiere of Schuman's *American Festival Overture* on 6 October 1939.

Schuman's Symphony No. 1 dates from 1935. Thirty minutes long, it had its premiere with Jules Werner and the Gotham Symphony on 21 October 1936. Aware that it was an immature work containing many weaknesses, Schuman withdrew it subsequently. Although he would also withdraw his Symphony No. 2, this second effort met with some approval from composers including Aaron Copland and Leonard Bernstein, even if its style was indebted to Harris. Finished in 1937, the symphony was played for the first time at a WPA concert, presented by Edgar Schenkman and the Greenwich Orchestra, on 25 May 1938.

Despite the many reminders of Harris, the music showed the beginnings of an individual style. A few passages sound overly austere. The handling of counterpoint comes across strangely. One or two angular ideas return again and again with negligible development. Elliott Carter commented, after attending this performance, that its plan was too obvious, its ideas uninteresting, and the music too repetitious. Composed in one fairly short movement (eighteen minutes), it is built on three long pedals. The music gains "its effect by the hammering in of little fragments and tonalities."[33]

At the premiere and at a 1939 performance given by Koussevitzky and the Boston Symphony Orchestra, audiences found the sound unpleasant, the melodies unsympathetic, the rhythms irritating, and the dissonances unceasing. Two years after the premier of his Second Symphony, Schuman became his own man with the *American Festival Overture*. The composer said it was based on a call to play from the streets of New York City, the cry "wee-awh-hee," a descent and rise of a minor third. The music is dressed in more contemporary harmonies. The melodic element is of better quality. The fugal writing is spirited. The entire piece has passages of bracing sweep and power. He allows the music to sound almost improvised (an effect not often found in Schuman's music). No program is supplied.

By 1940, Schuman was far more set in his own style. The Third Symphony would demonstrate a newfound independence. The Harris influence still lingers in the predisposition to employ polyphony and to write in broad, monolithic arches of sound. Yet Harris's full, radiant resonances of low brasses and strings are absent. Sharp-edged instrumental timbres prevail. In his symphonies, Schuman is especially fond of the characteristic quality of sound imparted by brasses and soaring strings. Spiky collisions within and between chords occur. Even if the chordal configurations are essentially tonal, they serve no functional purpose. Since the music is chiefly linear, the dissonant harmonies result from a mix of individual tracks.

Diversity in rhythm is the rule in his symphonies, although the underlying beat may remain the same, particularly when the music is moving at a slow pace. On the other hand, the passages above the basic beat alter their rhythmic shapes incessantly. Portions of a measure that are normally unaccented are stressed time and again. Here, one hears evidence of the influence of jazz. Without doubt, a great deal of energy surges through his movements. This energy and a certain brashness that accompanies it indicate what is American about Schuman.

Peter Korn hears "a certain synthetic quality" in Schuman's music, as if it is "conceived in a spirit of emotional detachment . . . of symphonic gestures rather than of symphonic content."[34] The composer may reveal more head than heart; more that is man-made than inspired. He may share little about himself with his audience. Unvarying seriousness permeates the symphonies. No folk or popular music and no cheery dance tunes invest his symphonic measures to help lighten the tone. Melodies can lack warmth and grace. However, these observations do not necessarily apply to the non-symphonic works for orchestra, such as the *William Billings Overture,* the *Circus Overture, New England Triptych,* and the orchestral arrangement of an Ives organ piece, *Variations on "America."*

There is no question that the Third Symphony represents Schuman at his best. It was composed in 1940–41 and given its premier in Boston just a few weeks before the United States entered the war. At the time, a few native composers believed in all sincerity that they could create music that portrayed the American character and delineate its bold and generous spirit. This was the premise that Schuman acted upon when he wrote the symphony. To some extent, the listener can still detect an acknowledgment of his teacher, Roy Harris, in the prominent brasses, changeable rhythms, continuous vigor, forceful expression, and penchant for Baroque polyphonic procedures. Otherwise, Schuman is heard striking out on his own.

In 1940, as Schuman commenced composing his symphony, the war raged on. The Nazi *blitzkrieg* was set in motion, gobbling up the Netherlands, Belgium, and Luxembourg and forcing the evacuation of British troops at Dunkirk. Paris fell. The French government surrendered in June. The Battle of Britain started in July. Significantly, the British army began to rebound in December of that year, starting its first major offensive in North Africa. By the end of 1941, the attack on Pearl Harbor had taken place and the United States was in the war.

About this time, Walt Disney released his famous musical film *Fantasia,* and Igor Stravinsky heard his Symphony in C premiered in Chicago. In some ways Stravinsky's most traditional work, this modified neoclassical symphony adheres to the usual four-movement plan, in the customary succession of movements: fast, slow, scherzo, finale. I do detect some of its dry manner here and there in Schuman's Third Symphony.

Schuman's Third Symphony was completed in January 1941 and premiered by Koussevitzky and the Boston Symphony Orchestra on 7 October 1941. No direct evidence of a war connection exists, whether in the words of the composer or the flow of the music. It sounds like a giant flexing his muscles, like an America ready to cope no matter what. The symphony is muscular and potent. Its gestures are given kinetic force and impress the listener deeply. The score's projection of authority and strength may possibly be Schuman's unconscious response to the enemy forces clamoring at the American gates. He powers up the music with a huge orchestra—twelve woodwinds, thirteen brasses, three percussionists, and a full complement of strings. In his printed score Schuman writes that, though they are "optional," he believes it "very desirable" to add five more woodwinds, four more French horns, and piano.[35] Without question, the instrumentation gives great communicative punch to the symphony. Generally apparent is Schuman's attentiveness to the capabilities of the orchestral instruments. His predisposition is to think of the orchestra in terms of three main choirs—woodwinds, brasses, and strings—with each a distinct block of color.[36]

What is most likeable about the composition is the composer's willingness to allow strong feeling to enter its pages. The musical style is not simply national but more cosmopolitan. The symphony reveals knowledge of and willingness to employ forms and procedures inherited from Europe, past and present. Basically, the work is tonal, and although the measures frequently remain harmonically ambiguous and are flooded with discord, we should keep in mind Schuman's admonition: "My music is all melody. . . . I guarantee to teach you to sing the principal melody of my symphony in half an hour."[37] The music generates extreme expressive tension jacked up by forceful unbalanced rhythms. His frequent resorting to polyphony introduces a large amount of intricacy into the structure.

The Symphony No. 3 arrives in two parts. Part I is a slow Passacaglia and a spirited Fugue (*vigoroso*). Part II is a moderately slow Chorale (*andantino*) and a light and swift Toccata (*leggiero*). The redeployment of his Passacaglia theme in the next three movements adds greatly to the structural unity. Unity is also promoted through the use of rising semitones, especially in the imitative entry of instrumental voices. The beginning of each section grabs our interest, if only because one line alone is heard, however briefly. Yet the employment of strict contrapuntal forms, though used freely, can sound rather academic. It also contributes to artificial inflections of the melodies. The dangers are monotony arising from the unvarying use of one idea, absence of thematic conflict, and lack of variety in the expressive design. Nevertheless, the many virtues of the Symphony No. 3 more than offset the liabilities.

The symphonic plan is quite original. The Part I: Passacaglia theme, a handsome seven-measure melody, unfolds in grave triple time. From it emerge all the themes in the composition. It starts in quasi-canonic fashion: moderately soft in the violas; rising a semitone when taken over by the second violins; rising another semitone when heard in the cellos; still another semitone as the first violins take over; and a final semitone when it is given to the contrabasses and low woodwinds. The independent lines increase canonically from one to five, as does the complexity of the texture. An initial variation has the trumpets play the theme against a background of frenetic strings scurrying through eighth-note triplets. The second variation is given to the woodwinds. The volume increases to *fortissimo.* The altered theme is represented by fast-moving triplet figurations while strings, low woodwinds, tuba, and timpani pound away at a brief rhythmic figure. This is followed by a few measures of jittery high strings that introduce the third variation. This variation starts with running sixteenth-note figures in the cellos as the violins play an augmented variant of the theme. Trombones take up the melody. Suddenly the strings erupt with agitated trills on six quarter notes as prelude to the Fugue.

The Fugue, in 4/4 time, begins loudly and robustly in the horns and lower strings. The spiky subject, which is related to the Passacaglia theme, leaps dramatically about. Its notes are attacked and released abruptly and without resonance. One cannot help but wonder if the fugue of Harris's Symphony No. 3 lurked in the back of Schuman's mind. The subsequent entries are free and do not by any means go by the book. After the opening presentation, which mounts to a large climax, a series of different treatments follow that vary the subject and textures. This second section can be interpreted as a collection of loose variations on the opening subject, which, as has been said, is drawn from the Passacaglia theme. The close is a weighty and thunderous statement of the subject in an augmented presentation that continues for thirteen measures. The last three measures illustrate a point that Walter Piston used to make in his composition seminar,[38] that with enough dissonance and tonal disorientation, any dissonant chord coming before the final triad can sound like a dominant—in this instance, a B-flat seventh chord before the final B major triad.

The Part II: Chorale, Schuman said, represents the spirit of the entire composition.[39] It begins with divided violas and cellos singing serenely and smoothly for twenty-one measures of 4/4 time. A solo trumpet enters with a quiet variant on the Passacaglia theme, while a flute adds embroidery above it. The strings continue with the melody and lead into a grand account of the chorale in the full orchestra. After the climax is achieved, the volume dies to a whisper of muted horns and then trumpets. Eventually the music ceases its movement.

At this point, the Toccata begins *alla breve,* a snare drum rattling off light, rhythmic drum taps for fourteen measures. Starting with the bass clarinet, the woodwinds now join the snare drum; still later a xylophone is included. The sound drives on boldly as it strives on to an immense climax. The audacity continues with the passage that follows. The passage sounds much like a cadenza for the cellos, and then for the violins, and after that for the entire string section. A fresh treatment of the Chorale theme comes next. Many virtuosic demands are made on the players. The symphony ends with a solemn, thunderous peroration. Schuman lets the listener know that the composition has ended by a succession of emphatic *sforzando* E-flat chords heard over the span of six measures.

Symphony No. 3 became the most played of all Schuman's symphonies and went on to win an award from the Music Critics Circle of New York City. The composer Vincent Persichetti sums up the entire composition by saying, "The vigorous Third Symphony is the most brilliantly written work of Schuman's early period. A robust athleticism has built its unique architecture; its virility extends even to the lyricism, which is strong and nonsubjective."[40]

Schuman's gloomy, fervid, and astringent Symphony No. 4 came on the heels of the previous symphony and seems a more obvious product of the war than the previous symphony. Completed in 1941, it received its first performance with Artur Rodzinski and the Cleveland Orchestra on 22 January 1942—six weeks after the attack on Pearl Harbor. Regrettably, the audience at the premiere showed little enthusiasm for the composition, and later audiences have rarely warmed to it.

Several correspondences occur between it and the Third Symphony, not least being the grandiloquent gestures that would no longer be in fashion after 1950. In three movements, the Fourth Symphony starts (quarter note = 72) with a cheerless English horn solo above a single string bass—which establishes the atmosphere for the entire piece. The first movement gets a free ternary treatment, with fugal touches in the middle section and, otherwise, developmental variations on the principal subject. The music, however, needs a more solid shape and character. The slow movement, marked "tenderly, simply," is the warmest and saddest of the three. It is also the most attractive, owing to greater refinement and grace. Its calm, muted first subject is a lyrical variant on the previous movement's opening theme. A passionate flare-up in the middle leads back to a recapitulation of the earlier melody. The last movement (quarter note =

144) brings forward a well-turned-out new thematic idea that is heard above a striding bass line from the first movement. It provides the theme for several variations that are dealt with contrapuntally. Unfortunately, the movement seems to pursue a discursive course with too many aimless windings. Ultimately the composition manages to conclude optimistically and is brought to an end on an exultant C major chord.

The forebodings of the Third Symphony had led to a Fourth that was mostly anguished, despite its upbeat ending. By the time of the Symphony for Strings (Symphony No. 5), Schuman seems worn down by the war—one moment there is vehement protest, at another there is nervous exhaustion, at still another there is sardonic laughter. It was written on a commission from the Koussevitzky Foundation and received its premiere in Boston on 12 November 1943. (In 1943, too, Schuman's cantata *A Free Song* would receive a Pulitzer Prize.) The symphony impressed audiences as being on the dry side. It is not as convincing a work as the Third, nor, for that matter, quite as persuasive as the Fourth Symphony. Though it was praised by the Boston critics, the critic of the *New York Times* and the audience found it inordinately hard to assimilate, formal in layout, and not very open in its expression.[41] The latter verdict has prevailed.[42] The first movement, *molto agitato ed energico,* is just that. An extremely loud opening theme consists of excited repeated notes and numerous leaps. It introduces us to a sonata-allegro movement full of rhythmic turmoil and harsh harmonies. Much time is spent on the expansion of the opening theme. The second movement, *larghissimo,* starts boldly, but much of it is muted. Occasionally the music touches on the personal. Some polytonality occurs. The last movement, *presto leggiero,* ends the symphony in a light and playful manner. The structure is that of a rondo. The listener hears hints of jazz in the main subject and at one fleeting moment an allusion to Tchaikovsky's Fourth Symphony.

Schuman's administrative abilities came to the fore in 1944. While still on the faculty of Sarah Lawrence College, he became Director of Publications for the music publisher G. Schirmer. The following year he became president of the Juilliard School of Music in New York. Along with innovations in teaching, he was active in the creation of the renowned Juilliard String Quartet. In 1962, he found himself the first president of Lincoln Center, a post he occupied until 1969, when a heart attack forced his resignation. Before and after his heart attack he worked ceaselessly at educational reform and advancing the cause of classical music in the nation.

He continued to find time to compose music, his strongest abstract composition for orchestra, besides the Third Symphony, being his Violin Concerto of 1947. Other works that have found favor with critics and the public are the *American Festival Overture* (1939), the Sixth Symphony (1948), the ballet *Judith* (1949), *New England Triptych* (1956), and, most particularly, the colorful arrangement of an Ives work, *Variations on "America"* (1963). He died in 1992.

In general his music's characteristics were similar to the impression that Schuman made on his acquaintances—busy, active, confident, forceful, and almost larger than life. One might say that his "Americanism" emanated from the personality itself. Schuman is quoted as saying, "If my music should eventually prove a failure, I want it to be a great big failure, not a little piddling failure."[43] He creates with bold strokes such things as wide-ranging melodies, jagged harmonies, and assertive rhythms. For him, writing a symphony was a serious activity. It allowed no room for frivolity, for loosening up. The act of composing required taking considerable care. A composition had to represent him at his serious "best." This may go part way to explaining his refraining from anything resembling the dance rhythms and popular tunes that had formed a large part of his earliest musical experiences.

Steinberg writes, "Schuman composed some of our best music, music of hard-edged, deeply felt Romanticism. He wrote in many forms and genres, and with notable success for dance and chorus; it is, however, the series of [10] symphonies that has particularly ensured his place as the sonorous rhetorician, the great Public Orator among American composers. His music can be muscle-bound and loud-mouthed, but the best of it is tender, rich, fiercely athletic, funny, imposingly forthright."[44]

THE CIVIL SYMPHONY: CARPENTER

John Alden Carpenter, who was thirty-four years older than Schuman, had had a long record of accomplishment before he worked on the two symphonies yet to be described. He had ventured into impressionism, exoticism, Spanish and Latin American sounds, quasi-jazz effects, and a style featuring Stravinsky-like rhythms and harmonizations. By the 1940s, when the two symphonies came out, he was perhaps creatively less intent on proving himself as a composer, as was the much younger Schuman, and more intent upon taking stock of and summing up his career, war or no war. His two compositions would be quiet and serene in sound, and knowledgeable and sophisticated in method. Both are well mannered. They have the polish and suavity one might regard as characteristic of the cosmopolitan social life led by the composer.

Just before his death in 1951, Carpenter looked back over his career as a composer and remarked about the roles of music and art in his and American life, "Their task is to nourish and sustain people. The day of American leadership has dawned and it is necessary for us to become spiritual leaders. It is not enough to deal with things. In addition, we must express our ideas and ideals. It is the role of music and the arts to be the medium for this expression. . . . They speak to the best that is in us."[45] When he wrote his two symphonies in the early forties, Carpenter observed the guidelines he would set down for himself. In a time of mental and emotional stress, he saw it as his calling to reassure his listeners, bolster their confidence in humanity, and entertain them at the same time.

It is most curious that in passing judgment on the merits of a music composition, commentators may be suspicious of popularity and fear being considered deficient in taste and judgment if they approve such music. This suspicion applies in particular to works that seem insufficiently somber—that is to say, too much given to what may be defined as trivialities or of slight worth. For these reasons, Carpenter's symphonies have remained suspect. Carpenter himself was uninterested in pontificating in his symphonies and in claiming exaggerated authority for them. Nevertheless, his symphonic works have their own cogency and do remain convincing on rehearing.

He was urbane and cultured; his music, well mannered and well crafted. His compositions gave pleasure. His style was mostly traditional, at times moderately modern, and infused with impressionistic techniques. The music rarely threatened to go off the deep end. Yet Carpenter managed to make his mark on America's cultural history and leave behind works of worth.

He was born in Park Ridge, Illinois, in 1876, into a wealthy family. His father operated Carpenter and Company, a ship chandlery located in Chicago; his mother was a singer and was passionately fond of music. After receiving his first music lessons from his mother, John Alden Carpenter studied music theory and composition with John Knowles Paine at Harvard College. He graduated in 1897. After leaving Harvard, he entered his father's business and would serve as vice-president of the firm from 1906 to 1936. Following his return to the Chicago area he continued his music studies under the noted music theorist Bernard Ziehn. He also took a few lessons with Edward Elgar in Rome. For his entire adult life, he worked as an officer at Carpenter and Company, finding time to compose music only when at leisure.

Even though saddled with business duties, John Alden Carpenter managed to become one of the leading American composers of the first two decades of the twentieth century. He gained high respect for his songs, many of them sensitively capturing the mood of the poetry in a personalized impressionistic manner. Especially fine are two song cycles that lean toward the exotic: *Gitanjali,* a setting of six poems by India's Rabindranath Tagore (1913), and *Water-Colors,* a setting of four ancient Chinese poems (1916). Delicate melodies, subtle rhythms, and unusual harmonic colors evoke variegated moods and impressions.

Prominent conductors and orchestras of the early twentieth-century decades performed his orchestral music. His first big success, *Adventures in a Perambulator,* was composed in 1914 for the Chicago Symphony Orchestra. The depiction of a day in the life of a baby, inspired by the composer's only child, Ginny, presents an unusual scenario. Carpenter called the piece a symphony in six descriptive scenes: "En Voiture," "The Policeman," "The Hurdy-Gurdy," "The Lake," "Dogs," and "Dreams." Although Carpenter's early work reveals to some degree the influence of Germanic models by way of his teacher, Paine, the *Adventures in a Perambulator* proves he also had acquaintance with French and Russian sources as it suggests a sort of domesticated *Pictures at an Exhibition,* flavored with Fauré and Debussy.

After World War I, demand grew for classical music compositions employing jazz elements. Louis Gruenberg responded with *The Daniel Jazz* (1923), George Gershwin with *Rhapsody in Blue* (1924), George Antheil with *Jazz Symphony* (1925), and Aaron Copland with *Music for the Theater* (1925) and Concerto for Piano and Orchestra (1926). In Chicago, John Alden Carpenter knew the work of the outstanding jazz trumpet players "King" Oliver and Louis Armstrong. His contributions to the Jazz Age were the Concertino for Piano (1915), which came before all of the above-named, the "jazz pantomime" *Krazy Kat* (1921), and the ballet *Skyscrapers* (1924), which had originally been planned for Diaghilev's Ballets Russes.

In no work does he pretend to write "authentically." "Jazz" is a stylistic device that merges in his mind with ballroom dance. The unpredictable Concertino mixes liberal dollops of Latin American sounds with the rhythms and tunes of ragtime, blues, and early jazz. The screwball humor of George Herman's cartoon character is captured in *Krazy Kat,* a piece that influenced Gershwin when he wrote his *Rhapsody. Skyscrapers,* "A Ballet of Modern American Life," which likened jazz to American skyscrapers, was first exhibited on the Metropolitan Opera stage and had a triumphant run of two years. Here, Carpenter revealed his most daring, energetic, and high-spirited self in his depiction of urban men and women at work and play. A high incidence of clashing sounds and aggressive, Stravinsky-like rhythms runs through the music.

Other works, such as the ballet *The Birthday of the Infanta* (1918), the Whitman-inspired *Sea Drift* (1933), and the Violin Concerto (1936), employed a less up-to-date, more turn-of-the-century language. *Birthday* revels in romanticized Spanish idioms treated a bit like Ravel. Indeed, throughout his career, Carpenter delighted in introducing Hispanic elements into his pieces. *Sea Drift,* a symphonic poem based on lines from Walt Whitman's "Out of the Cradle Endlessly Rocking," gives the sense of an almost unvaryingly slow, melancholic, vaguely defined impressionistic "drift" from the first sound to the conclusion. It is the darkest and one of the finest compositions that Carpenter wrote. The Concerto is also a first-rate work, giving the soloist ample room for full, open-throated lyricism.

In summary, Carpenter's style is eclectic. Blues, jazz, and Hispanic inputs have already been noted. All three are filtered through the composer's mind and restated to serve artistic purposes. French Impressionism left a permanent mark. Additionally, the tunefulness of popular song and the catchiness of ballroom dance rhythms attracted his attention. In his scores, we find occasional musical excursions to the Far East, to India, and to North Africa. His orchestration leaves nothing to be desired.

In 1917, he composed a three-movement orchestral piece, *Sermons in Stones,* which he called his Symphony No. 1. Its title came from Shakespeare's *As You Like It.* The deposed duke, exiled in the Forest of Arden, says:

> Sweet are the uses of adversity;
> Which, like the toad, ugly and venomous,
> Wears yet a precious jewel in his head:
> And this our life exempt from public haunt
> Finds tongues in trees, books in the running brooks,
> Sermons in stones, and good in everything.

When Frederick Stock, conductor of the Chicago Symphony, requested a new composition to celebrate the orchestra's fiftieth birthday, Carpenter decided to rework *Sermons in Stones.* This he did, dropping the descriptive title, reconstituting the music as an eighteen-minute one-movement composition, and naming the new work simply Symphony No. 1. No explanatory program was attached. He used material from the first two movements of the earlier piece and hardly any from its finale, except for the coda.[46] The result was a trimmer and sparer work. Troubled by the war raging in Europe, he described the symphony as "peaceful music, and in these days, perhaps, that is something."[47] The premiere took place 24 October 1940.

A few weeks later, Stock took the Chicago Symphony and the Carpenter composition to New York City. Francis Perkins reviewed the performance for the New York *Herald Tribune,* writing that the symphony does indeed contain peaceful music. He went on to observe that it "does not err . . . on the side of too consistent placidity. . . . [It] avoids sonorities which might be received with disaffection by conservative-minded concert goers." Perkins decided the symphony had "sincere and appealing music generous in melodic content, well knit and concise in form, ably wrought in its scoring and in the employment of its ideas."[48]

The Symphony No. 1, like most of the previously discussed symphonies, calls for a large orchestra: woodwinds by threes, eleven brasses, expanded percussion, harp, piano, and strings. The composition is in five sections, each evoking a different mood: *Moderato-sostenuto, Moderato grazioso, Moderato, Moderato,* and *Largo.* The opening material infuses all sections. The style mirrors that of the earlier *Sermons in Stones* of 1917, especially in its inclination toward French Impressionism. It differs from the earlier work in its greater sophistication, increased gravity, structural strength, and rich interweaving of elements. Moderation is the watchword, whether in emotion, harmonic innovation, or demands made on the listener. Carpenter avoids any hint at forceful modernism. He reins in dissonance. Ingratiating lyricism attracts the ear. He handles instruments knowingly. Textures are clear. Colorings are remarkably varied. An emphasis on percussion, including celesta and glockenspiel, enhances the colorations and adds backbone to the symphony. There is much that the listener can enjoy.

The first section starts off with the uninterrupted singing of violins, with horns in the background. A minute later, some excitement is generated as motifs from the opening theme are fragmented and developed by brasses and strings. Next, the music grows quiet. Gentle wisps of melody are heard. When the brasses sound again, they seem to intone a chorale. A loud climax lasts for a brief moment and the sound dies down to nothing.

The second section resorts to more definite pulsations and a play of ideas among strings, brasses, and woodwinds. The brasses increase their boldness. Then suddenly the sounds become hushed. A wistful tune whispers to the ear and thrice increases in volume only to fall back and resume its wistfulness. A seamless linkage to the third section is now realized. Vigorous rhythms, chattering woodwinds, bouncy strings, and brass calls characterize the new section until a harp arpeggio heralds the return of quietness. This noticeable turn to softness is a feature in all sections thus far.

The fourth section opens with high woodwinds and strings sharing a delicate melody. The sound dies to nothing. A brief elegiac English horn is quickly silenced with the start of a quicker tempo and the contrast of instrumental blocks. The final section's main division begins. The music turns serious. The pace is slower. The strings enter. Before long the full orchestra joins them. Chorale-like phrases come from the brasses. A full climax emerges and a brass chorale is heard from beginning to end. At the close a persistent drum beat and brief brass exclamations get softer and softer. The symphony ends with a low, almost indistinct murmur.

This First Symphony provides quantities of charming and serious moments. The appeal is to the imaginative and delicately emotional side of human experience. Elegiac solos from the woodwinds conjure an atmosphere of nostalgia. Wide-ranging string lines generate a little excitement. Chipper segments that combine jabbering woodwinds and clanking percussion illustrate Carpenter's command of colorful instrumental combinations. Lengthy brass chorales produce a suggestion of nobility. A member of the audience may come away unable to recall any particulars, but he certainly remembers the kaleidoscopic array of tone pictures.

In 1941–42, Carpenter worked on and finished a Second Symphony, which Bruno Walter and the New York Philharmonic Symphony premiered on 22 October 1942. Carpenter's starting point was a Piano Quintet composed in 1937, which he transcribed for orchestra. The scoring is for an ensemble of similar size to that of the First Symphony. Both Quintet and Symphony were revised in 1947. Fritz Busch and the Chicago Symphony would premiere the revised symphony.

The Symphony No. 2 is more novel, balletic, and expressively varied than its predecessor. Carpenter shows his latest style to be an amalgamation of everything that has gone before, now synthesized into a new whole. Interestingly, the music does come through as quite fresh. Measures are filled with swinging rhythms and lilting song. The work comprises three movements, each lasting a little over six minutes: *Moderato, Andante,* and *Allegro.*

The first movement is economically configured, injects some nonconventional dissonances into the fabric, and covers a ground shifting emotionally from larger-than-life to agreeably jesting. It starts dramatically with a menacing rhetorical gesture in the brass and percussion, which gets a cheerful response from the strings. (I am reminded of the flower-children of the 1960s responding to the armed militia confronting them.) A march-like theme establishes itself, but not for long. This theme alternates with more subdued lyricism and allusions to the opening in an intensive development. A recapitulation of the opening leads to a diversified return of previous ideas, with some measures given a fresh Spanish inflection. The movement finishes in a jaunty, even capricious, mode.

The second movement alternates drama with desire. It proceeds nervously and unfolds over a steady beat. The start is a downward sliding parallel-chord stream straight out of Debussy. Next, tones reaching into the lower regions support an unhurried principal theme that lasts almost two minutes. A brief, ominous interruption from the brasses intrudes and then ceases. It allows the lyricism to continue in a broader, richer, and more expressive vein. A harsh, declamatory climax is reached but lasts only a short while. The end is solemn but calming. A second spicing of Debussyan harmony adds piquancy to the close.

The third movement draws supposedly on an Egyptian melody, although what is Egyptian about the movement is impossible to detect. Nor does Carpenter say. It begins on a sauntering march-like theme, which is taken up by various sections of the orchestra. There is an added presence of raucous brasses and percussion. Fleetingly, the music reminds us of Ralph Vaughn Williams's heated and scary Symphony No. 4, in F minor (1935). A more heartwarming tune gradually engages the attention. The two themes are subjected to a short development, before the second one makes a more expressive return. A makeover of the symphony's opening rhetorical gesture then inspires a fervent close. The ending is a reminder that the symphony is not a matter of fun and games. The final sounds are militant drumbeats and an abrupt trill. The audience may wonder whether the martial tones are a put-on, as if, the composer's seriousness notwithstanding, he means them as a satirical poke at militarism and what it stands for.

During the thirties, Carpenter had voiced a growing alarm over the increasing militaristic strength of the Nazis and Fascists. After World War II started, he steadily opposed American isolationism and labored on behalf of British Relief. After the United States entered the war, he assisted in the sale of war bonds and allowed his Lake Shore Drive mansion to be used as housing for nurses. What time he had for music composition was spent mostly making revisions of older works. The principal compositions of his final years were *The Anxious Bugler,* a symphonic poem, written in 1943, *The Seven Ages,* an orchestral suite after Shakespeare, written in 1945, and the *Carmel Concerto,* for piano and orchestra, of 1948.

Carpenter's music hardly ever touched on the heroic or starkly dramatic. His palette normally featured more muted emotions. Even so, he managed to fill an important musical niche occupied by no one else.

AFTERTHOUGHT: THOMSON AND COWELL

Three eminent American composers have been neglected in this discussion: William Grant Still, Virgil Thomson, and Henry Cowell. I would advance two reasons for the neglect. None of the three was interested in composing a grand American symphony, one impressive in size and effect. Their aims were otherwise. Furthermore, none wrote symphonies in the late thirties and early forties that were as attractive to critics and the music public as the ones discussed in this book.

William Grant Still (1895–1978) was an African American composer, arranger, and conductor devoted to advancing the cause of his own people. His *Afro-American Symphony* was composed before our time period and given a first performance by the Rochester Philharmonic, with Howard Hanson conducting, on 28 October 1931. Later it was taken up by the New York Philharmonic, the Chicago Symphony, the Boston Symphony, the Los Angeles Philharmonic, the Berlin Philharmonic, the London Symphony, and the Tokyo Philharmonic, among others. It features music based on spirituals, jazz, and the blues, especially the blues of W. C. Handy. George Gershwin was also an influence—witness the quote from "I Got Rhythm" in the third movement. African American issues are on Still's mind. African American tunes are given symphonic weight and expert orchestral treatment. The symphony was highly enjoyable, proved popular, and was given performances by several other orchestras. Four other compositions called symphonies came later from Still, but none of these made any real headway with orchestras and public. Even though he won renown within African American society and the *Afro-American Symphony* had widespread success, America's white music historians and commentators left Still mainly unnoticed. Only in the last years of the twentieth century did interest pick up.

Virgil Thomson (1896–1989) remained himself no matter what he composed. His symphonic efforts were idiosyncratic and ingenious. The earliest, *Symphony on a Hymn Tune* (1928, revised 1945), dates from Paris and came into being shortly after he studied with Nadia Boulanger. It is hands-down one of his finest compositions. Discontinuous in layout, it rarely pursues a course anyone can anticipate. Dissimilar ideas are being thrown together: hymn, waltz, tango, fugue, blues, and other touching, entertaining, and surprising sounds.

Thomson's two other symphonies are outwardly more like conventional works and are not nearly as interesting as his First Symphony. Symphony No. 2 was a rewrite of the Piano Sonata No. 1 (1929) and was finished in 1930. It was revised in 1941, because Thomson thought more contrast and color were needed. Some of the composer's planned illogic is present, as also are poetry and cheer. Regrettably insufficient contrast and a monochrome palette still characterize it. His Symphony No. 3 (1972) is an orchestral arrangement of the String Quartet No. 2 (1932), composed in France. It is unlike most of Thomson's other, rather impersonal, compositions in that it hesitantly makes an effort for intimacy in expression. The result is not persuasive. The music harbors important weaknesses as a quartet and, especially, as a symphony.

Henry Cowell composed three symphonies during our time period: Symphony No. 2, *Anthropos* (1938); No. 3, *Gaelic Symphony* (1942); and No. 4, *Short Symphony* (1946). All three sound tentative, investigatory, and even, at times, naïve. With Cowell, one never knows what sort of work will emerge. It may be American-oriented, or center on the idiom of an Asian culture, or revolve around an abstract concept. His music was sometimes sparkling and pioneering. This was rarely the case, however, in his symphonies. The symphonies often lack force and fail to hit their mark. In the three symphonies from within our time frame, Cowell appears uncomfortable with symphonic structures and unable to enlarge naturally on his material. Every one of Cowell's ideas has a short musical life. Normal development and the integration of dramatic segments are out of his reach. The compositions remain dull and whatever they put forward is negligible.

The symphonies that were written in the late thirties and beginning forties by five American composers—Barber, Hanson, Harris, Schuman, and Carpenter—have received the greatest emphasis in these pages. They all came to life before the United States went to war. All of the composers, one way or another, were acutely aware of the many problems besetting the American people, the belligerent stances of the dictatorial regimes in Germany, Italy, and Japan, and the dark war clouds in Europe. No two of their symphonies sound alike. Each, in its own unique way, offers a commentary on the human condition.

Samuel Barber speaks in impassioned, deeply personal tones. He frequently sings nostalgically or with longing. At the same time, he is too fastidious to allow mawkish sentiments to prevail. In contrast, a kind of spiritual hunger pervades the music of Howard Hanson. I sense it underlying his choice of the persons or events that may serve as models upon which to base his symphonies. This hunger is behind the meaning of the "Nordic" and "Romantic" labels he gave to his first two symphonies, and behind the "reverence for the spiritual contribution . . . of northern pioneers" that inspired his Third Symphony. Roy Harris is a different composer from Barber and Hanson and needs to be reckoned with on his own terms, according to what he stipulates he is. He claims to embrace America, all of its defects and imperfections notwithstanding. In reality, I find him more comfortable with people from the past and the rural present.

Harris is rural; William Schuman is urban. Despite the fact that Schuman was Harris's student, he sings a different song than his mentor. The bustle of city streets in daytime and the mystery of empty streets in nighttime emerge from Schuman's scores. The music's strength lies in the no-nonsense honesty of his communication, often with a degree of abruptness or brusqueness. Lastly, there is John Alden Carpenter, who can be seen as a composer of music that usually falls pleasurably on the ear and is generally intended, as he said, to entertain. In their own time, his Piano Concertino, *Krazy Kat,* and *Skyscrapers* were all original in their own ways. That the symphonies are less daring was a choice the composer consciously made. They deserve consideration on their own merits. They did achieve the goals that Carpenter set out for them.

3

SYMPHONIES OF
THE WAR YEARS

It is important to keep in mind a few details of the war years, since they formed a background of critical importance to the creative activities of American composers, regardless of whether the composers acknowledged their influence. The United States plunged into war when the Japanese attacked Pearl Harbor on 7 December 1941. In early 1942, Japanese armed forces advanced southward on the Asian continent, in the Philippines, and on island after island in the seas off Southeast Asia. Slowly the Japanese armed forces advanced toward Australia. The struggle to stop them grew ferocious. During the entire year and into the next, the United States and Japan engaged in a series of sea battles for control of the Pacific from which the United States eventually emerged victorious. By February 1943, after fierce fighting, the Japanese advance toward Australia had been halted.

Some composers, such as Walter Piston, became creatively paralyzed as they witnessed the mayhem, and ceased writing for a while. Others, including George Antheil, Samuel Barber, and Marc Blitzstein, wrote with the wartime struggle in mind. David Diamond and Leonard Bernstein would show their concern indirectly in their symphonies.

In 1942 and 1943, as these men composed, the Axis armies were trying to hammer the Soviet Union into submission. Crucial battles took place at Leningrad and Stalingrad. Leningrad remained under siege until early 1944. The Axis advance into western Russia met with defeat in Stalingrad in January 1943. After the Battle of Kursk, in the summer of 1943, the Axis would no longer be able to take offensive action on the Eastern Front.

These artists read about American troops landing in North Africa in June 1942 in order to assist the British against the German and Italian forces there. After contention over control of the wide expanse of desert land, the Allies gained the upper hand and forced the Axis armies to surrender in May 1943. Two months later, an invasion fleet left Africa for Sicily. In September, the Allies landed in southern Italy and the recovery of the continent began. Meanwhile, through 1942 and 1943, the butchery of Jews and other people the Nazis deemed undesirable escalated, and a murderous rule of the European continent was implemented.

Alive to this tragic swirl of history, some composers joined the American armed forces or worked in other ways to help the war effort. They thought it imperative to continue composing. Colleagues who remained at home saw it as an obligation to continue writing. These composers thought it was their responsibility to affirm mankind's capacity for civilized behavior despite the brutalizing activities of wartime.

Adding leaven to the American musical scene were the many outstanding European composers who had come to live in the United States, whether permanently or temporarily—among them, Bloch, Stravinsky, Schoenberg, Bartók, Hindemith, Britten, Milhaud, Wolpe, and Weill. Some had come before the war had started, driven out of central Europe by Nazi oppression. Others came later, to escape homelands now turned into battlegrounds or suffering oppression as occupied territories. Most of these artists set themselves up as teachers in composition. At the same time, they continued their creative writing. Few had a real stake in sustaining the American attempt of the thirties and forties to realize a musical identity. They would influence the postwar generation of American composers significantly, through their teaching, their opinions, and the works that they wrote.

WARTIME ATTITUDES

The European composers who arrived in America found a people who, though welcoming, were subject to divisions based on education and money. A large number of white Americans were biased racially and ethnically. Witness the dispossession and segregation of Americans of Japanese descent, the conditions that provoked black Americans into several race riots, and the more subtle discrimination against Jews. Americans tended to hold conformist beliefs and voiced hardly any political opinions. Movies, popular music, and radio programs were their chief entertainment, especially if sentimental, funny, overly dramatic, or full of action. As a group they were not particularly cultivated or cosmopolitan. On the other hand, they were not dummies. Therefore, they tried to understand the reasons for the war and to apply practical judgment to the fighting of it. They were wise enough to let the rants of those leaning to the political far right and far left go unheeded. Nor would they act to banish music composed by German and Austrian composers, which intolerant Americans had tried to do during World War I.

Americans felt that maintenance of domestic liberty during wartime and a successful conclusion to the war would show how right their democratic beliefs were. William O'Neill has pointed out that in several ways they were right. Elections took place when due despite the strain of wartime conditions. O'Neill writes that the United States fought ostensibly without a desire to annex territory, to exact war reparations, or to take revenge. He claims, "Americans could be proud of themselves, not only for winning the war but, by and large, for the way they won it." That is to say, if eyes were kept shut about the treatment of Japanese Americans and African Americans, the wage discrimination experienced by women, and continuing signs of anti-Semitism.[1]

Passengers perished when ships were torpedoed. Americans viewed with horror the relentless bombing of urban areas. Husbands and sons died on the battlefields. The persistent ebb and flow of contending armies devastated rural areas and laid waste cities and towns. Oppressed by the ugly reality of wartime, more and more people looked to music for consolation and aesthetic satisfaction, or as a way of fortifying themselves emotionally against a threatening world. This held true for soldiers as well as civilians. A survey of white soldiers, conducted by *Broadcasting Magazine* and published in October 1942, stated, not surprisingly, that almost all of the young men favored popular music, particularly songs that reminded them of distant loved ones and took them back to familiar places. What was surprising was the finding that one-third of them wanted to listen to classical music.[2]

In his biography of Aaron Copland, Arnold Dobrin writes, "It was 1942, the first year of America's participation in World War II. As the holocaust went on, people began to have a greater interest in the arts—but with an emphasis that was different from that of the previous decade. Destruction was sweeping across many parts of the world and people who were now confronted with news of death and violence whenever they read a newspaper or turned on the radio began to search for some deeper meaning in life. They hoped to find it in art forms. . . ."[3]

Some of the finest music has seen birth when composers remain faithful to beliefs held in common with their society and humanity in general. History implies that the best creative activity takes place during periods when conflicting convictions coalesce and one set of principles emerges about which people and composers are in agreement. This coalescence was taking place during the war.

The composer Douglas Moore reported, in 1943, that symphonic music had taken on "exaggerated importance in the mind of the public" and that opportunities for performance had increased. There were more premieres of orchestral compositions, and new works traveled from orchestra to orchestra to be reheard in various parts of the country. Audiences, he claimed, were quicker "to respond to our native music . . . with the increase of national pride which has followed automatically in the wake of the war." These "same audiences grow apparently more understanding and cooperative." The result was that composers were encouraged to write more than before and with confidence that what they wrote would be performed. Their scores now gave evidence of an abundance of artistic maturity and technical competence, Moore said. Unfortunately, most young composers were in the armed forces and could neither continue their studies nor write music.[4]

The American government needed the input of composers as never before, declared Copland. He explained, "On the home front, for instance, they can stimulate and inspire love of country. To Latin-America they can demonstrate that not all U.S. energy and talent goes into manufacturing and the selling trades."[5] Arthur Berger made particular mention of the Boston Symphony Orchestra programs and their confirmation of the wave of patriotic sentiment that had reached American composers. He cites Roy Harris's Fifth Symphony, William Schuman's *A Free Song*, and Aaron Copland's *A Lincoln Portrait*.[6]

Native classical composers received greater and more repeated exposure than heretofore had been the rule. Copland and Barber were the names most frequently encountered in the orchestral programs. Schuman, Piston, Diamond, Antheil, Thompson, Creston, and Hanson were not far behind.[7]

At least four explanations might make clear why music waxed strong in wartime. First, it helped fight the war by stirring up patriotism. Roy Harris's Symphony No. 6, *Gettysburg*, fits this description. Second, music was an excellent vehicle for disseminating information and sentiments sympathetic to the democratic cause. Two examples are George Antheil's Symphony No. 4, *1942*, and Samuel Barber's Symphony No. 2, "dedicated to the Army Air Forces." Third, music provided distraction from the burdens of wartime existence. Carpenter's Symphony No. 2 had this effect. Fourth, music reminded people of what and whom they loved. Surely, Hanson's Symphony No. 4 (*The Requiem*) did just that. However, the larger number of symphonies had no direct connection with the war, although their content in some fashion had germinated in emotions and thoughts called up by wartime conditions. The Second symphonies of David Diamond and Walter Piston come to mind.

No claim can be made that any of these symphonic compositions was the focal point of an outstandingly new style. Usually each composer went his own way. Not all of this new American music was entirely without flaws, and none would be transformed into a twentieth-century model type that future composers would necessarily emulate. Some had hoped that Copland's work would achieve the desired result, but that did not happen. However, it can be claimed that during the war period, as composers increased their creation of symphonies, they were signaling the nonstop expansion of a vital musical era in America.

THE COMMEMORATIVE SYMPHONY:
ANTHEIL

When we consider George Antheil's life and activities, creative and otherwise, we encounter a host of incredible occurrences, enough for several television docudramas. He had adventures from birth to death like a character in a picaresque novel. One improbability follows on another. Vast social, economic, and artistic and ups and downs mark his career. He is, without doubt, one of America's most unusual and intriguing composers. Like Roy Harris, he thought big and followed his own star. Furthermore, though his methods were slapdash, he thought that his quickness in learning and creative capacity would leave the door open for realizing his goals, variable as they might be. During his lifetime, his star fluctuated between luck and misfortune and between triumph and disaster.

He was born in Trenton, New Jersey, to German-American parents, in 1900. His father operated a shoe store and earned only an adequate living. George began piano lessons at the age of six, initiated his study of theory and composition at the age of sixteen, and had the composer Ernest Bloch accept him as a student at the age of nineteen. He persuaded Mary Louise Curtis Bok, the founder and president of the Curtis Institute of Music, to aid him financially and left for Europe to try to win fame as a concert pianist. Berlin and then Paris became his principal places of residence while in Europe.

Almost immediately, he met and came under the influence of Igor Stravinsky. He became enamored especially of Stravinsky's brittle, mechanistic, rhythmically aggressive, and purportedly nonexpressive constructions in music. Writing about this influence, he said, "Stravinsky's music, hard, cold, unsentimental, enormously brilliant and virtuous, was now the favorite of my post adolescence. In a different way it achieved the hard, cold, postwar flawlessness which I myself wanted to attain—but in an entirely different style. . . ."[8]

Antheil followed Stravinsky's lead. His motto, after Danton's, could have been the revolutionary maxim "pour les vaincre . . . il faut de l'audace, encore de l'audace, toujours de l'audace." He started off trying to vanquish the musical world with his audacity. Because he burned to conquer, he wrote and hammered out daring piano works: *Airplane Sonata* (1921), *Sonata Sauvage* (1922), *Death of Machines* (1923), and *Jazz Sonata* (1923). The music was recklessly bold and defied convention.

Blocks of sound, each block supplied with its own rhythmic design, follow one after another without benefit of transitional material to smooth out a composition. Counterpoint is absent; ostinato passages, chromaticism, and tone clusters assail the senses. It was as if he wanted to pound his audience into submission. He himself admitted that his aim was fame and notoriety.

In Paris, his recitals incited riots. He cultivated the image of an untamed American, gangster-style, by packing a .32 automatic, wearing it under his arm, and ostentatiously laying it down on the piano before starting to play. The Parisian avant-garde went all out for the music and the "tough guy" who played it. Antheil himself admitted that he was "the Bad Boy of Music." Artistic forward-lookers including Ezra Pound, James Joyce, Ernest Hemingway, Pablo Picasso, Fernand Leger, William Butler Yeats, and Erik Satie acted as friends to him. Futurists, Fauvists, Dadaists, and other ultra-moderns saw him as one of their own. They admired his violent machine-factory sounds, his abrupt juxtaposition of glaringly vivid tone-colors, and the incongruous effects the music produced. "I envied George his freedom from academic involvements, the bravado of his music, and its brutal charm," wrote Virgil Thomson. "All were fascinated by Antheil's cheerful lack of modesty. He was in fact the literary mind's idea of a musical genius: bold, bumptious, and self-confident."[9]

The culmination of his unorthodox, cutting-edge period came with his *Ballet Mécanique* (1923–25), written for a large percussion ensemble. The *Ballet Mécanique* is a rhythmic, harsh, and ferocious work, requiring great coordination among its performers. The first instrumentation was for sixteen player pianos, two conventionally played pianos, four bass drums, three xylophones, a tam-tam, seven electric bells, a siren, and three airplane propellers. However, owing to technical difficulties in performance, Antheil revised the piano parts. The new version, using ten conventionally played pianos, was heard in Paris in 1926.

Regrettably, when *Ballet Mécanique* was put on in Carnegie Hall, New York, in 1927, the airplane propellers created such a powerful blast that they blew the first-row attendees out of their seats. The concert was a complete and ignominious failure, musically and in composer-audience relations. Hardly anyone believed any sort of "music" had been heard. Both the general audience and the American avant-garde rose up against Antheil. Press coverage was widespread. Mockery mingled with condemnation. The *New York Press* headline (April 1927) was "Making a Mountain Out of an Antheil"; the *Denver Colorado News* (12 April 1927) gave the concert top billing: "Terror-Stricken Women Flee Cubist Music"; the *Baltimore Sun* (17 April 1927) issued the final verdict: "Critics Call Antheil a Flat Tire."

He was labeled a charlatan and was forced to retreat to Europe. All the while, the New York fiasco haunted him like a nightmare. His reputation remained in ruins. The *Ballet Mécanique* would wait over a century for another performance. Meanwhile, he was reconsidering his creative stance.

Perhaps because he thought that he had reached a stylistic dead end with *Ballet Mécanique* and found it necessary to propitiate the music public, he abandoned his brutalistic ultra-modernity and cultivated a more moderate approach to writing, as in the *Symphonie en fa* (1925–26), the Piano Concerto (1926), the operas *Transatlantic* (1928) and *Helen Retires* (1930–31), and the Symphony No. 2 (1931). In them we find a slow but perceptible changeover from his take on Stravinskian neoclassicism to a warmer palette. Musical structures remained modular, consisting of self-contained units that were added onto, one after another. Rhythms out of jazz and tunes modeled on popular music were attempted. However, nothing he was composing really could be termed a genuine success. In part, the failures may have come because the music world was down on him. Looking over these works today, one can find a great deal to admire. They should not have been put on the shelf.

Financial problems arose, despite Mrs. Bok's continuing to send him money from time to time. Usually it was his own fault. He had never been able to husband his resources. In order to earn money, Antheil investigated non-musical avenues. In 1930 he published a mystery novel, *Death in the Dark*, printed through the offices of T. S. Eliot. Oddly enough, seven years later Antheil was the author of a book on endocrinology entitled *Every Man His Own Detective* and subtitled "X marks the gland where the criminal's found." He also wrote a syndicated column, "Boy Advises

Girl," in *Esquire* magazine, giving advice to the lovelorn. Curiously, in June 1939 he published a book, *The Shape of War to Come,* that foretold the happenings that would take place in World War II with amazing accuracy. For a while, he would also find employment as a war correspondent. His autobiography, *Bad Boy of Music,* would be completed in 1945. It narrates an inflated tale about Antheil's genuine and fabricated deeds in America, Africa, and Europe.

Perhaps Antheil's most extraordinary, and almost unbelievable, non-musical activity was his work on torpedo guidance technology, which was conducted in partnership with the beautiful actress Hedy Lamarr. The invention protected torpedo guidance systems from being jammed or taken over by the enemy. Antheil and Lamarr's work culminated in U.S. Patent 2,292,387, "Secret Communication System," granted on 11 August 1942. Antheil made no money out of the patent.

He had moved to Hollywood in 1936, where he gained a reputation as a reliable movie composer, another of the many hats he wore. Here, he composed notable music for some much-praised films: *The Plainsman* (1936), *Specter of the Rose* (1946), and *Knock on Any Door* (1949), among others. Meanwhile he had begun an intensive study of the symphonic scores of Beethoven, Mahler, and Sibelius. He was soon adding the scores of Prokofiev and Shostakovich to his list for study. He took inspiration and guidance from them when he created his new orchestral works.

It has often been written that Antheil's later style, as heard in the Symphony No. 4, to be discussed shortly, was derived from Shostakovich in particular. Antheil himself insisted that whatever sounded like Shostakovich really originated in his own earlier compositions, which had preceded Shostakovich's. He cites, for example, many pages from his opera *Transatlantic,* especially those in its last act.[10] What is certain is that he consciously turned to tonal, triadic writing with only a modicum of dissonance. He tried to please listeners with attractive, whistleable melodies and up-tempo dance and march rhythms. As might be expected, the orchestration was done by a master. His untamed, exaggerated, and wrenching phase was completely a thing of the past.

Two impelling urges drove him to write symphonies: First, his fixation on producing a work that could be considered "the Great American Symphony." Second, his desire for vindication by his peers and reinstatement in the ranks of admired composers. After World War II ended, he would write of how highly he prized the symphony as a vehicle for creativity:

> I believe, first of all, that the symphony of all times and periods is a spiritual as well as an abstract musical canvas, and that any "symphony" written to present purely abstract musical values is a misnomer. In other words, I believe that every symphony ever written could be subtitled "The Life of Man" as seen by the composer of that particular period while writing that particular symphony. It is like a great novel which shows some complete large section of life and has some deep spiritual moving comment upon it. This makes me reject many modern symphonies which, although they may be admirably constructed, or filled to the brim with exciting musical ideas, sounds, or constructions, yet miss in the fundamental reason for being the "grand symphony."[11]

Antheil's Symphony No. 3, composed during 1936–39, is obviously an American symphony. It is not the America of the past that is featured in its four movements, but the America yet to come—brave, heroic, and innovative in spirit. It tramps or dashes along with a jazzily syncopated, in-your-face kind of bravado. The four years of its crafting corresponded with Antheil's getting to know life in America again. Antheil says, in a letter to Mary Louise Curtis Bok dated 8 March 1938, "It is an 'American' symphony, but it does not pull out all the old darky stops and tremolos. It is the America of the future, bold, fearless, new, and coming from the very breath of the new continent. It has been written after I have written two large picture scores about old America, *The Buccaneer* and *The Plainsman*. . . . The movies have been good to me, however; they have taught me (a) how to write quickly and surely; (b) how to write melodies that people all over the earth understand; (c) good showmanship and actual and continuous contact with a large public."[12]

He speaks of a prolonged road trip by automobile that coincided with his writing the composition. It started with a visit to Clearwater, Florida, where he began the first movement and brushed up on Brahms, Beethoven, Mahler, and Sibelius in order to shore up his technique. As I listen to the fast-moving opening movement I cannot help but feel that

Antheil surely had some program in mind. One idea follows another in headlong haste. A sense of excitement pervades the measures.

The first entry is a short motif played by a jazzy, syncopated trumpet. Quickly, the strings intervene with a genuinely American-sounding tune. Sometimes the tune seems related to Appalachian folk song; sometimes it veers toward popular song. Next, Antheil occupies himself with fragments of the tune mixed with the motif, mostly at a soft level but with a brief climax. The development of these ideas is almost continuous. A restless quality permeates these measures. A recapitulation of the opening and an abrupt coda close the movement.

He reached El Paso, Texas, and sojourned on a nearby ranch belonging to an acquaintance. While there, he produced the moderately paced second movement. For the most part it proceeds as a quiet and fetching march, attractively varied and complete in itself. A touch of Latin American flavoring spices the stylistic mix. For a minute a horn joins the strings on an incipient tune. Next, the melody takes on a more definite shape, sounding like a slow march, one that resembles the slow march in Gustav Mahler's First Symphony. Once in a while, the brasses add a sardonic touch to the proceedings. The end comes with a soft trill on the piccolo.

The third movement, "The Golden Spike," was influenced by his music for the film *Union Pacific*. Antheil claims there is a more direct relationship to the golden spike driven in at Promontory Summit, Utah, on 10 May 1869, to commemorate the finish of the first transcontinental railroad link. One finds an extroverted rowdiness in the music, which strikes the ear as an old-time hoedown tune, somewhat like that in Copland's *Rodeo* (and occasionally like the chugging-along of a steam locomotive). It is as if the listener is attending a rural community dance party featuring square dancing. An animated backwoods tune is played on fiddles. For a couple of moments the tune hints at minstrel songs out of the 1850s. Thrice, also, a passage appears that Antheil borrows from the end of the Sibelius Fifth Symphony. On balance, the hoedown tune bears a distinct resemblance to Antheil's *Hot-Time Dance,* which he would compose in 1948. The final measures are loud and emphatic. The movement ends with a bang.

The finale, "Back to Baltimore," supposedly takes us eastward, in a swift *Presto* tempo. However, something West Coast–like resides in the rambunctious, scampering figures that dash pell-mell from beginning to end. The music has parallels in sound with the music of Shostakovich, but Antheil's style goes back to the opera *Transatlantic* (premiered in 1930), an Antheil composition written when Shostakovich was just appearing on the horizon. The coda receives a "we will conquer all" emphasis as a brassy march treads forward to the conclusion.

Two things this symphony is not—intimate and passionate. The work is primarily concerned with things outside the self, not derived from within Antheil's own feelings. I must also add that the work does not convince me that it is a symphony. Integration is lacking. Each of the four movements is like an independent tone poem with the program suppressed. Each movement is complete in itself and has little connection to the other three movements. If the listener accepts the composition for what it is, a series of colorful pictures, he finds many measures that he can find delightful and refreshing. Hans Kindler and the National Symphony Orchestra premiered the third movement, "The Golden Spike," alone on 28 November 1945. Antheil never heard the complete symphony performed. Although he revised it in 1949, he was at no time satisfied with the composition.

Antheil tried to do better with his next symphony, which is our primary interest. The Fourth Symphony, subtitled *1942*, is quite a different state of affairs from the Third. Romanticism has replaced neoclassicism on its pages. Warmth has ousted coolness. Feeling has supplanted whatever mechanistic objectivity may have lingered from his early years. The scoring is for the expected full orchestra: woodwinds by threes, eleven brasses, timpani and five other percussion, piano, banjo, and strings. All stops are pulled out to catch the attention of an audience.

The symphony is replete with emotion, even passion, although at times it may resemble a human-centered news report about the war, told in music. The composition is one of several vital symphonies written by Americans during World War II, when the armed forces of the United States, the Soviet Union, and Great Britain were considered the rescuers of the world from the Axis powers. In fact, it is one of the most war-oriented of all the symphonies examined in this book. In essence, Antheil's Fourth Symphony, *1942*, is about the will to triumph over the evils of fascism. It is commemorative because it was meant to serve as a memorial to those who had suffered through the war, and as a reminder of the horrors they had endured.

Antheil also directs the audience's attention to the uncertainties of war—war's tensions, viciousness, stupidity, and vicissitudes. The result is an impressive composition that repays repeated hearing. He said of it,

> I composed my Fourth Symphony in between a good deal of typewriter-pounding. Indeed, some of it was written at my desk in the offices of the *Los Angeles Daily News* during the period of the battles of El Alamein and our invasion of Morocco. At the time I was in charge of war-analysis. The war, therefore, has undoubtedly deeply influenced this symphony. Composed during a period when the entire future of the world hung in balance, its first movement undoubtedly reflects my tense and troubled state of mind while writing it; I had no actual "program" in mind, but, every day, I was watching the news, from Stalingrad, from Africa, from the Pacific. The second and third movements also reflect this state of mind, for the second [movement] is tragic—news of [the massacre of men, women, and children at] Lidice and the horrors in Poland had just come in—while the third, the scherzo, is more like a brutal joke, the joke of war. The Fourth, written after the turn of the tide at Stalingrad and our landings in Morocco, heralds victory. For me, it was as if the world had now come to a new turning in its road of destiny, and with the first dawn of a great, wonderful hope up ahead, not too far distant to be visible.
>
> This is exactly how I felt, although I should not like anyone to attempt a more definite "war analysis" of it than that which I have given—for the emotions which beset the composer while composing are seldom literal; they are rather beyond words. That is the reason one writes music.[13]

The composer was anxious to relieve his feelings through music. At the same time he wanted to reach his listeners, bring home the war to them, and bolster their confidence about its outcome. Other American composers, including Aaron Copland, Roy Harris, Mark Blitzstein, and

Samuel Barber, were doing the same. Antheil trusted that his symphony would live on after the war and have a more permanent meaning for audiences, war or no.

Antheil gives more than an occasional bow to two Russians, Shostakovich and Prokofiev, as a show of respect. His colleagues were more subtle if and when they made use of Russian sounds, and this use would evaporate soon after the war's end.[14] Despite this homage, the Fourth Symphony's movements are American in their exuberant or dejected ambiances, loudly brassy or soft lamenting states, and slow or quick march-propelled progressions toward the victorious conclusion. He throws in waltzes, dance tunes, jazz, marches, and the tread of the Red Army in his treatment of a recurring motto meant to integrate the entire work.

As usual the subdivisions stand in strong contrast to each other. They are laid out in a mosaic design. When one idea ends, another begins without pause. Smooth transitions are nil. In his attempt at intensified expression, Antheil comes close to biting off more than he can chew. Somehow, he manages to achieve his purpose. After he worked on the symphony throughout 1942 and 1943, he completed it early in 1944. He gave it to Leopold Stokowski, who presented its premiere on 13 February 1944. Contemporary listeners, hungry for fine tunes, bracing rhythms, and heightened emotional experience, embraced the work completely. At last, Antheil could bask in the praise of audiences and feel reinstated into the ranks of his peers.

An abrupt declarative passage by the unison brasses, echoed and extended by the strings, marks the first appearance of the dramatic and hard-to-forget motto, which will recur throughout the work. This opening to the first movement (*Moderato*) suddenly becomes soft, and a march begins with the tune in the woodwinds and then the strings. The march grows broader, pushed along by basses and snare drums. The rhythm is given a derisive stride that rams the melodic fragments forward. At the end a dissonant climax in the full orchestra is achieved. The motto rings out once again over a timpani roll, and this time it initiates a freely managed recapitulation of the opening. The music grows loud and ominous. After a while, the sound melts away into a hushed but uneasy conclusion.

A melody that might be mistaken for something written by a Russian begins the second movement (*Andante*). At the same time, it harks back to the opening of the previous movement. The structure of this movement appears to be a set of fantasy-variations on the motto theme. The mood is tragic; the motion, in general, is that of a funereal procession. However, a variety of tempos occur. Strings first intone the tune. Second, a soft re-statement of the melody dispenses with the slow-march pulse altogether. The slow-march then returns, only this time over a persistent bass figure in the background—one detects a kinship to Sibelius. A tender middle section briefly replaces the impression of a tragic procession with more personal measures of aching lament. This also derives from the motto theme. A militant blast of the motto bursts forth to interrupt the lament. The tragic mood of the movement's beginning is reinstated, with the ini-tial theme occurring above a constantly repeating bass figure. A piccolo makes a brief, quiet allusion to the motto and the movement fades into silence.

A jarring and wrathful scherzo fills out the third movement. Not un-like the sort of scherzo that Shostakovich liked to write, it looses a fast march. After the brasses bellow out an acerbic salute, the music scurries along in brittle fashion. Every attempt at a legato episode is pounced on and obliterated. Before long a new start is made, with the motto treated fugally. A quiet, fleeting, lyrical version of the motto follows. Antheil soon puts an end to it and substitutes a distorted, dance-like passage, which en-larges into a singular, eccentric, and moderately paced march. This con-cludes this division of the work.

Immense alterations in tempo and modifications of mood create an exciting jumble of motifs, bits of melody, and instrumental colorations in the final movement. It starts raucously in the brasses and percussion. Severe march fragments are put side by side with exultant full-orchestral shouts. The tempo fails to stabilize for a while. Again the motto from the opening movement returns, now heard in all the instruments. The music turns stately; the tempo settles into a moderate gait. The symphony con-cludes in grand, triumphant fashion. The addition of piano, xylophone, and woodblock shape the ending and give a unique conclusion to this mostly militant music. Without question the Fourth Symphony, *1942*, is an imaginative piece expressing the individual stance of a greatly stirred, emotionally excited artist.

Critics raved about the symphony after they had attended its premiere. The composition was heard in city after city. When Virgil Thomson reviewed it in the New York *Herald Tribune,* he wrote, "The Symphony is about the most complete musical picture of an American success that has ever been made. There is everything in it—military band music, waltzes, sentimental ditties, a Red Army song, a fugue, eccentric dancing. . . . It is bright, hard, noisy, busy, bumptious, efficient and incredibly real. It is 'Columbia the Gem of the Ocean' orchestrated in red, white, and blue. . . . And its tunes can all be remembered."[15]

Despite his artistic success, Antheil continued to have financial problems, though not as acutely as before. He had to maintain his connection to Hollywood in order to earn his living. At the same time, he went on to write two more symphonies: the Symphony No. 5, *Joyous,* and the Symphony No. 6, *After Delacroix.* The Delacroix painting *Liberty Leading the People* inspired the latter work. The symphonies received their first performances on 21 December 1948 and 10 February 1949, respectively. Both are admirable works. They are American to the hilt, bristling with solid tunes and containing many striking passages. The Symphony No. 5 holds together far better than its immediate predecessor. What flaws there are stem from Antheil's awkwardness in developing ideas and his persistence in stretching out movements by means of block after block of sound that remain fixed in nature and that fail to enlarge any of his ideas. His Symphony No. 6 contains a first movement that throws forth an intense wartime image plus a suggestion of "The Battle Cry of Freedom." A welcome *Larghetto* comes next, and the finale transforms the mood with the cheery, often cheeky, sound of syncopated popular music. One should keep in mind that although inspired by Delacroix's painting, Antheil goes his own way with his music.

Concerning all of his symphonies, confusion persists about what he wrote and when he wrote it. He also went on, after the Fourth Symphony, to compose two ballets, four operas, two serenades, a suite, and miscellaneous orchestral works of modest length. George Antheil died in 1959.

THE AESTHETIC SYMPHONY: DIAMOND

The term "aesthetic" applies to the symphonies of David Diamond because these compositions came from an artist with a discriminating and cultivated palate and an appreciation of the sensuosity in sound. Admittedly, this aesthetic claim could be made for other composers. However, what strikes me the most is that in Diamond's music especially I come into contact with what seems an abstract expressiveness, a design that draws the listener toward the music as an end rather than a means. Whatever the emotional reaction, it seems to derive from a perception of the Diamond composition as a thing in itself.

He was concerned with balancing pure feeling with intellectuality. The emergence of feeling resulted from a developed sense of what was musically fitting. It found outlet in his employment of established genres such as the symphony. He meant the contents of his symphonic structures to transcend ordinary experience in their expression, whatever the immediate circumstances that caused a work's creation. His careful attention to the relevance of the musical portions of a movement to the overall design was quite acute. Leonard Bernstein echoed the opinion of several commentators when he wrote that he considered Diamond's music to be a restatement of "the most lasting aesthetic values."[16]

Diamond believed in retaining, not rejecting, the substantial stylistic contributions of previous periods. Composers, he said, should build on them, not put them to one side. To do otherwise, he believed, was not prudent. The *Music Journal*, in 1964, quoted him as saying, "Technical proficiency or skill in composition can never replace imagination or fantasy, yet imagination run rampant can destroy musical values. . . . A composer's greatness is gauged by how he enlarges and extends spiritual communication between himself and humanity." He believed in emotive, "romantic inspired contemporary music, moderated by reinvigorated classical technical formulas."[17]

David Diamond was born in Rochester, New York, in 1915, started music study at the Cleveland Institute of Music, and went on to enroll at the Eastman School of Music, where Howard Hanson was the head and Bernard Rogers was his composition teacher. Unsatisfied with the conservative stance of his two teachers, he departed for New York City, where he became a student of Paul Boepple. However, Diamond soon made up his mind that Boepple was conservative, too. He also studied with Roger Sessions, who, he discovered, was decidedly more adventurous.

In New York, poverty was Diamond's lot. He worked as an odd-job laborer to keep himself afloat. In 1936, funds from a patron, Cary Ross, enabled him to go to Paris, where he met the composers Maurice Ravel, Darius Milhaud, and Albert Roussel, and the conductor Charles Munch. He found himself drawn to the French approach to composition. Ravel, especially, was his ideal. (Soon after Ravel's death in 1937, Diamond composed an *Elegy* in his memory. The first version, for brasses, percussion, and harps, he would later arrange for strings and percussion.)

The following year he studied theory and composition with Nadia Boulanger and met and fell under the influence of Igor Stravinsky. During 1936–37, he completed his first major productions: the Concerto for String Quartet, Violin Concerto No. 1, and *Psalm for Orchestra*. The *Psalm* had first been shown to Stravinsky, who had suggested revisions in the score. Diamond was in Paris on a Guggenheim Fellowship when World War II broke out and forced his return to the United States for the duration.

His Symphony No. 1 was written in 1940–41 during a stay at the Yaddo art colony, a community inhabited by artists and located on a 400-acre estate in Saratoga Springs, New York. The symphony was premiered by Dmitri Mitropoulos and the New York Philharmonic in 1941. On the whole, it turned out well for a first essay into the form, although it also exhibited some of the limitations that went with an early attempt. About twenty-two minutes long, it was scored for the large orchestra usual for this time: woodwinds by threes, eleven brasses, timpani and percussion, and strings. Diamond had written two previous symphonies, fledgling student works, whose immaturities were so obvious that he suppressed them. Of the First Symphony, Diamond said, "I worked hard to get that opening motto. But I am very proud of the cyclical relationships among all three movements, based on that B, D, E. The second movement begins with a G minor version; the last movement, of course, is the fulfillment of the very opening first movement's motto. So it is a very tight piece indeed."[18]

This three-movement symphony fits together fairly closely. Diamond organized and realized all of its ideas with some success. The music sounds modal and, for much of its length, blustery. The motto that dominates the symphony reaches our ears repeatedly in stormy and often noisy gusts. Yet the expression remains amorphous. It is really neither dramatic, nor angry, nor in the grip of an overpowering feeling. One keeps on wishing the thematic material was stronger and more distinctive. Hardly ever does Diamond venture to sacrifice internal order and balance in favor of openly emotional writing. In all movements he opts for simple, strongly contoured subject matter. Youthful vigor and spirited delivery come through. Striking ideas are in short supply. Diamond is still in the process of coming out from under the cover of Stravinskian neoclassicism.

I suspect that the finding of his own voice so preoccupied him that he allowed little else to intrude. Yes, the world was in turmoil, but he appears more concerned with an inner tussle to build himself a solid creative base.

The first movement, an *Allegro moderato con energica* in sonata-allegro form, builds upon the ascending three-note motif mentioned above, which is introduced in a vigorous opening. It conducts us to the presentation of the main subject, divided between the oboe and violins. The subject receives generous treatment and is heard together with the three-note motif. The effect is more rhythmic than lyric and in the vein of the Copland ballets, only somewhat more dissonant. The secondary subject begins in angular fashion and goes on to a development featuring, for a change, a sustained lyricism mostly in the strings. The opening material returns but is treated somewhat more freely. The rhythmic propulsion has increased, and it increases even more in the coda, which is based on the opening motif.

The second movement, *Andante maestoso*, transforms the motto and incorporates it into a well-balanced and completely realized melody. The song-like tune treads in regal steps from beginning to end, its volume swelling and subsiding several times. No real break in the forward movement takes place. No contrasting section materializes. The expression does intensify here and there, but no genuine climax is reached.

The final movement, *Maestoso-Adagio-Allegro,* starts with the motif, stated by the brass. Suddenly the pace picks up. Brief staccato melodic-rhythmic fragments based on the motif are tossed around. Thrice, quietly singing interludes intervene, but they are short-lived. A thunderous peroration concludes the symphony. The composer has demonstrated the proper credentials to be taken seriously as an artist to be noticed. The music proves proficient and likable.

Meanwhile Diamond made a bare living on money from awards and prizes. When these ran out, he was pushed again into abject poverty and the need to work at any menial job he could find that would allow him some freedom to compose music. From 1943 to 1945, he would play violin in radio's *Hit Parade* orchestra. He would associate living in the United States with hardship and the denial of free time to be creative. Owing to his outspoken tendencies and opinionated remarks, he would also put people off who might otherwise have aided him.

The earliest sketches for the Symphony No. 2 were made at the beginning of 1942. He completed the symphony in February 1943. Serge Koussevitzky and the Boston Symphony Orchestra gave it a first performance on 13 October 1944.

With this symphony, Diamond reaches a point where he functions competently and consistently. As an artist, he is comfortable with himself. He can give his music substantial expressive content. The talent exhibited in this composition is exceptional. Like Copland he not only proves his music can be emotionally moving but also reveals an accurate ear for the poetic gesture that captures an American ambiance. While composing, Diamond occupied himself with as effective a sculpting of his subordinate, as of his primary, subject matter. The work indicates a sharpened understanding of his craft, far more advanced than might be expected in a relative newcomer to the symphony. The promise in the First Symphony now reaches fulfillment in the Second Symphony. Here, one finds unforced counterpoint, deeply perceived lyricism, lucid organization, and outstanding technical skill. The scoring is for full symphony orchestra: woodwinds by threes, eleven brasses, timpani and percussion, and strings.

He had no program in mind, although he said that his symphony saw light during a time of great nervous strain owing to the world conflict. He acknowledged that a composer's feelings and awareness of what was happening in the world had a hand in the end result. However, he said, "It was always the [musical] material that remained foremostly important to me in my working stages."[19] All the same, the gloomy, pessimistic ruminations in the first and third movements, the fierce agitation of the second movement, and the optimistic American assertiveness of the finale would seem to have a connection with contemporary world events.

In fact, Diamond admitted that when he was composing the symphony, he was emotionally upset by the war and considered what he wrote to be his "war symphony."

When the Second Symphony was first heard, some critics complained about its length (forty-three minutes). More positive comments were made about its high-flying violin melodies, rich harmonies, use of open sonorities (owing to plentiful fourths and fifths in chord structures), and vital bass lines. They said the audience reacted sympathetically and was especially gratified by the music's accessibility. Diamond was summoned to the stage three times.

One commentator, Charles Mills, found the symphony "well scored and broadly colored" when he heard it. Furthermore, the work was "surprisingly effective despite its four imposing movements comparable to Shostakovich in dimension even in certain orchestral attitudes and protracted gestures. Fortunately, it has the continuity needed to sustain such large structural outlines if they are to be other than pretentious. This is the first Diamond score, in my opinion, which has been as gratifying in content as in style and manner. There is conclusive evidence of a genuine and deeply felt lyric expression, essentially religious in spirit."[20]

The first movement, *Adagio funebre,* lets loose a resonant fourteen minutes of plaintive singing. (By 1943, many composers had felt it incumbent upon them to include a mournful movement in their symphonies.) It starts solemnly with an introduction in the violas and cellos. This is followed by a slow-treading subject that could be designed to accompany an ancient processional. Initially, the violins present a solemn melody of great length as the subject, against a recurring melodic fragment in the cellos and basses. Occasionally, the full orchestra joins the violins. Twice, the brasses dominate the measures loudly and shrilly, but not for long. A second subject enters, an especially expressive tune for solo oboe accompanied by viola trills. After some developmental treatment of ideas from the introduction and two subjects, the recapitulation begins. If anything, the orchestra becomes more ardent and louder in its lamentation, mounting to special intensity when very high violins take over. Instead of the oboe, the English horn delivers a restatement of the expressive second-subject tune. The ending is quiet and puzzlingly cryptic.

The second movement, *Allegro vivo,* is a scherzo in effect. It opens with a thunderous bang from the timpani. Its primary thematic element is a scrap of a rhythmic phrase derisively thrown around between cellos and basses and one bassoon. This melodic crumb, which governs the rest of the movement, is taken from the secondary material in the first movement. Impudent brass barks and hammering timpani pierce through the fabric on several occasions. No real trio appears. The most important contrasting material is the portion allotted to the brass in octaves backed by timpani, and later to the strings in unison, also backed by timpani. Curiously the ending is again quiet, as if suddenly the orchestra had run out of breath.

The third movement, *Andante espressivo, quasi Adagio,* is almost fourteen and a half minutes long and is the most emotionally candid portion of the symphony. It strikes the listener as an extension of the first movement. From this point of view, the second movement takes the shape of a five-and-a-half-minute interlude that provides diversion and prepares the way for this *Andante*'s great show of feeling. In fact, all of its themes are derived from the first movement. It starts off with a reference to the introduction of the symphony's opening movement. Then a broad lyrical melody spreads out over many measures. It may be plaintive, warm, loving, or reflective in turn—but constantly and explicitly emotional. At three important dividing points we hear, first, mournful violins singing a somber high-pitched tune without any accompaniment; second, a lonely solo flute vocalizing by itself, thus emulating the violins; and third, a solo trumpet doing the same. The main melody is metamorphosed as it spins itself out, growing more intense and reaching a major but brief climax about eleven minutes along the way. Sometimes the music is fugal, sometimes chorale-like, and sometimes a wailing cry. Certainly the main weight of the symphony is lodged in this and the first movement. Both are threnodies over the tragedy that man inflicts on man.

The finale, *Allegro vigoroso,* is eight minutes long and starts off like a spirited American dance—fast, loud, and syncopated. One might describe it as a lively old-time barn dance. The dance marks time now and again in order to allow calmer melodies to intervene. The first intervention is an attractive episode featuring a folk-like tune. Its kin is found on the pages of the Copland "Western" ballets. Perhaps it is the pentatonic shape of the melody that produces the similarity. In truth, tunes based on the pentatonic scale happen with some frequency in this finale. A later episode is given over to pizzicato strings. By the end of the movement, a loosely woven rondo has revealed itself as the design.

All in all, hearing the Second Symphony is three-quarters of an hour well spent. The Romantic spirit is clearly detectible in the composition, in its directness, personal commitment, eloquence, and ties to a tonal system. This traditional directness is offset by the complexity of a more modern approach. We hear intricacies involving more adventurous harmonies, rhythms, and use of other up-to-date resources. The music is a moving exposition of the sorts of anxieties and conflicting emotions besetting men and women of the time.

Between the Second Symphony and his next symphonic ventures, Diamond composed one of his most well-liked compositions, the *Rounds for String Orchestra*. Dmitri Mitropoulos had commissioned it with the appeal, "These are distressing times. Most of the music I play is distressing. Make me happy." The public first heard it played by Mitropoulos and the Minneapolis Symphony on 24 November 1944, and it quickly won a wide following. Its melodiousness and cheerful character were found engaging. It won the New York Critics Circle Award. After some months, the composer was wearied by the popularity of *Rounds,* believing his other serious compositions were being ignored because of it. One other composition would catch the public's fancy, the *Orchestral Suite for Romeo and Juliet,* composed in 1947.

Diamond worked almost simultaneously on his Third and Fourth symphonies. Both date from 1945. The Third Symphony, dedicated to his parents, waited until 3 November 1950 for its first performance, which was given by Charles Munch and the Boston Symphony Orchestra. It is scored for the customary full orchestra with plenty of percussion. A cyclic structure is realized by employing similar subject matter in all four movements.

Like the Second Symphony, the Third is tonal and employs romantic speech. In it, one comes upon fine melodies and smart rhythms. Diamond's orchestration, as usual, demonstrates the expertise of the composer. The harmonic language continues to be resourceful and, at the same time, easy to assimilate. The first movement, a lengthy *Allegro deciso,* follows tradition by resorting to sonata form and engaging in a thorough development of the main thematic ideas. The *Andante* that comes next is so delicately orchestrated that in many measures it sounds suited for performance in a room rather than a large concert hall. Especially effective is the section with three unison flutes accompanied by harp and piano, which paradoxically has both a medieval and a contemporary feel to it. It is the most elegant division of the symphony. Without pause, the music goes on to the third movement, *Allegro vivo,* which rushes along in the strings assisted by woodwinds and a rhythmic figure in the snare drum. The last movement, *Adagio assai,* sings an elegiac ballad, and has a fine interlude where the oboe and clarinet come forward. The finale is more pensive than gloomy.

The Third Symphony was originally in five movements. After the premiere, Diamond did away with the concluding *Allegro,* thus opting to give the ending a sense of incompleteness. Lovely as the final movement is, the music is left up in the air. The listener is left in an unsettled state of mind.

The Koussevitzky Foundation commissioned the Fourth Symphony, which is dedicated "to the memory of Natalie Koussevitzky—*Magni Nominis Umbra* [the shade of a great name]." The Foundation presented him with $500 and paid for copying the parts, but otherwise Diamond found money in short supply. Because Koussevitzky felt unwell, his protégé, Leonard Bernstein, gave the premiere with the Boston Symphony Orchestra, on 23 January 1948. The scoring was for a huge orchestra: woodwinds by fours, fourteen brasses, a large percussion group, two harps, piano, and strings. Later, on the recommendation of Erich Leinsdorf, Diamond issued a reduced version of the scoring, with woodwinds by threes and twelve brasses. Diamond has said that thoughts of mortality dominated his mind as he wrote the symphony: "The entire symphony was created with the idea of life and death, Fechner's theories of life and death as, I—a continual sleep, II—the alternation between sleeping and waking, and III—eternal waking. Birth being the passing from I to II, and Death, the transition from II to III. More than this I cannot interpret for the listener. The rest he must ask of himself."[21] Be that as it may, Diamond later disavowed any programmatic underpinning to the work. He also denied that it contained anything specifically American, since he saw himself as an international composer, not as an "arranger of folk tunes." However, he does admit to an American "feeling" in the final movement.

Koussevitzky had requested a compact composition; therefore this work, in three movements, is only about seventeen minutes long. Within this time frame, the music penetrates deeply into the realm of feeling. Movement I is an *Allegretto;* II, *Adagio—Andante;* and III, *Allegro.* The movements last five and a half minutes, a little over six minutes, and six and a half minutes, respectively. Originally, Diamond had intended to start the symphony with a prelude, followed by a fugue. He abandoned this idea, but would use some music from the abandoned fugue in the second movement. The music has the fervor of the young at heart and, despite the conciseness, gives an impression of unhurried motion. "The undercurrent is grave but the vitality and freshness of ideas are compelling," writes Howard Taubman in the *New York Times,* 10 January 1958, after a performance given in New York City. Its diatonicisms, adherence to tonality, attractive modal hues, and enticing melodies helped send the symphony from city to city and created a demand for its constant performance.

The *Allegretto* movement, given a firm sonata form, contains a bucolic first subject, heard in muted and unmuted strings, and a cheerful second subject played by the oboe and then the violins. A long development of both these subjects eventually culminates in a protracted climax that combines both ideas. A recapitulation of the first subject and a coda based on the second subject complete the movement.

The second movement starts with a slow, dignified brass chorale (*Adagio*) that proceeds to a long lyrical melody in the violas (*Andante*). A new idea, stated by clarinets followed by violins, is worked out carefully until a climax is reached. The chorale returns (in the clarinets and then the trumpets), as does the first subject, now given to the violins with background figurations in harp and piano.

The last movement, an *Allegro* in a rondo format, is high-spirited and at times strikes the ear as a contrapuntal scherzo, alongside its rondo features. Brasses vociferously announce the theme. When they are almost through, a rhythmic figure in the percussion intrudes, as it will continue to do during the movement. The episodes, which supply breathing space, are chorale-like and therefore stand in stark contrast to the main theme. The finale sounded "American" to some critics. Indeed, Copland had mentioned that many of Diamond's fast movements tended to give this impression. However, Diamond insists that, although he loves American folk songs and dances, he never has thought of quoting one.

After the war, Diamond fled America to take up residence in Italy. A Fulbright professorship at the University of Rome and, afterward, a stay in Florence kept him abroad until 1965. His compositions grew more and more chromatic, even impressing some listeners as being atonal. Yet tonal centers were not entirely abandoned, and recognizable melodies were normally present for audiences to discover. The reinstated American avant-garde of the postwar years, whether of twelve-tone or aleatory persuasion, tried to ostracize him. He refused to buckle under, saying that one had to write honest music that might be loved and that there was no point in composers writing only for each other. (Just before he died, in 2005, he said that he had always believed in strong melodies, clear rhythmic articulation, and some degree of consonance.)

During the fifties, he would receive few commissions for new works and performances of his music would become negligible. However, when he returned to the United States, he found that he had won some esteem in important New York music circles. In order to celebrate Diamond's fiftieth birthday, an enthusiastic Leonard Bernstein and the New York Philharmonic performed his Fifth Symphony. Bernstein had nothing but praise for Diamond's symphonies, calling them serious, weighty, intelligently thought out, and skillfully executed.

Unfortunately for Diamond, the sixties and seventies left his orchestral music unnoticed. The up-and-coming conductors, in particular, did not schedule his compositions. At last, in the eighties and nineties, the tide changed; tonal systems and more traditional practices were again in favor. He was rediscovered.

Meanwhile, he had to make a living. Diamond found work as an instructor at the Manhattan School of Music from 1965 to 1967. Later, in 1973, he began teaching at the Juilliard School of Music; he continued at the school until 1997. By the time of his death on 13 July 2005, Diamond had completed eleven symphonies, a formidable number for the postwar period. He was also the composer of ballets, concertos, chamber music (including ten string quartets), one opera, piano compositions, and numerous songs and choral pieces. None of the symphonic works surpassed the Second and Fourth Symphonies, both finished in the war years. Even so, all are worth knowing. Diamond is a composer in whom Americans can take pride.

THE DRAMATIC SYMPHONY: BERNSTEIN

Leonard Bernstein admired Diamond's symphonies, but his own symphonies would not emulate them. For one, Bernstein was first and foremost an orchestra director and was wrapped up in the contrasting and conflicting give-and-take of instrumental sections and individual soloists that constituted much of the symphonic rhetoric. He conducted as if mesmerized by the churning emotions that the music, from Beethoven through Mahler, called forth. Another side of him was his writing musicals for the Broadway stage. He loved it when *On the Town* and *West Side Story* won him popular acclaim. He often had to work in haste, because conducting duties and various public appearances allowed little time for composing. By temperament, he was sympathetic to the outsize gesture and the assertion of personality. He wrote message-symphonies, not abstract ones, meant to communicate non-musical thoughts. As an artist, he could not help but be different from Diamond.

The term "dramatic" points to theater. It indicates conflict made vivid through a variety of striking effects and activities meant to intensify a work's expressive power. In the foreword to Symphony No. 2, *The Age of Anxiety,* Bernstein wrote: "I have a deep suspicion that every work I write, for whatever medium, is really theater music in some way." In a few works he makes it plain that his music is linked to drama and theater. For example, his 1971 composition *Mass* (a blend of the traditional Catholic ritual and non-traditional annotations and questionings) is a "Theatre Piece for Singers, Players and Dancers," not a mass per se. His musical passages are set down with an ear for dramatic effectiveness, whether in the depiction of character or in the interplay or conflict of ideas.

Copland spoke of the immediate emotional appeal of Bernstein's music and the warmth that speaks directly to the audience. At its best, Copland wrote in 1949, Bernstein's music contains "vibrant rhythmic invention of irresistible élan, often carrying with it a terrific dramatic punch."[22] In his Symphony No. 1, *Jeremiah,* as in his other two symphonies, Bernstein composes music in which the drama is generated by a seeker in search of elusive faith. The musical depiction of the search is analogous to theater in that it can be interpreted as a series of dramatic scenes.

Bernstein's father, Samuel, was a rabbi's son and had some familiarity with Talmudic studies and a respect for Jewish tradition. He came to America from Russia at the age of sixteen, started working at menial jobs, and gradually made his way up the business ladder to become a well-off businessman. By age thirty, he was a top salesman in the barber-and-beauty-supplies trade and worked in the Boston area. Samuel Bernstein's son, Leonard, would owe a lasting debt to grandfather and father. His grandfather's membership in the rabbinate, his father's grounding in Jewish law and tradition, and the drive that pushed his parent from lowly fish-cleaner to successful entrepreneur were all reflected in Leonard Bernstein's personality during every decade of his life.

In his adulthood, Leonard was proud of his Jewish background, a strong supporter of the state of Israel, and a composer whose compositions often gave notice of his Jewish orientation. As for the father's drive, it was manifested in the son's endless energy and uninhibited behavior. Leonard Bernstein ventured into a bewildering variety of activities. His huge ego was all-embracing. He composed, conducted, entertained, taught young and old, and performed admirably on the piano. He wrote books and articles. He backed liberal and humanitarian causes. Most people found him irresistible. Some, he infuriated. Because he worshipped music, Bernstein believed that everyone should be made to love it.

He was born in Lawrence, Massachusetts, on 25 August 1918, and raised in the Greater Boston area. While young he took up piano study and in adolescence already showed his affection for the theater, especially musicals—even producing his own versions of *The Mikado* and *Carmen.* He attended the academically rigorous Boston Latin School. From there he went to Harvard College and studied music theory, composition, and orchestration under Walter Piston, Tillman Merritt, and Edward Burlingame Hill. His piano teachers were Helen Coates (later his secretary) and the highly regarded Heinrich Gebhard. At Harvard, he quickly won the admiration of students and faculty for his piano-playing ability.

He attended a Boston Symphony performance conducted by Dmitri Mitropoulos when he was nineteen years old. The music and conductor bowled him over. That experience and a subsequent invitation to spend some time with the conductor caused the young Bernstein to pursue training as an orchestra conductor. He attended the Curtis Institute in Philadelphia, where Randall Thompson was his teacher in music composition, and Fritz Reiner, in conducting. Later he worked with Serge Koussevitzky at the Berkshire Music Institute at Tanglewood.

Koussevitzky, Gershwin, and Copland would be important influences on Bernstein's music career. Serge Koussevitzky promoted him to his leading student conductor and prepared him to be his successor.[23] Aaron Copland took Bernstein under his care and helped set the younger man's feet on the road to success as a composer. Bernstein reciprocated by absorbing Copland's musical style and, after winning prominence as an orchestral conductor, promoting his compositions. George Gershwin gave him the courage to enter both the popular and the artistic areas of the music world. Bernstein studied popular music, jazz, blues, and Broadway musicals and incorporated their lessons into his future music-making. He became equally adept at writing works for the Broadway theater and the symphony stage.

After he finished his study with Koussevitzky, he floundered about for a conducting position and at last, through the offices of Koussevitzky, was appointed assistant conductor to the New York Philharmonic. A stroke of fortune occurred in November 1943. He stepped in to conduct when Bruno Walter, the regular conductor, became ill, and Arthur Rodzinski could not substitute. The occasion was a subscription concert that was also to be broadcast over national radio. Instead of just going through the motions, Bernstein offered an original and exciting interpretation of a difficult program: Schumann's *Manfred Overture,* Rosza's *Theme, Variations and Finale,* Strauss's *Don Quixote,* and Wagner's *Meistersinger Overture.* Audience, critics, orchestra players, and radio listeners reacted enthusiastically.

From then on his progress in music was steadily upward. His services as a conductor and pianist were frequently called upon. He would guest-conduct throughout Europe, including at Milan's La Scala—the first American to do so. In 1958, he would make his debut as the principal conductor of the New York Philharmonic, a position he would hold until 1969. He won praise for his advocacy of twentieth-century music, especially that of Americans including Barber, Harris, Schuman, and Copland.

Bernstein would also make a name for himself in the popular sphere with compositions including *Candide* and *West Side Story,* the score for *On the Waterfront,* and the ballet *Fancy Free.* The original 1957 Broadway production of *West Side Story* ran for close to 750 performances, and then went on tour. It was later made into a hit movie. These works reveal him to be knowledgeable about ragtime, jazz, blues, dance-rhythms, and every variety of popular song.

As an educator, he was most famous for his ability to reach a mass television audience with the *Omnibus* show, beginning 14 November 1954. Then came his award-winning *Young People's Concerts with the New York Philharmonic* in January 1958. No condescension marred his communication with an audience of millions. Men and women, boys and girls, were won over by his enthusiasm, explanations, and live-music illustrations. He taught them to recognize the worth of classical music. Not least was his proselytizing for music through his writing, especially *The Joys of Music* (1959) and *The Infinite Variety of Music* (1966). He would also take on teaching stints at Brandeis University and Tanglewood.

The first ventures into classical composition comprise the Piano Trio of 1937, Piano Sonata (1938), incidental music to Aristophanes' *The Birds* (1939), Violin Sonata (1940), and Clarinet Sonata (1941–42). Only the last was ever published. The Bernstein style that would emerge in his classical music was much beholden to Copland, Stravinsky, and Gershwin. Other composers would also have some impact on him, not least being Gustav Mahler, Paul Hindemith, and Dmitri Shostakovich. His eclectic style was usually a synthesis of classical, jazz, popular, and Latin American influences. His effervescent temperament directed the music in a potent theatrical direction and also gave it a forceful slant. There was also the body of Jewish music that he had inherited from his family and that he loved throughout his life.

Most of his compositions contain muscular cross-rhythms, syncopations, and, oftentimes, asymmetric meters. His melodies, which often veer toward Broadway, can appear to be angular in score but are usually constructed for ready assimilation. Long movements may start off with a brief basic motif or a defining intervallic design, which undergoes expansion throughout the movement or entire composition. He was a steadfast champion of tonal music, yet was awake to serial techniques. Twelve-tone themes would appear in one or two works, but usually within tonal contexts. Interestingly, he rarely conducted the works of the atonal or twelve-tone composers. Nor would he find sympathy for the postwar experiments in musical indeterminacy.

He himself was busy trying to go in several directions at once. As a result, he composed everything under pressure-cooker conditions. Now and then, the results of his creativity were a little too facile. Despite this, Bernstein was a musician of bottomless energy who operated most competently when big and competing demands were made on his time and attention.

Bernstein conceived the Symphony No. 1, *Jeremiah,* while he was still struggling for recognition and apparently getting nowhere. The years 1942 and 1943 found him living in one room in New York City and trying to make ends meet by giving music lessons, playing piano occasionally for ballet classes, and making arrangements and transcriptions from jazz recordings for a popular-music publisher. He heard about a music-composition contest sponsored by the New England Conservatory and hastened to compose and submit his First Symphony. He had already written a version of a *Lamentation,* for soprano and orchestra, in the summer of 1939, and had shelved it for two years. He needed only to revise it to serve as the last movement of the symphony. Finished at the last minute (31 December 1942), the completed score was taken to Boston and hand-delivered by the composer. He failed to win the prize.

Then the breakthrough in his career came with his November 1943 crash appearance with the New York Philharmonic. His conducting triumph on that occasion smoothed the way for the First Symphony's first performance. At last, the premiere of the symphony took place on 28 January 1944, with the composer conducting the Pittsburgh Symphony Orchestra, and Jennie Tourel as soloist. It was followed by performances by the Boston Symphony and the New York Philharmonic. The New York Music Critics Circle voted Symphony No. 1, *Jeremiah,* the outstanding new classical work of the season, and the NBC Symphony Orchestra broadcast it nationwide via seventy radio stations.

The war was much on his mind when he composed the music. As

background to the First Symphony, Bernstein cites his identification with Europe's Jews and their persecution under the Nazis. The composition grew out of his emotional reaction to the war, the stimulus of his Jewish heritage, the Hebrew passages he studied as a child, and the cantillations he had heard at Boston's Temple Mishkan Tefila.[24] The symphony would take on a special meaning for the Jewish people as the war went on and details about the Jewish holocaust emerged.

The score calls for twelve woodwinds, eleven brasses, timpani and percussion, piano, strings, and mezzo-soprano solo. The three movements are I. "Prophecy," *Largamente;* II. "Profanation," *Vivace con brio;* III. "Lamentation," *Lento.* The music tends toward the rhapsodic. It can be loosely knit, prolix, ebullient, or ecstatic. The orchestration is brilliant. The movements contain numerous subtleties and unanticipated twists and turns. The composition captured the fancy of classical music audiences from the first year it was performed. Certainly one of Bernstein's most deeply felt works, the symphony is free of grandstanding and communicates straightaway with the music public. The composer said that he never intended to follow any story literally but wanted to capture feeling—the feeling attending the "crisis of faith." About the Symphony No. 1, the composer commented further, "I have been writing all my life about the struggle that is born of the crisis of our century, a crisis of faith. . . . The faith or peace that is found at the end of Jeremiah is really more a kind of comfort, not a solution."[25]

The first movement, like the two movements that follow, was designed for its emotional impact. The object is to provide the equivalent in music of the intensity in the prophet's appeals to his people. Bernstein's realization is imaginative, deftly orchestrated, and ecstatic in tone. The main musical thought, announced initially in the horns, is from the Jewish liturgical service—the traditional *Amen* heard during Passover and a cadence employed in High Holy Days. The initial ideas direct the development of the entire movement. The meter is irregular. Strings predominate, but crude brass sounds push through on several occasions. Moments of tranquility mask the agitation concealed underneath.

The second movement depicts the devastation and anarchy that result from paganism and its corrupting influence. Yahweh, the one and only God, and His precepts are abandoned as people take uninhibited pleasure in sensual gratification and material possessions. The music employs a dramatic, almost cinematic range of expression, which comes through by means of a constantly uneven pulse and belligerent, discordant sounds. Bernstein's sense of upheaval and his overflow of feeling is successfully conveyed. An Ashkenazic cantillation opens this movement, followed by measures that make the most of wild dance rhythms. This is a "scherzo" immersed in blasphemy. An intense climax arrives when horns offensively blast forth the "Prophecy" theme during the height of orgiastic turbulence.

The last movement expresses the grief of Jeremiah as he weeps for his much-loved and devastated Jerusalem. We hear his cry of lamentation over his beloved city, now ruined and defiled, despite his frantic effort to rescue it. Once more, Ashkenazic cantillation is introduced, and, in a while, the "Prophecy" music returns. The cantillation is based on a sequence of motifs derived from the dirges chanted on The Ninth Day of Ab, the holiday of mourning for the lost Temple. It is actually the traditional melody used to intone the Book of Lamentations on the eve of *Tisha B'Av*, the fast commemorating the destruction of the Temple.[26]

The "Lamentation" begins:

> How doth the city sit solitary,
> That was full of people! . . .
> She weepeth sore in the night
> And her tears are on her cheeks;
> She hath none to comfort her.

and ends:

> Wherefore dost Thou forget us forever,
> And forsake us so long time?
> Turn Thou us into Thee, O Lord,
> And we shall be turned:
> Renew our days as of old.[27]

The close of the symphony offers some consolation, reasserts faith in God, but presents no way out. The predicament remains unsolved. An amazing accomplishment for one so young, this third-movement "Lamentation" is one of the finest pieces that Bernstein ever wrote.

The symphony's music employs nonfunctional dissonance, bitonality, and inventive rhythms—all with an ear for resonance and what the music public might accept. The dazzling orchestration and the engaging melodies gave tremendous pleasure at the premiere and have continued to please listeners in subsequent performances. In many ways this is the best of his three symphonies. The twenty-five-minute composition exhibits enough intricacy in rhythm, harmony, and melody to place it firmly in the twentieth century. The heartrending subject and the music that makes it real are so potent they bring home the tragedy to the listener. One feels that Bernstein has arrived at a high point of excellence and, through the words of Jeremiah, sings with persuasive force and strong inner belief.

The dual musical personality of the composer comes to the fore when one looks at the works written between his first two symphonies—the ballet *Fancy Free* (1944), the musical *On the Town* (1944), and the "choreographic essay for orchestra" *Facsimile* (1946). The first two are lighthearted pieces, with magical rhythms and winning tunes out of jazz and popular song. *Facsimile* is a different story. It forms a link between the first two symphonies. Written for Jerome Robbins, its subject is the search for meaning in the wake of World War II, when humanity was lost in a spiritual wilderness. However, its music, for all its dramatic moments, boasts vibrant melodies that hint at *West Side Story,* still to be written.

Bernstein's thirty-eight-minute Symphony No. 2, called *The Age of Anxiety* after the poem of W. H. Auden, was scored for orchestra and a prominent piano, and was first performed on 8 April 1949, with the composer conducting the Boston Symphony Orchestra. The music would be revised in 1965. Auden's poem, published in 1947, effectively portrays the flaws in man that make fruitless his quest for the meaning of self. The existential subject is contemporary, as is the music. In the program notes that Bernstein provided for the concert, he states, "I imagine the idea of writing a symphony with piano solo emerges from the extremely personal identification of myself with the poem. In this sense, the pianist provides an almost autobiographical protagonist, [one who] attains an orchestral mirror in which he sees himself, analytical, in the modern ambience. . . . The essential line of the poem (and of the music) is the record of our difficult and problematical search for faith." The work is in due order lonely, peaceful, hysterical, brutal, glitzy, and ultimately a thoughtful spiritual voyage in music.

This symphony is too deliberately planned and, paradoxically, more slackly put together than the *Jeremiah* Symphony. The meticulous musical itemization of a wide-ranging poetic story generates an awkward and discontinuous musical dialogue. The music remains unconvincing to the ear. As with all of Bernstein's works, wonderful moments do materialize. However, the efforts to combine a stripped-down delineation of anxiety with grandiosity close to bombast fail more than they succeed.

Between the Second and Third symphonies came the satirical opera *Trouble in Tahiti,* the musical *Wonderful Town* (1953), the film score to *On the Waterfront* (1954), the comic operetta *Candide* (1956), and the musical *West Side Story* (1957). They point both to the composer's versatility and to the scattering of his attention and energies as he tries "to do it all." Yet, each is an engaging composition. The breezy and satirical *Candide* is at the opposite end of the spectrum from the symphonies. *West Side Story* takes the Shakespearean love tragedy into the world of today—story, music, and all. It was also incredibly popular.

Bernstein's Symphony No. 3, *Kaddish,* was begun in 1961 and finished on 22 November 1963, the day that President Kennedy was assassinated. It was created during a period of acute anxiety over nuclear warfare; its completion coincided with the violent death of a beloved president. Almost forty minutes long, it requires a large orchestra, mixed chorus, boys' choir, speaker, and soprano solo. The premiere, given by Bernstein and the Israel Philharmonic Orchestra, took place in Tel Aviv on 10 December 1963. It would be revised in 1977, at which time Bernstein eliminated some of its overly sensational text.

The Third Symphony, like the *Jeremiah* First Symphony, emanates from a crisis of faith, the composer's own. Also like the earlier symphony, it originates in the Jewish religion and requires the human voice to complete the message. Kaddish is a mourner's prayer recited after the death of a parent or other close relative and on subsequent anniversaries of the death. Here, Bernstein has the speaker choose to recite Kaddish, the speaker's own Kaddish, troubled that no one will remain to say it at the speaker's death. God receives a scolding for not keeping his pledge never to put the world to an end. At the very end comes reconciliation, and the speaker again utters praises of God. The symphony is in three sections. First is the "Invocation" along with Kaddish I.

The symphonies are lengthy, complex, and meant for the serious listener. They do not offer the kind of music that would please an audience whose liking goes to brief pieces that move along crisply. As has been shown, other, simpler Bernstein works address such an audience. What is of significance about these symphonies is that they embody the serious core of his creative persona. Bernstein's Jewish orientation and search for meaning and faith would continue in the *Chichester Psalms* (1965), the *Mass* (1971), and the ballet *The Dybbuk* (1974).

He wrote the symphonies with earnest intent during a period of continuous crisis in the United States. He poured his concerns into them. They tell the audience about what troubled him in the current world, what in Judaism kept him going, and whatever else weighed on his mind when he was not preoccupied with his conducting chores. He created the compositions to reinforce his message by using the considerable talents with which he was blessed. Sometimes the result is music lacking in freshness and effectiveness; much of the time it hits its mark. Whatever the difficulty that comes up in listening to the three symphonies, they are worthy compositions, the Symphony No. 1, *Jeremiah*, especially.

THE MASTERLY SYMPHONY: PISTON

A masterly symphony is one that evidences the thorough knowledge and superior skill of a talented creator who is worthy of note. Such a person was Walter Piston. Born 20 January 1894 in Rockland, Maine, he was acknowledged during his lifetime as the most authoritative musical craftsman alive in the United States, and as a designer of fresh approaches in filling out the classical musical forms. As evidence of this, he has left us orchestral and chamber compositions distinguished by their lucidity, precision, and balance. His was a formidable intellect that retained a profound knowledge of all stylistic periods.[28]

Piston's style rests on a neoclassical base. It shows a respect for classical tradition and structures. His musical compositions are characterized by the assimilation of the controlled expressive elements and formal restraints of the Classic and late Baroque eras into his contemporary manner. Behind this approach is his conclusion that "New ways of musical speech find more ready acceptance when they are understood as new aspects of musical meaning. The radically new has difficulty in finding acceptance because its connection with the common ground of musical meaning is not easily discerned. . . . It is a fact of experience that . . . all music intended to be atonal, that is without key, comes sooner or later to be heard tonally."[29]

His teacher, Nadia Boulanger, and the composer Igor Stravinsky were early influences. When the forties arrived, Piston allowed himself more emotional latitude. His harmonies became less brittle and lost their sharp, hard quality. They became more widely spaced, in a manner similar to that which characterized Copland's "American" style. March-like episodes and long, quiet ruminations occasionally hint at Shostakovich's symphonies.

He was also a master educator at Harvard, where he taught music theory and composition for thirty-four years. Among his students were the well-known composers Elliott Carter, Leroy Anderson, Arthur Berger, Gail Kubik, Irving Fine, Harold Shapiro, Leonard Bernstein, Daniel Pinkham, John Harbison, and Frederic Rzewski. Piston would also write four noteworthy books for music instruction: *Principles of Harmonic Analysis* (1933), *Harmony* (1941, revised edition 1962), *Counterpoint* (1947), and *Orchestration* (1955).

Walter Piston was the grandson of Anthony Piston (an Americanization of Pistone), a sailor from Genoa, Italy, who settled in Rockland, Maine. The Piston family moved, in 1905, from Rockland to Boston, where young Walter would enter the Mechanical Arts High School to train as an engineer. After graduating, he decided engineering held no interest for him, and he enrolled in the Massachusetts Normal Art School in order to study painting and architectural drawing. (Here he met Kathryn Nason, who would become his wife.) At the same time, he had taken sufficient instruction in piano and violin to find some work playing in local dance bands and theater orchestras.

During World War I, he served in the U.S. Navy, playing saxophone in a Navy band. (He had learned to play the saxophone in seven days.) After the war, he decided on going completely into music. He enrolled at Harvard and studied composition with Edward Burlingame Hill, a composer with French stylistic leanings. While at Harvard, he conducted student orchestras and served as a factotum to several of the teachers, winning their good will.

Upon graduation *summa cum laude* from Harvard in 1924, and subsidized with a John Knowles Paine Traveling Fellowship from the college, he traveled to Paris, where Nadia Boulanger and Paul Dukas instructed him in composition. He came to a Paris in the grip of musical neoclassicism—that is to say, the desire to return to rational models in the arts and diminish attempts at emotional expression. The resultant music was leaner, more reserved, more organized, and less heated than had been the case when the extreme emotionalism of Romanticism had prevailed. Piston was provided examples to emulate as diverse as the music of Gabriel Fauré and that of Igor Stravinsky.

His neoclassicism caused him to honor balanced forms and unsentimental musical language. He mastered pre-nineteenth-century techniques and structures. On the other hand, Piston continued to utilize contemporary instrumental practices and advanced harmonic procedures. On his return to America in 1926, he began his long teaching career at Harvard and put his Paris training to creative use. For him, teaching was not a chore. He enjoyed academic life.

Piston's compositions were, from the beginning, tastefully conceived, technically confident, splendidly constructed, and emotionally guarded. They would have a regard for older practices and shun extremes. He wrote instrumental works almost exclusively, casting most of them in the multimovemented classical structures of symphony, concerto, sonata, quartet, and quintet. The movements of his compositions have tonal orientations. He liked to expand upon basic motifs of three or four notes. Yet he was equally fond of writing melodies in long arches, especially in his slow movements. Harmonies can run the gamut from simple triads, to fourth and fifth constructions, and more rarely to complex pileups of tones. His harmonies are not inserted haphazardly or only for the sake of tone color but are meant to act functionally. They proceed logically and contribute to the coherent organization of an entire movement. So also do his rhythms, which sound appropriate however irregular or syncopated they may become. No loudness or softness occurs for its own sake; it always follows a definite reason in his design. When it is needed, he turns to counterpoint, whose technical details are indebted to the procedures of Bach and Handel. However complex the mingling of lines, nothing ever sounds muddy. The texture remains transparent.

The composer's writing for instruments was so idiomatic that players welcomed his scores. Piston accounts for this by saying, "I've always composed music from the point of view of the performers. I love instruments, and I value the cooperation of the players."[30] The instrumentalists he had most in mind were the members of the Boston Symphony Orchestra, with whose capabilities he was thoroughly familiar. As he wrote in the program notes for the premiere of his Symphony No. 6, "I was writing for one designated orchestra, one that I had grown up with and that I knew intimately. Each note set down sounded in the mind with extraordinary clarity, as played immediately by those who were to perform the work."[31] In turn, Koussevitzky and the orchestra would reciprocate by premiering five of his symphonies.

On his return from Paris to the Boston area, Piston met Serge Koussevitzky, recently installed as head of the Boston Symphony Orchestra and already dedicated to advancing the cause of American composers. They began a long friendship, during which Koussevitzky willingly programmed not only the symphonies but a majority of the compositions that Piston wrote for orchestra. Among the first works premiered by the Boston Symphony Orchestra were the Suite No. 1 for Orchestra (1929), the Concerto for Orchestra (1933), and the Symphony No. 1 (1937). Piston conducted the first performance of the symphony with the Boston Symphony Orchestra, on 8 April 1938. Like Johannes Brahms, he joined the ranks of symphony composers at a late age. He was forty-three years old when he felt confident enough to write a symphony. The Symphony No. 1 stands at the end of Piston's early stylistic period.

The First Symphony is an earnest, aspiring, and precisely crafted composition. At the same time, the listener may find its severity of manner unpleasant. The stress on formal relationships seems to exclude warm melodiousness. In this symphony, Piston remains true, for the final time, to his neoclassical tendencies. Unfortunately for the composer, many in his audience may have come away thinking that they had heard the premiere of a composition of slight appeal to them. They had listened to abrupt announcements of the themes, complicated entwinings of different lines, and disagreeable collisions in the harmonies. Some longed for an outpouring of lyricism. This had not happened. It remained buried within him.[32] However, the symphony has a distinctive flavor of its own. One discovers striking vigor, rhythmic strength, and other signs indicating that a first-rate mind is at play.

Like Barber and Hanson, Piston abstains from any conscious attempt at Americanisms. He worried that the self-conscious Americanism practiced by composers such as Harris might lead to a sameness in style that would cancel out any individuality. He insisted that "ours is a big country, and we are a people possessing a multitude of different origins. . . . If a composer desires to serve the cause of American music he will best do it by remaining true to himself as an individual and not by trying to discover musical formulas for Americanism."[33] In the Boston Symphony Orchestra program book for 31 January 1941, the date his Violin Concerto was performed, Piston says an American school of composition "will be built by those men, living in America, knowing it and partaking of it, who are true to themselves. . . . If the composers will increasingly strive to perfect themselves in the art of music and will follow only those paths of expression which seem to them the true way, the matter of a national school will take care of itself."[34] However, every once in a while one hears a fleeting touch of jazz syncopation and American-leaning melody that reminds the listener of Piston's earlier experience as a member of dance and theater bands.

A slow preamble commences the First Symphony and acquaints the audience with the thematic kernels that will inform the entire work. From the orchestra comes a soft sound of timpani, pizzicatos from low strings, and the main motif played by the bassoon. The fast movement that quickly starts up is cast in a concise sonata form, whose ending arrives unexpectedly, with no warning at all. The slow movement, an *Adagio* in A B A form, sings in grave fashion and Spartan plainness, especially through the voice of the English horn. The spirited final movement roams through a set of free variations that are resourcefully and fascinatingly handled. The urgent closing measures complete this painstakingly constructed work with an angst-ridden reassertion of the preamble from the first movement. Curiously, the symphony ends with the more promising sound of a major triad, as if to reassure the audience that things have changed for the better.

As I listen to the unfolding of the movements, I sense a detachment from worldly matters and a neutrality of feeling. One would not know from this symphony that there was another, utterly different side to Piston. This poles-apart aspect came to view a month after the symphony's premier, on 30 May 1938. That evening, music of *The Incredible Flutist* ballet was first performed at a concert of the Boston Pops Orchestra to the wild acclaim of audience and orchestra. *The Incredible Flutist* was written at the request of the Pops conductor Arthur Fiedler for Hans Weiner who, with his dance troupe, was working and appearing with Fielder and the Boston Pops orchestra. (For the most part, Pops is the Boston Symphony Orchestra in disguise.) The tale involves a circus that comes to town along with the Incredible Flutist and his enchanting flute. The audience hears delightful tunes, like the sleek "Tango of the Merchant's Daughters," the boisterous "Circus March" (including "wrong" notes and vocal sound effects—a crowd cheering and a dog barking), a quaint Minuet, a sensuous Spanish Waltz, a Siciliano, a Polka, and the Impressionistic weaving together of harmony and melody when the Flutist appears. The charming suite derived from the ballet became so popular that Piston became somewhat unhappy that the public knew him only through its sounds and not through his symphonies and chamber music.[35]

At the least, *The Incredible Flutist* proved that, when he wished, Piston could become liberal with his melodies and generous with his consonances and congenial expressions. Indeed, this was the direction in which he was going, as he left behind his complete allegiance to an international style focused on neoclassicism. Along the way, he composed a Violin Concerto (1939), a *Sinfonietta* for chamber orchestra (1941), and a *Prelude and Allegro* for organ and strings (1943). From 1939 to 1943, Piston's music was sounding more and more "American" to his fellow musicians.

The Violin Concerto, for example, does hint at rhythms and tunes from the popular realm. More straightforward triadic harmonies are found in it, especially in the slow movement, which clearly swings over toward the personal. Elliott Carter wrote that Piston's footsteps at the time were taking him along the road to simplicity and directness. Carter confirms also that Piston's music was beginning to have distinguishable American qualities in phrases and rhythms out of jazz and popular music and in a feeling of spaciousness in the slow movements.[36]

The war greatly disturbed Piston, and when America joined the conflict, he grew despondent. He sent a letter to Arthur Berger in 1942, saying,

> As a composer, I had a slump for the first year of the war, feeling that writing music was about the most futile occupation. What got me out of it chiefly was getting letters from men in the armed forces who said they hoped I was keeping on composing because that was one of the things they were out there for. I have now completely recovered a sense that it is important and that I am meant to do that job (along with other things like teaching and civilian defense). I am now on my second symphony, commissioned by the Ditson Fund in Columbia University.[37]

The war had an impact on Piston's music during the first half of the forties, even when not obvious. It was a factor in his turn to an expressive lyricism that more often than not was elegiac and to a vigorous language indicative of firm resolve. The accusation, though false, of icy-hard intellectualism, which was thought to be evidenced in his previous works, now had no relevance whatsoever. He had developed into a composer less guarded about showing his feelings.

The Symphony No. 2, which reveals these changeovers, would convey his perspective on the war. Nowhere does the audience hear the tramping of soldiers' feet, the clashes of battle, the dirges for the fallen, or the stimulants that incite courage.[38] He does not hit the listener with sledge-hammer blows in order to demonstrate his patriotism. This is a symphony written in time of war that wants us to remember what is important in human life. He does not wax nostalgic and resurrect folk tunes and country dances, nor moon over the separation of lovers, nor croon to us of happy days to come. His meaning is more subtle. A newfound Piston version of Americanism is present in all three movements. They give out sounds that come from his experience and are not secondhand acquisitions. If there are hints of the nightclub scene or of a Fourth of July parade or of a pastoral Vermont meadowland, they allude to the bands he had played with, the home events he witnessed on a regular basis, and the New England countryside he loved retiring to during summer vacations. These are the sorts of things native to him. They can also be taken as examples of what is important in our human lives; these are what the fighting was all about.

All of what was just said about Americanism notwithstanding, caution is advised in applying the term to Piston's music. Not every melody built on a pentatonic scale becomes ipso facto an offshoot of American folk song. Not every syncopated rhythm by its very nature owes a debt to jazz. It is only after repeated listening to a work like the Second Symphony that one comes away convinced that no one but an American could have written it. For one, it sounds far more like the music of Copland, Harris, and Diamond than it does like the music of Prokofiev, Shostakovich, Milhaud, Bartók, and Stravinsky. Whatever the Americanism in the music, it is an integral part of the whole composition.

The Symphony No. 2 was written in 1943, when the Allies were gaining the upper hand over the Axis powers and everyone fervently prayed that victory was in the offing. As he composed the music, Piston had to be aware that it was a crucial year, in which a decisive change in the war was impending. The radio commentator Edward R. Murrow was reporting that the struggle had reached a critical phase. The composition was Piston's personal commentary, indirect as it may have been, on the war. Some writers claim, as does Michael Steinberg, that one gets "the most touching glimpses of the deeply sentimental Italian inside the shell of the Harvard professor."[39] Yet although his music had grown more melodious, he had not necessarily become more Italian, and sentimental he decidedly was not. He was far removed from the Italian grandfather he had never known in real life and much closer to all his other family members and ancestors, who were all Yankee.

Hans Kindler and the National Symphony Orchestra premiered the Symphony No. 2 on 5 March 1944. It earned Piston the New York Music Critics Circle prize. The symphony was immediately taken up by other American orchestras and made familiar to audiences throughout the nation. Assuredly, it is an impressive work, deserving to occupy the highest rank among American symphonies. Twenty-six minutes long, the symphony is scored for the usual instrumentation—woodwinds by threes, eleven brasses, timpani and percussion, and strings. The designations given the three movements are I. *Moderato;* II. *Adagio;* III. *Allegro.*

Without doubt, the Symphony No. 2 is one of the most tonal and least dissonant instrumental compositions that he ever wrote. Whatever may be academic and intellectual in his approach to composing has been saturated here with warm romantic feeling. No longer does Piston appear to be made uncomfortable by emotion or luscious tunes. He wants to reach a broader audience than he has with anything he has written in the past, save for *The Incredible Flutist,* and he does.

The symphony's first movement has a skillfully planned sonata-form design. It starts in 6/4 meter, with an intensely lyrical melody in A minor given to the cellos and violas and lasting for nineteen measures. Its eloquent diatonic flow is a new departure for Piston. Listeners can imagine they are listening to an elegiac poem. The violins take up the melody and enlarge on it until a broad climax is reached. Next, the movement moves over to the subordinate theme in C major, a springy, cock-of-the-walk, syncopated dance that lurches along in the woodwinds until the strings and then the full orchestra take over. Something circusy permeates the music. The development section concentrates on the first theme. The music builds and builds and finally culminates in a moving recapitulation of the principal melody, now presented by the entire strings section *fortissimo.* In due course, the subordinate theme returns in all its jauntiness, followed by the coda. When the movement ceases, on a *pianissimo* intoning of the A minor triad, the listener is left feeling that, striking as it is, the movement has left matters unresolved and needing completion by music to follow.

That completion begins with the slow movement's exquisite tune, marked *dolce espressivo.* It emerges tranquilly, first in a clarinet solo and then in the other woodwinds. The movement is not divided into contrasting sections but instead devotes itself to a long spinning-out of the tune. The middle does become a little excited. However, the music calms down again to resume its pastoral musing until the close. The last five measures offer a satisfying ending, with a wisp of melodic phrase from the bass clarinet and then from the B-flat clarinet, immediately followed by muted strings that send forth a frisson of dissonance before resolving to a G major triad. This was the movement that Leonard Bernstein chose to have the New York Philharmonic play in remembrance of Piston at the time of his death.

The last movement is the necessary completion of what has gone before in the symphony and is as close as Piston ever got to sounding heroic. However, it is much too chivalrous and elegant (and occasionally light and droll) to be described as truly heroic.[40] The opening consists of a call-like first theme, briskly stated by the horns and cellos against the repeated rat-a-tat of eighth notes in the violins, followed by a march-like diversion heard first in clarinet and bassoon, and then a legato melody, *espressivo,* initiated by the clarinet and English horn. The symphony ends as it began, in A minor, after some full-voiced passages in the brasses and an immense climax.

The listener has heard a powerful piece that tries not to be overly grand or to hold an exaggerated opinion of its own importance. If anything, it is a discourse on civilization, or rather on what it means to be human. War or no war, Piston seems to express in music the need to commit ourselves to a belief in the humanity of all men and women. Admittedly, this is a highly subjective statement, and Piston would back away from saying the symphony was anything more than music. However, I am not alone in believing that the symphony is marked by compassion, especially in its opening theme and slow movement. It also lifts the spirit—as in the subordinate theme of the first movement and the last movement.[41] The audience at its premiere, so aware of the war raging in Europe and the Pacific, could have read into the finale the promise of success after the strenuous war effort.

Nothing much was written for orchestra between this and the next symphony. Piston managed to complete a *Fugue on a Victory Tune* (1944) and a *Variation on a Theme by Eugene Goossens* (1945), both of them minor compositions. There were also five chamber works, the most important of them being the Quartet No. 3 for Strings (1947).

The Symphony No. 3 was commissioned by the Koussevitzky Music Foundation, dedicated to the memory of Natalie Koussevitzky, completed in 1947, and premiered on 9 January 1948 by Koussevitzky and the Boston Symphony Orchestra. It went on to win the Pulitzer Prize. Piston composed the symphony in four movements (slow, fast, slow, fast). The music advances with solemnity in the first movement, *Andantino,* which does get chromatic and opaque in texture. There are moments when the movement veers toward tragedy, perhaps recalling the war. Next comes the unbuttoned abandon of the scherzo movement. It sounds alternately jazzy and hoedown-like, as if Copland had helped write it. The third movement has a variation structure and appears lost in thought, much of it sad and gloomy. The finale seems to express happy satisfaction at the war's end. At the least it is carefree and frolicsome.

Mention should also be made of the Symphony No. 4, although it is outside our time period, since in several ways it is much like the Symphony No. 2. It was commissioned for the Centennial Celebration of the University of Minnesota and first played by Antal Dorati and the Minnesota Symphony Orchestra on 30 March 1951. The movements are labeled *Piacevole, Ballando, Contemplativo,* and *Energico.* Like the Second Symphony, the Fourth tends toward the diatonic, is clearly tonal, favors simple triadic harmonies, and abstains from overdosing on dissonance. In a letter sent to Donald Ferguson in 1954, Piston makes a comment on this symphony that can be applied to the Second Symphony as well. He writes, "It is not intended to convey other than musical thoughts, although I think you will agree that this leaves more freedom to the listener to bring to the music what he will. . . . I feel this symphony is melodic and expressive and perhaps nearer than my other works to the problem of balance between expression and formal design. It should not prove complex to the listener in any way."[42]

Piston went on to write four more symphonies, all of them of the highest rank in excellence. His symphonic works surpass those of Harris in their elegance of feeling, taste, and workmanship, Schuman in their appeal and the quality of ideas, and Bernstein in their sense of proportion and what is fitting. Other fine compositions calling for an orchestra include the Concerto for Orchestra (1934), Concertino for Piano and Chamber Orchestra (1937), *Sinfonietta* (1941), *Serenata for Orchestra* (1957), Violin Concertos Nos. 1 and 2 (1939, 1960), and a Viola Concerto (1958). He wrote next to nothing for voice. *Carnival Song* (1940) and *Psalm and Prayer of David* (1958) are his only compositions that call for singing.

THE AMBIVALENT SYMPHONY: BARBER

Although my decision to do so may be subjective, I have given Samuel Barber's Second Symphony a separate entry for reasons given in the previous chapter. I recognize that I do not give a similar concession to any other composer. I do consider that it deserves this particular treatment because it was written during and inspired by wartime. A Barber work associated with events in progress is unusual. Also unusual is the composer's altered musical style, which reveals noteworthy differences from that of the First Symphony.

I consider Samuel Barber's Symphony No. 2, *Airborne,* to be ambivalent because the composer felt uncertain about what sort of music to write when he created it for the Army Air Forces. He injected this uncertainty into its measures. At the time that he composed it, Barber had a simultaneous desire to do two opposite things—he wanted to continue to compose warm, lyrical music, as he had in the past, but he also felt impelled to write in a harsher manner that reflected the contemporary world of warring nations and conflicting values. He knew that he had excelled as a melodist working within the tonal parameters of Romanticism, but he also thought that he should make freer use of the more chromatic and dissonant techniques propagated by the Stravinskian neoclassicists. Harsh criticism of his conservatism had rankled Barber for several years, and, though upset, he may have wanted to propitiate his critics. At the same time, he wanted to look at his method of composing from a fresh perspective and without fixed ideas.

The symphony shows him drawn in opposite directions owing to the persistent coexistence of positive and negative feelings toward what he was composing. He tried to create a musical interpretation of war's hard reality. He also tried to remain true to his softer private emotions. This is the way his musical thoughts of planes in flight and the space in which they fly are to be understood in this symphony—we must keep in mind their outward and inward significance. The symphony was meant to direct his persona externally to encompass his relationships with the military world. Yet, even as he did this, he protected his inner core from the taint of violent conduct. In short, the symphony follows no program connected with the Air Forces, although it may represent feelings engendered by his association with the Air Forces. It is music first. No scene is described; no story is told. The composer has concocted no program.

As reported in *Newsweek,* 13 March 1944, "Though Barber flew often during the symphony's writing, he made no attempt to tell a narrative or descriptive story through his music—although a screaming trumpet and crashing percussion in the third and final movement suggest the block-busters of an air raid. In the second movement, an electric 'tone generator' simulates the radio beam, but Barber insists that it has a purely musical meaning. The difference between the rather old-fashioned romanticism of Barber's first symphony and the harsh and rugged lines of the new second is undoubtedly what being in the Army would do."[43]

Between the First and Second symphonies, Barber had arranged the *Adagio for Strings* (1936) from his String Quartet, and composed the *First Essay for Orchestra* (1937), Violin Concerto (1939), and *Second Essay for Orchestra* (1942). The *Adagio for Strings* was ubiquitous in concert programs worldwide, becoming one of the most admired compositions written by any twentieth-century composer, American or European.

In these years, the popularity of his music had increased by leaps and bounds. He was a famous American composer who enjoyed enormous success while still young and maintained that fame as he grew older. He also won an international following. Early in 1943, Samuel Horan reported in *Modern Music*, "According to the analysis made by ASCAP of symphonic programs for the season of 1941–42, Barber was more often played than any other American symphonic composer. At the present age of thirty-three he is a private in the United States Army."[44]

The music public had loved his melodious music early on; music critics had pounded his wary approach to stylistic change. He liked to write impulsively and rhapsodically; writers advised that he should rein himself in and eliminate the effusiveness. The censure soon led to lack of confidence in the reliability of his thinking. He feared that he was neglecting musical developments that contemporary composers were exploring. He wished not to be seen as out of the loop as an artist. Cautiously, Barber introduced a few innovations that had come into existence during the twentieth century. He acted slowly to modify the overflowing lyricism and nostalgic emotionality that distinguished his past compositions. However, they would not disappear.

By the time he wrote the Violin Concerto, Barber was ready to do some experimentation with a twentieth-century idiom. His music began to include more of the more strident discord and rough rhythmic vigor that characterized the works of his forward-looking contemporaries.

The attempt to update his style and reconcile its backward- and forward-looking aspects continued with the *Second Essay*. The *Essay* states a musical idea that the composer spins out from beginning to end like an essayist expounding on his subject. About the work, Barber said, "Although it has no program, one perhaps hears that it was written in war-time."[45] He was inducted into the United States Army on 2 September 1942. The *Essay* was premiered by the New York Philharmonic on 23 October 1942. Barber was transferred to the Air Forces in Fort Worth, Texas, on 30 August 1943. With the transfer, he developed a strong desire to make an immediate contribution to the war effort.

One of his first creative actions after his induction was to compose the *Commando March* for band, which was given a first performance by the Army Air Forces Band conducted by Barber, now a corporal. Additionally, Barber sent a letter to his uncle, Sidney Homer, written almost two weeks after his transfer, which spoke of his great interest in flying and flyers and of his intent to compose a symphony incorporating this interest. He submitted a written description of his symphonic plan to his superior, Barton Kyle Yount, who was the Commanding General of the Army Air Forces Training Command. Yount was familiar with the young composer's accomplishments. He approved the plan, commissioned Barber to write the symphony, and, so the story goes, had the young composer flown about from airfield to airfield in order to let him get the feel of flying. He gave Barber leave to return to his home at Mount Kisco so that he could complete the task. While at Mount Kisco, Barber reported to a colonel at West Point who, to Barber's surprise, enjoyed contemporary avant-garde music. The colonel requested that he incorporate a modern device or two into the music—hence the inclusion of an electronic tone-generator, built by Bell Telephone Laboratories, to replicate the sound of a radio beam.

Undoubtedly, Barber was aware of at least three "airplane" compositions that had been written earlier in the century. Between 1913 and 1918 Leo Ornstein had composed one of his most notorious piano pieces, *Suicide in an Airplane*, which made free use of tone clusters. George Antheil had composed his discordant, tempestuous, jazz-seasoned *Airplane Sonata* for piano around 1922–23. Kurt Weill and Paul Hindemith then put out the radio cantata *Der Lindberghflug* for chorus, with or without solo voices, and orchestra, in 1929. The text, by Bertolt Brecht, celebrated the first successful flight of Charles Lindbergh over the Atlantic Ocean in the year 1927.

By March 1944 Barber had completed a symphony with an ambiance suffused with conflicting emotions and nervous tension. This unsettled atmosphere resulted from angular melodies, terse motifs, constantly recurring dotted rhythms, ever-shifting tonalities, polyharmonies, and high levels of dissonance. The tonality was obscured. However, the symphony ends on an F sharp harmony, and the tone F sharp is probably the underlying tonal center.

Serge Koussevitzky and the Boston Symphony Orchestra gave the Symphony No. 2, *Airborne,* its premiere on 3 March 1944. The score bore the heading, "Symphony Dedicated to the Army Air Forces." The U.S. Army directly sponsored the work and broadcast it to all the armed forces. Immediately, as would appear inevitable, the general public read into it depictions of aircraft taking off and landing, dogfights between war planes, dive-bombing, air raids, and so forth. These interpretations simply served to puzzle the composer.

The first movement, *Allegro ma non troppo,* was meant as music first and only secondly to indicate the vigor, power, and stir of feeling attached to flying. In sonata-form, the movement's attention-grabbing first theme in the woodwinds and piano and then in the strings jars the ear with repeated second and seventh intervals. The motif turns into a subject that is expansive and powerful. A lengthy subordinate theme reveals Barber's more lyrical side and is heard in the oboe first. The direction is to play it *espressivo.* The music mounts to a major climax. Soon, plummeting strings, piercing brasses, and skewering percussion allude to the unsettled, tumultuous conditions of the current time. The clashing seconds and sevenths return, and violent ostinatos dominate the proceedings. Lyricism is in abeyance. Eventually the music calms; the subordinate theme returns. Yet calmness does not remain for long. A coda based on the first theme follows and overflows with passion. The movement closes with the violins ruminating on the initial theme.

This first movement is riveting from beginning to end. The listener finds it edgy, closely ordered, and possessed of unusually strong and vigorous ideas. The nontriadic harmonies and discordant collisions of the opening are fortunately ameliorated by the easier-on-the-ear subordinate subject.

The affecting second movement, *Andante un poco mosso,* is, first of all, a musical night piece, a variety of composition known as a *notturno,* which had existed without the need for a program for over two hundred years. Of inessential importance is its delineation of a solitary solo flight at night. The listener can enjoy the plain A B A structure without the picture of a pilot alone and aloft flying through the dark skies. We hear the lonely sound of an English horn (said to be the pilot isolated in his cabin) soaring above muted cellos and brasses. A solo horn sings the tune a second time. The music moves on to the flutes and clarinets, surrounded by bluesy strings that, to some commentators, replicate the feeling of empty space and clouds. A crescendo mounts to a climax. This is the point when the radio beam sounds. Commenting on this movement, Barber speaks of "a lonely sort of folk-song melody for English horn, against a background of string-clouds, [which] might be called solo flight at night."[46] The listener is left with pensive, melancholic recollections not unlike those inspired by *Dover Beach* (1931) or *Knoxville: Summer of 1915* (1947).

The bold and ingenious third movement, *Presto senza battuta—Allegro resoluto,* reveals Barber taking creative risks. It begins on a swiftly spiraling string figure (supposedly representing spiraling aircraft) cut short by the brasses playing a contrasting idea. Violins and violas lunge upward and plunge downward. Horns intone a theme in longer notes, which rise and fall between the tones E and G-sharp and furnish a little stability to the opening. The two ideas intermingle to form an introduction to the rest of the movement. The main section constitutes a set of variations, expressive more of determination than of militancy. A brief fugato section follows. The spiraling figure rematerializes at the end.

The Second Symphony dwells in a different world than the First. Its speech is harsher and more arid. The expression seems distant, more objective than that of the earlier work, even though it does have its lyrical periods. The listener may wish he could experience some deeply felt melody, but he is held more at arm's length. Barber's world is that of danger, hazards to be endured, and individuals alone trying to cope with come-what-may. It allows small room for tenderness, intimacy, and crooning in a never-never land. One finds the difference in the dynamic, forceful gestures, the driving rhythms, the acerbic harmonies, the melodies struggling to free themselves of their melodiousness, and the impressive and open discourse.

Both journalists and audiences greeted the composition eagerly. Music circles made it a prominent subject for discussion. Many listeners considered it the embodiment of their feelings during these perilous years. The Second Symphony had the benefit of many performances during the months that came after. Nonetheless, Barber kept on making revisions to it. (This was something he did a lot following his first hearing of any work.) In 1947 he revised the entire composition, doing away with much of its programmatic content, adding to the dissonance, and bringing some further polytonality into play. He eliminated the tone generator and replaced it with an E-flat clarinet, and called the revision Symphony No. 2, without the *Airborne* heading.

He was still unsatisfied with it. Perhaps its ambivalent stylistic and expressive character and the attempts at grandeur, which went against his nature, disturbed him. At any rate, in 1964, he decided it was not a good work and tried to destroy it. By then, he was probably fed up with the relentless attacks of the serialists and the adherents to indeterminism. He was weary of hearing himself described as overly romantic in his music. Most hurtful, he found conductors one by one denying him a place in their programs. Obliterating the symphony may have been the outcome of despondency, a despairing response to the negativity he was encountering daily.[47] He would salvage only the slow movement, reissuing it as the tone poem *Night Flight* and remarking, "Times of cataclysm are rarely conducive to the creation of good music, especially when the composer tries to say too much. But the lyrical voice, expressing the dilemma of the individual, may still be of relevance."[48]

It was only after his death, in 1981, that the 1947 revised version of the symphony was reconstructed from a set of parts that still existed. They had lain hidden in an English warehouse. The work was revived, performed again, and recorded. A reevaluation of the symphony took place. Many listeners discovered music that did not deserve its long hiatus. They enjoyed its firm, vigorous, and scrupulously thought-out sound. Critics turned benign and discovered merit in its pages. A new consensus seemed to be developing. It deemed that the Symphony No. 2 deserved to be ranked with the best symphonies that Americans had produced.

Barber composed no more symphonies. All the same it is worth glancing at his major works from over the next few years, if only to examine more thoroughly the ambivalence that dominated his thinking. His principal efforts would go into two operas—*Vanessa* (1957) and *Anthony and Cleopatra* (1966).[49] In both his lyrical and bolder manners are in equilibrium and act to deepen his expressiveness. A third opera, *A Hand of Bridge* (1953), is a lesser work. In 1946, an excellent ballet, *Medea,* was completed for Martha Graham. For the most part lyricism is replaced by the muscular paraphernalia dear to the Stravinskian neoclassicists, plus an injection of tough emotion that they would have frowned upon. *Medea's Meditation and Dance of Vengeance,* extracted from the ballet, has led an independent life in the concert halls.

The *Capricorn Concerto* (named for the home in Mount Kisco) took its stylistic cues even more from Igor Stravinsky and neoclassicism. It is a triple concerto for oboe, flute, trumpet, and string orchestra composed in 1944. Its three movements are modeled after Johann Sebastian Bach's *Brandenburg Concerto* No. 2. Barber's Cello Concerto (1945) is a more ambitious work. It was composed for the Russian cellist Raya Garbousova, who first performed it with Koussevitzky and the Boston Symphony Orchestra on 5 April 1946. The musical world acclaimed the composition as one of the finest cello concertos written in the twentieth century, and it enjoyed the same popularity as his Violin Concerto. Unlike in the Violin Concerto, full-sized romantic melodies and outgoing expression are absent.

Next came what was without question one of the finest works that Barber ever composed, *Knoxville: Summer of 1915* for high voice and orchestra (1948), on a text by James Agee. The dichotomy between his two manners has changed. His lyrical, consonant bent is now exercised to the full in order to represent an American age of innocence recalled in words and sound. His angular, discordant leanings find a logical outlet where appropriate in the events contained in the Agee text. For a while Barber was able to escape the bugaboo of being of two minds. The Agee prose

poem fired his imagination, and writing for voice brought out his forte—
an outpouring of melody. The music brings out the yearning for the security and happiness residing in a former place and time.

Two more major works for the concert hall were written after *Knoxville*, the Piano Concerto (1962) and the *Third Essay* (1978). Both illustrate Barber's contradictions. Both compositions contain magnificent measures but also measures that prevent either work from crystallizing into a coherent whole.

On balance, heartfelt melodies and romantic impulses are invariably conspicuous in much of the music he composed. He hardly ever sounds deliberately "American." Like Piston, he felt no affinity to folk music. Nor did he feel an attraction to jazz or popular song and dance. However much he employed dissonance, he disliked its free or gratuitous use. It was for this reason that he could not stand Charles Ives's music. To his ears, Ives's pieces sounded needlessly unpleasant and not well constructed. He was most comfortable when composing for the human voice. Not surprisingly, his best purely instrumental compositions exhibit prominent vocal qualities in the conduct of the melodic lines. In 1971, he tried to explain himself, saying: "I'm writing music for words; then I immerse myself in those words, and let the music flow out of them. When I write an abstract piano sonata or a concerto, I write what I feel. I'm not a self-conscious composer. . . . It is said that I have no style at all but that doesn't matter. I just go on doing, as they say, my thing. I believe that takes a certain courage."[50]

The accusation of having "no style at all" refers to two arguments about Barber's writing. First, it references the assumption that anyone who had the effrontery to write in an older style considered exhausted ipso facto could not write anything fresh or individual. Second, there was the accusation that when Barber did attempt to modernize his style, he still retained his conservative methods, thus canceling out his effort. With neither one nor the other accusation can the unbiased listener agree. Barber did write distinctively and communicated a fresh sound that was wholly his own. The ambivalence spoken of refers more to the creative process rather than the finished result. The Symphony No. 2, for example, may demonstrate the composer's ambivalence about the sorts of materials he should and did introduce, but the composition itself exhibits finished workmanship and the highest degree of excellence in expression. This is the result of Barber's "doing, as they say, my thing." And doing his own thing did require "a certain courage"—to keep himself going, doing what he knew he did best despite the urgings of those who wanted him to act against his nature. We are fortunate that he did have this courage. One regrets that no symphony came after the Second. Barber died in 1981.

THE THEATRICAL SYMPHONY: BLITZSTEIN

Of all the symphonies taken up in this study, Marc Blitzstein's *Airborne Symphony* is the least symphonic and barely deserves to be called a symphony. It is more a dramatic cantata, and similar to several influential shows that Norman Corwin had written for radio during the thirties and forties. Corwin, known as America's "poet laureate of radio," wrote and produced radio programs that combined romance, fantasy, travelogues, history, lampoons, life stories, and political and social commentary. People nationwide watched them avidly. The *Airborne Symphony* has a connection also with the documentary movies and the newsreels of the day.

Marc Blitzstein was born in 1905 to well-to-do parents. Marc's musical talents were manifested early, through attempts to play the piano at three years of age and to compose at seven. Study at Philadelphia's Curtis Institute of Music, and then with Arnold Schoenberg in Berlin and Nadia Boulanger in Paris, prepared him for his career in music. At first, he seemed to be going the usual way for young American composers under the thrall of the Boulanger-Stravinsky neoclassism of the time, with his Piano Sonata (1927), String Quartet (1930), and Piano Concerto (1931).

Another direction was more than hinted at with his operatic farce *Triple Sec* (1928), opera-ballet *Parbola and Circula* (1929), and operatic satire *The Harpies* (1931). His flair for the stage became obvious. He had also learned to admire Kurt Weill, Bertolt Brecht, and Hanns Eisler and thought highly of their concern with social conditions and the welfare of society. This admiration and, after marriage to Eva Goldbeck in 1933, the prodding of his left-wing wife kindled his devotion to the cause of the laboring classes and his love for writing stage dramas that would win over the ordinary Joe. He openly declared himself to be homosexual, but his wife did not seem to mind. She died in 1936 from breast cancer.

A revolution took place in the composer's thinking during the thirties. It came as he reassessed his creative life and what gave him artistic satisfaction. He especially craved an association with a public different from his tiny special society of intellectuals and fashionables. Blitzstein soon discovered a fresh purpose for his life and a new understanding of how he wanted to proceed as a composer. To be able to give himself to an audience and know his devotion was reciprocated was the path he wished to pursue. To take up the cause of ordinary men and women, to give and take with them freely, to become more involved and share in their concerns caused him to feel invigorated.

He won notoriety in 1937, when Orson Welles and John Houseman, under the auspices of the Federal Theater Project, tried to mount his socially significant *The Cradle Will Rock,* a striking stage musical. The music drama had been written as homage to his deceased wife and her hunger for justice. The advice given to him in a discussion with playwright Bertolt Brecht had been the spark that ignited Blitzstein's creativity. When the composer had told Brecht that he was debating composing a stage musical about prostitution, Brecht had recommended that he include all kinds of prostitution, sexual and otherwise.

The Cradle Will Rock skillfully interlaced musical and spoken stories into sketches that mounted an assault on the greed and exploitation of labor inherent in the capitalist system. It was a searing drama about the organization of a union in "Steeltown." The play found the streetwalker innocent and the panderers to the ruthless munitions manufacturer Mr. Mister—police, minister, newspaper editor, artists, drugstore proprietor, doctor—the true whores, selling away their ideals and selling themselves for money to "whoever would pay the most." Bigwigs in the government and business tried to kill the show, which had the sponsorship of the Federal Theater Project. They had the production locked out of the Maxine Elliott Theatre. But Welles and Houseman led the cast and audience to the available Venice Theater nearby, where *The Cradle Will Rock* was put on to wide acclaim. It would also have a considerable influence over the direction that Leonard Bernstein and Stephen Sondheim would take later, when they wrote music for the stage.

John Houseman, in *The Night the Audience Walked Out,* says of *The Cradle Will Rock:* "It was described by the author, Marc Blitzstein, as a

Labor Opera—in a style that falls somewhere between realism, romance, satire, vaudeville, comic-strip, Gilbert and Sullivan, Brecht and agitprop." In several ways, *The Cradle Will Rock* was a forerunner of the *Airborne Symphony.* With it, he learned to manipulate comedy and tragedy, bombast and restraint, propaganda and truthfulness. The music could be any style—popular, folk, artistic, conservative, or modern—so long as it drove the message home. Advocacy and agitation for the cause of the common worker would become advocacy and agitation for the cause of the Allies on behalf of the common people of the world.

He further honed his dramatic skills with scores to movies such as *Surf and Seaweed* (1931), short films such as *Hands* (1934), documentaries including *Valley Town* (1940) and *Night Shift* (1942), and polemical films including *Native Land* (1942) and *True Glory* (1945). In these films, music had to be tied to action, whether visual or understood. No prolonged disquisition was available. The linkage required instant connection.

After *Cradle,* Blitzstein continued to enlarge his dramatic-stage experience with his opera *No for an Answer* (1939). The musical style was to some degree a continuation of the merger of diverse popular and artistic modes found in the previous work.

Two years after *The Cradle Will Rock* and before the debut of *No for an Answer,* the war had begun. By 1944, victory for the Allies was in sight. The Soviet armies liberated Leningrad in January 1944. In June, the Allied Expeditionary Force landed in Normandy. Two months later, Paris was free of the Nazis, and the Soviet forces had arrived at the Austria-Prussia border. In April 1945 the long presidency of Franklin Roosevelt ended in death, and Harry Truman was sworn in as the thirty-third president. In October, General MacArthur and the U.S. Army had returned to the Philippines. December's "Battle of the Bulge" was the last major counterattack that the Nazis could organize. At last, in May 1945, Germany surrendered and World War II ended in Europe. The atom bomb was dropped on Hiroshima in August with horrific results. Japan surrendered on 14 August 1945. The war in the Pacific was over.

Meanwhile, Blitzstein received Guggenheim fellowships in 1940 and 1941. Rage grew within him over the senseless and merciless murder of innocent men, women, and children by the Nazis, not least being the massacre of Jews in their thousands. In August 1942, like Samuel Barber, he found himself in the Army Air Forces. The Eighth Air Force in England became his base. Blitzstein zealously joined in the fight against Nazi totalitarianism and wanted to make a telling contribution. The Air Force designated him as an expert in entertainment and had him compose music for shows in canteens and on radio, and for short films.

To Colonel Beirne Lay he had proposed composing a symphony, citing the overwhelming success of Dmitri Shostakovich's Symphony No. 7 (*Leningrad*), not only in the Soviet Union but the United States. Blitzstein argued, "The results [of the symphony's enthusiastic reception] more than justified the effort. The symphony, symbolizing, even representing courage in the face of withering fire and destruction, was responsible for an immense worldwide wave of enthusiasm and admiration for the people of the USSR and their fighting forces. Music was on the map as a positive weapon in winning the war."[51] After an interview before a board of high officers, he received the commission to write a major composition. This was to turn out to be the *Airborne Symphony* (1946), for narrator, soloists, male chorus, and orchestra. Its subject was the history of flight beginning with the failed attempt of Icarus. Its diverse input included Shostakovich, movies, stage shows and musicals, popular song, and the *Living Newspaper* (current events presented as theater). They guided the text that he prepared and inspired the music that he composed.

Like Barber, he was aware of the three "airplane" compositions that had been written earlier in the century. To these three should be added the contemporary Barber score of Symphony No. 2, *Airborne*. Blitzstein would also know about the several Hollywood films involving airplanes and flight.

At first, Blitzstein's airplane composition was envisaged as a score for a film to be shot for the Eighth Air Force. A leftover of this plan lingers in the narrator's speech, which directs the audience's attention to different parts of the story. Work on the composition kept on being deferred because other duties continued to demand his full time. The completion of the music and its premiere had to await the end of the war. On his return to New York in 1945, Blitzstein played what he could recall of the music for Leonard Bernstein, who became so enthusiastic over what he heard that he insisted on scheduling a first performance for the next April.

Unfortunately, a trunk containing the music and text of the symphony was mislaid during its transatlantic passage from England. The composer set about writing a second version of the work, incorporating as much as he could remember of the previous score. As luck would have it, the mislaid trunk was found in Boston with the composition inside it. On the other hand, Blitzstein preferred his new version, which was ten minutes shorter and, according to Blitzstein, "a heck of a lot better piece." It was this fifty-five-minute version that Leonard Bernstein performed on 1 April 1946, with Orson Welles as narrator, the Robert Shaw Collegiate Chorale, and the New York City Symphony.

The *Airborne Symphony* is in three sections:

Movement I:	The Theory of Flight
	Ballad of History and Mythology
	Kittyhawk
	The Airborne
Movement II:	The Enemy
	Threat and Approach
	Ballad of the Cities
	Morning Poem
Movement III:	Ballad of Hurry-Up
	Night Music: Ballad of the Bombardier
	Recitative
	Chorus of the Rendezvous
	The Open Sky

The writing adheres to the standard major and minor scales. A great deal of melodiousness ameliorates any harmonic dislocations. While the poetry may be trite, the music is expressive and clear, and directly communicates the text's meaning. The style is variable, depending on the manner of the communication. An assortment of stylistic approaches, popular and artistic, are stage-managed to realize unambiguous expressive goals. The narrator is tempted to engage in histrionics; the music on occasion tends to the overbearing.

The symphony received a mixed response from critics, some of whom were puzzled by its claim to symphonic status. Donald Fuller, reviewing the work in *Modern Music,* wrote that the *Airborne* "stands quite by itself, direct and affecting in its appeal." Regardless, it had imperfect features, many theatrical effects, and proved not to be really a symphony, Fuller wrote. In addition, he found no "long-range form with a clear dramatic curve. Yet the score encompasses a huge canvas with great daring and frequent success. The audience reaction was instantaneous."[52]

The audience, as Fuller indicated, seemed to take to the work. Moreover, *Airborne Symphony* won the Music Critics Circle Award and the Page One Award of the Newspaper Guild of New York. A prize-winning recording was made soon after the first performance. However, the *Airborne* failed to gain a place in the concert repertoire. The accusation that Blitzstein was a communist weighed him down. The Cold War and the suspicion of anyone on the political left were beginning. They served as a damper on Blitzstein's artistic hopes.

Unlike Samuel Barber's Symphony No. 2, *Airborne*, Blitzstein's *Airborne Symphony* is dated and tied almost completely to the war period, especially in the role allotted to the narrator. On the other hand, the symphony contains a great deal of fine-sounding and stimulating music, from the rousing introduction, through individual pieces such as the "Ballad of the Bombardier," to the convincing ending.

The first movement celebrates mankind's yearning to fly, the failures and the success: "Wings on the brain, wings on the brain, / Mad for to fly and walk the sky." The second movement describes the terrors of attack from the air and the senseless cruelty of the Nazis—the devastation of entire cities owing to the bombings, which he knew through personal experience: "Wounded cities, hold out. . . . / All dust and rubble, / Wounded cities, hold out." The concluding "Morning Poem" lauds the airmen's struggles against the enemy but in the main concentrates on the excitement of flying: "Those clothy clouds, / Unlit by the early sun, are pavement now. . . . / The craft upon its bell, on its side; / And mounting almost vertical, and stopping / To change its mind and float."

The third movement first gives a description of the pilot's daily routine—the nervousness and boredom while waiting to go into action; the worry that some part of the apparatus will malfunction: "In the Air Force / It's hurry up, hurry up, hurry up—and wait." Extremely quiet, plain, and lovely music describes a bombardier longing for his "Emily" while away from her for a long time, as he writes a letter home. The rest of the movement celebrates the defeat of fascism and the painfully won triumph of the good. It also warns of the terrors awaiting men and women in the future.

Blitzstein explained: "I have taken a risk in the ending of the Airborne. Most symphonies, you know, end on a single note, maybe triumph, maybe tragedy. But a symphony about our times cannot have that luxury—you cannot do that and be honest with yourself. No victory is unqualified victory; no glory is unqualified glory. So the Airborne ends in conflict. There is a great paean of triumph over the enemy sung by the chorus, but a single voice—the narrator—begins to jab in the note of warning! Warning!"

The *Airborne Symphony* does warn that though the war is won, we may go on to generate new enemies if we are not careful. It warns about the danger of intolerance, of believing we and only we are right, and of closing our eyes to racial and other discrimination. The warning proved omniscient of the future. Over the horizon were McCarthyism, race riots, the Korean War, Vietnam, and Iraq.

When all is going right, the *Airborne Symphony* sounds like a masterly composition. The music is amazingly affecting and potent. The poetry, unfortunately, does not reach the timelessness and quality of the music. Is it a symphony? Strictly speaking, it is distant from the usual idea of a symphony. Although gathered into what are apparently three movements, each movement turns out to be a string of vocal numbers. None of them is arranged in a manner contributing to symphonism. Musical ideas are not stated as motifs, elaborated on, and integrated into a movement or from movement to movement. What integration occurs is left to the text.

On the other hand, the *Airborne Symphony* operates effectively as a dramatic cantata. Like a contemporary episodic theater piece, it seeks to provoke an understanding of the meaning of flight and war. It does so through a series of loosely connected scenes. The thread of the story is interrupted from time to time in order to allow the narrator to address the audience directly with asides that underline the principal subject. The musical cloth has been cut to suit Blitzstein's purpose. From this prospective, "symphony" goes back to its original meaning as a coming together or a harmony of sounds. In a previous chapter I spoke of the post–World War II period when a symphony was defined as anything the composer says it is. Blitzstein's *Airborne Symphony* anticipates this definition.

He went on to write a great deal of music for the stage, with the opera *Regina* (after Lillian Hellman's play *The Little Foxes*) being the most important. Commissioned in 1946 by the Koussevitzky Foundation and intended for the Broadway stage rather than the opera house, it was first mounted in 1949 and revised in 1953 and again in 1958.

Although it was enjoyed by the audience, *Regina* was supplanted in popularity by Blitzstein's translation and adaptation for the American stage of Kurt Weil's *Die Dreigroschenoper*, retitled as *The Threepenny Opera*, in 1952. Two other operas that he would start, *Sacco and Vanzetti* and *Idiots First*, were left incomplete on his death. The composer Leonard Lehrman would complete them later.

The purely instrumental concert pieces that came after the symphonic poem *Freedom Morning*, composed during wartime, were few—the suite *Native Land* (1946) and *Lear: A Study* (1958). A ballet, *The Guests*, was performed in 1948. He never attempted to compose a symphony other than the *Airborne Symphony*.

Blitzstein died on 22 January 1964 while spending the winter in Martinique. It seems that he was murdered. He had been drinking with three sailors who lured him into an alley and gave him a fatal beating. The loss to American music was great.

Blitzstein had one disappointment after another from the end of World War II on. As new works failed to succeed, he was pushed farther and farther into the background. Yet even then he stood for the social conscience of the theater and music world. No matter how much he was denigrated by the aggressive younger generation of composers, he remained a sophisticated and committed artist with considerable creative ability. It was no small thing for him to bridge the gap between the contemporary composer and the general public.

A last word should be said about the symphonies composed during World War II. Although the conflict may have been a spur to the writing of these symphonies, the compositions themselves, except possibly for Blitzstein's *Airborne Symphony*, avoid the cant of war—the hoopla, the superpatriotic paeans, the rattling sound of gunfire, the exploding-bomb effects, the heavy-booted tread of tramping soldiers. This music wants to go beyond such particulars, to find a deeper meaning in and universalize human feeling.

The three symphonies most obviously connected to the war—those of Antheil, Barber, and Blitzstein—also try to go beyond the links that tie them to their programs.

For example, Antheil makes clear that his Symphony No. 4 (1942), is not a narration about the war when he states that although the war influenced the symphony, the music reflected only his tense and troubled state of mind while writing it. He had no actual program in mind. He wished to capture in the symphony feelings of anxiety, tragedy, anger over man's brutality to man, and elation over the promise of the future. He wanted no attempt at a "war analysis" of the composition. The emotions that the music passes on to the listener are not literal but beyond words. One can easily listen to the symphony with no knowledge of its connection with World War II and come away satisfied that the experience was worthwhile.

Turning to Barber, note his unease about the programmatic allusions in his Symphony No. 2, *Airborne*. He revised the music, discarded the references, and removed the *Airborne* designation. He wished the symphony to be heard as music only. The symphony was recovered after he had tried to destroy it, decades after the war. New audiences heard it without the original trappings. For the most part, they found the writing solid, the music meaningful, and the composition pertinent. Whatever its weaknesses, these had to do more with the technical crisis that Barber was trying to resolve and less with the music's "airborne" associations.

Blitzstein's *Airborne Symphony* might be considered to be imprisoned by its text. Indeed, I have pointed out that it is more a dramatic cantata than a symphony. The music, when it projects optimism, longing, and determination, may do so accompanied by words connected with contemporary events but, at its best, has implications and meanings that break through the limitations of the text. Unfortunately the composition must inevitably include the text. For this reason, the symphony has come to be regarded as a part of its time and place. It has not aged well.

Antheil, Diamond, Bernstein, Piston, Blitzstein, and the wartime

Barber strike a note that that one way or another is responsive to contemporary conditions. Whether obvious or subtle, the expression in their symphonies replicates the concerns of an American people under great stress. Their symphonies, like those of the thirties, are meant to sound strong, firm in their message, clear in their meaning, and, in spite of the turmoil of the times, reassuring. In the main, the music is creativity at a white heat. The symphonies made their mark then and, we expect, will continue to do so into the future.

4

SYMPHONIES OF
THE IMMEDIATE
POSTWAR YEARS

The twentieth century furthered a global insanity that manifested itself especially in two world wars. At last, the Second World War was over. After living through the mayhem that had gone on for several years, the world was relieved by the end of hostilities. The euphoria over World War II's conclusion strongly affected the United States in 1946. Symphonies that showed feelings of relief over the arrival of peace, agreement over America's way of life and values, and trust in the future were completed. Propitious major events were taking place. The United Nations General Assembly met for the first time, on 10 January, in London. Preparations were already taking place to launch the Marshall Plan. The new divisions that would afflict the people of the world were still in the future.

It is true that some music people with advanced ideas wished that American composers would move in new directions. The composers themselves, however, were still attuned to the majority. The devastation left behind by the war still upset most artists. The horrors of the Nazi concentration camps haunted their minds. They knew there was much to correct in the United States.

At the same time, they could not help but experience the incredible elation that comes over men and women who are survivors. They could not deny their sense of marvel and release over the end to the killing. No matter what else critics might say of the symphonies finished in the year or so after the war, the music was a sincere and mostly consistent response to the occasion. Most composers focused on assimilating their contemporary musical offerings within the framework of American culture, if not smoothly then at least without inviting wholesale rejection. The artists, as they created, acted as humans rooted in the events experienced by humankind. For the time being, feelings of relief, confidence, and well-being were the rule. If and when human society showed signs of disintegration, composers would furnish testimony of this collapse through their musical responses.

On the other hand, the indications were many that the times to come would be anything but peaceful. Events were taking place that might not confirm the value of America's way of life or might undermine trust in the future. For the present, Americans chose to ignore the contrary signs. They preferred not to look at the bad news that was accumulating. Winston Churchill gave his "Iron Curtain" speech and Ho Chi Minh became president of North Vietnam in March 1946. Thus, the Cold War had begun and the future conflicts in Vietnam and Korea were seeded.

The U.S. Supreme Court declared racial segregation on buses unconstitutional in June, and President Truman ordered the desegregation of the Armed Forces in July. These were harbingers of the fierce battles for racial equality that would multiply and reach new levels of intensity. Senator Joseph McCarthy and the House Un-American Activities Committee accelerated their search for alleged communists and attempted to cow the country into a state of fearful conformity, beginning with an interrogation of the astronomer Harlow Shapley, in November. Even as these threats to our democracy increased, so also did the angry splitting-apart of liberal and conservative, one-worlder and superpatriot, internationalist and isolationist. Any bridges that might have existed between the two sides were destroyed. Unrest in Palestine between Jewish Zionists and Muslim Palestinians was building to the boiling point. Partition was in the offing, as was the creation of the new state of Israel. This would entrench the hostilities between Israelis and Palestinians and feed the anti-American attitudes of one-and-a-third billion Muslims, who saw the United States as supportive of Israel. Then would come the wars, not worldwide to be sure, but wars nevertheless—in Korea, Vietnam, Afghanistan, and Iraq. Men, women, and children would continue to die prematurely and, too often, for no good reason.

Events such as these made some thoughtful music people pessimistic. They were offended by what they saw as the simple-mindedness in contemporary symphonies. They were annoyed to hear melodies, in particular those most pleasing to concert audiences, feeling that they provided only escapist pleasures. To these critics, such tunes were allurements to never-never land. The idea that people wanted to be moved only by music they thought beautiful also gave offense. The general public for music, these critics claimed, wanted to feed on musical pablum rather than chew on more robust sounds.

That some major composers did not subscribe to this view was established by works such as Aaron Copland's Third Symphony, which seemed to sum up America's wholesome values and hopes for the future in music comprehensible to American audiences.

Simultaneously, a younger generation of composers was coming along who sought to displace the aesthetic values of their immediate predecessors, Copland among them. They sounded the trumpet call to abandon attempts to look outward and cultivate the general public. They chose to look inward and express themselves in nontraditional, venturesome compositions comprehensible, if at all, to a very limited public.

Neither side was right or wrong. The real problem was one of acceptance, of maintaining a balanced and objective attitude toward views and practices that differed from one's own. One side wished to remain connected to the American society and to write music meaningful to the majority of listeners; the other wanted to adventure into the novel and different, and to explore little-known territory no matter what the consequences. Both approaches could potentially make valuable contributions to music. Each needed the counterweight of the other to save it from its excesses.

However, reconciliation was not in the cards. The second of the two choices would be taken by many of the new composers, for most of whom the writing of symphonies was not of the first priority—Milton Babbitt, Charles Wuorinen, Ralph Shapey, Gunther Schuller, Andrew Imbrie, and Elliott Carter, among others. In a few years another group of composers would come along, who valued indeterminacy and composed "chance music." They employed the element of chance in the choice of tones, rests, durations, rhythms, and dynamics. The old order would be confronted with compositions that consisted of silence, street noises, electronic squawks, and performers allowed to play anything they wished.

Nonetheless, for a year or two after the war, compositions designed with conscious observance of musical styles honoring the past predominated, and estimable symphonies would come from Douglas Moore, Peter Mennin, Randall Thompson, Aaron Copland, Paul Creston, and Roger Sessions. These works are the subject matter of this chapter.

THE CONSERVATORIAL SYMPHONY: MOORE

Of all the symphonies taken up in this study, Douglas Moore's *Symphony in A Major* looks the most to the past. It demonstrates a reversion to traditional sounds that show Moore turning away from complexity in order to cultivate simple, homespun structures of considerable rustic flavor. He was fifty-two years old when he composed his work.

Moore, born in 1893, reverts deliberately to earlier forms of melodic organization, rhythmic design, and harmonic usage that he had grown up hearing and still prized. He wishes his music to exemplify an Americanism reflecting the qualities in American life and American traditions that he considered wholesome. His music is best understood as coming from a romantic idealist who, in looking back over American history, finds hope in the future. The operative words for him are optimism and unpretentiousness. The war was over and with its end, he felt, should also go any of America's despondency. His music is plainer than that of the younger Barber and of Thompson. His Americanism shows in almost every measure, whereas Barber's shows not at all.

Douglas Moore was born in Cutchogue, a village on New York's Long Island that dated back to colonial times. He was a descendant of the seventeenth-century Pilgrims and Puritans who had immigrated to New

England. The first ancestor to land on North Fork, Long Island, was Thomas Moore. He came from New England in 1640 and remained in the Cutchogue area. Two and a half centuries later, Moore's father would go to New York City, found the *Ladies World* magazine, and experience prosperity. He sent his son Douglas to the Hotchkiss School, an independent boarding establishment located in Lakeville, Connecticut. Eventually, Douglas Moore went to Yale University. He would constantly be aware of his roots.

As a boy, Moore had learned to play the piano and had discovered a love for music-making. Afterward, he decided on a music career. He studied at Yale University in the music department, where Horatio Parker, the teacher of Ives, was chairman and David Stanley Smith was a faculty member. Moore admired Parker and Smith but disregarded their Germanophile leanings in music. Parker's interest in writing for voice and his two operas, *Mona* (1910) and *Fairyland* (1914), were duly noticed by the young Douglas. He was also aware when *Mona* won an award of the Metropolitan Opera Association, and *Fairyland,* the first prize in a competition of the National Federation of Music Clubs. During the time he was a Yale student, however, Moore was far more interested in writing popular songs than opera.

Moore served in the Navy as a lieutenant during World War I. At war's end, he went abroad to Paris and became a student of Nadia Boulanger and Vincent d'Indy. Boulanger irritated him. He did not take willingly to her instruction. He had concluded that her preference was for students whose styles conformed to a Franco-Stravinskian viewpoint. D'Indy, on the other hand, spurred his interest in writing operas. D'Indy was sympathetic to a creative approach like Moore's, one that showed respect for music responsive to a folk and popular tradition.

Returning to the United States in 1921, Moore landed the position of curator of music and organist at the Cleveland Museum in Cleveland, Ohio. He learned that the Swiss composer Ernest Bloch was at the Cleveland Institute and went to him for further musical study (as did Quincy Porter, Roger Sessions, George Antheil, and Randall Thompson). He also found the time to do some acting at the Cleveland Playhouse, thus gaining stage experience. In 1926, he moved to New York City and joined the faculty of Columbia University, where he remained until his retirement in 1962. Moore proved to have excellent administrative abilities after he succeeded Daniel Gregory Mason as chairman of the music department in 1940.

Vis-à-vis school administrators and music faculty, Moore knew when to be charming or firm. Skillfully and shrewdly, he maneuvered the shark-infested waters of collegiate politics and succeeded in his aim to make the department stronger and of better quality. He also helped initiate and continued to be a steady backer of several national associations that promoted and gave support to native composers. He was president of the American Academy of Arts and Letters from 1953 to 1956, and director of the American Society of Composers, Authors and Publishers (ASCAP) from 1957 to 1960. A Pulitzer Prize was awarded him in 1951 for his opera *Giants in the Earth*. Moore tried to remain open-minded about all perspectives in music, from traditional to experimental, and expected open-mindedness in return.

Moore's training in music had been thorough. He was quite sophisticated and conversant with the various trends in musical composition taking place in Europe and America. Therefore he was completely aware of what he was doing when he chose a forthright, unpretentious, and down-to-earth musical style for himself. Moreover, although he worked in cosmopolitan New York City, his leisure time was spent in rural Cutchogue, where he composed much of his music and remained true to his rustic environs. In Ralph Waldo Emerson's words, he decided that his compositions should "smack of the earth and of real life, sweet, smart, or stinging."

Some aspect of America usually figures in his compositions, whether in story, country dance, or traditional ditty. His own talent was for melodic invention. He exercised this gift in the twelve operas that he wrote. The principal ones were *The Devil and Daniel Webster* (1938), *Giants in the Earth* (1949), *The Ballad of Baby Doe* (1956), and *Carry Nation* (1966). *The Ballad of Baby Doe* has continued to be one of the most performed operas in America, followed closely by *The Devil and Daniel Webster*. Moore saturates his stage works with tunes appropriate for the voice. The portions given over to group singing are attractive to the ear. The music can be folk-like or dramatic, and, when need be, in a popular mode. Flexible and nicely timed recitatives draw on native ways of speaking. The orchestral sounds are full and supportive. Stage-action is natural, never static. Page after page of his scores continuously gratify the senses and successfully conjure up the required atmospheric settings. All in all, Moore was a master of telling theater.

Most of his symphonic works also drew on American subjects, as in *The Pageant of P. T. Barnum* suite (1924), *Moby Dick* (1928), *Overture on an American Tune* (1932), the *Village Music* suite (1941), the symphonic poem *In Memoriam* (1943), the *Farm Journal* suite (1947), and *Cotillion Suite* (1952). The America he depicted was deep-seated in him—whether a countryside, a village scene, the circus coming to town, or farmers working in their fields. *Barnum,* his earliest success, refers the listener to the showman's boyhood in "Boyhood in Bethel," complete with band music on the village green and fiddler's music in the barn. Next, "Joyce Heth" allows the introduction of black spirituals. The movements that come after, "General and Mrs. Tom Thumb," "Jenny Lind," and "Circus Parade," all receive appropriate music.

The *Farm Journal* suite for chamber orchestra captures the moods of a farm family who are "Up Early" in "Sunday Clothes," by "Lamp Light," and raising a thankful "Harvest Song." These are touching scenes straight out of his growing-up years in Cutchogue. He views these matters through a refined lens. Easygoing tunes occasionally swell with lyric emotion. No sentiment is allowed to go out of bounds. The *Cotillion Suite* for strings captures rural folk at a barn dance—"Grand March," "Polka," "Waltz," "Gallop," "Cake Walk," and "Quick Step." The dance floor is crowded with agile country lads and lasses cavorting during a Saturday-night get-together. The point of view is of an insider observing friends and neighbors and capturing their festivities with genial, clear-cut, and honestly felt music. One composition is atypical: *In Memoriam* is filled with melancholic music but without any feeling of depression. It commemorates the war dead in sentiments that never verge on the sentimental.

The concert music, like the operas, was well received in its day and in the years after. One reason for the long-lasting esteem granted Moore's music is its alliance with the more decent features of the American temperament. His gives glimpses of the down-to-earth and companionable attributes of his fellow citizens. Alternately brilliant and romantically tender, a Moore composition normally calls to mind an idealized America.

One hears a merging of rural brusqueness and small-town suavity. His themes are evocative. Men and women work in fields or at home, stroll on Main Street, amuse themselves in their parlors, or gather for community socials. Opera subjects are drawn from folk memory or historical tradition. Their presented and hidden agendas are readily understood and appreciated. Each story tied to music rich in suggestion is invariably a winner.

Otto Luening confirms that Moore is principally a melodist. His music is normally free from complications, and only dissonant when contrast or dramatic tension is needed, Luening writes. When more than one melody is heard simultaneously, Moore spaces out his harmony so that each tune is heard clearly. The composer uses rhythms related to American marches, ragtime, hymns, and ballroom and folk dances. What syncopations occur derive from these sources.[1]

To this evaluation, Aaron Copland adds that Moore's music is a contrast to the grandiloquence of Ives and representative of a different aspect of America. After looking over what Moore and Virgil Thomson have composed, Copland finds "nothing in serious European music that is quite like it—nothing so downright plain and bare as their commerce with simple tunes and square rhythms and Sunday-school harmonies [that are] evocative of the homely virtues of rural America." Whether revivalist hymn, sentimental ditty, or country dance, these come from sophisticated musicians who have accepted a limited vocabulary as "gestures of faith in their own heritage."[2]

The *Symphony in A Major* is an optimistic symphonic composition and stands in arresting contrast to the mournful *In Memoriam* of two years before. The latter honors America's war-dead; the former reminds us of the decencies they fought to uphold. The symphony is an extraordinary affirmation of postwar faith in what America stood for and demonstrates trust in events still to come. Moore's expression of confidence is one meant to encourage and sustain. Eric Salzman speaks of the positive energy and optimism the symphony showed in the war's aftermath. He quotes the composer as saying that the music was "an attempt to write in clear, objective, modified classical style, with emphasis upon rhythmic and melodic momentum rather than upon sharply contrasted themes or dramatic climaxes. There is no underlying program, although the second movement was suggested by a short poem by James Joyce, which deals with music heard at the coming of twilight."[3]

The *Symphony in A Major* was composed at the request of the conductor Alfred Wallenstein in 1945, and dedicated to Stephen Vincent Benét. Benét was the American poet, novelist, and short story writer who wrote, first, the famous short story, and second, the libretto for Moore's opera *The Devil and Daniel Webster*. The symphony's premiere took place in Paris on 5 May 1946 in a concert given by the Paris Broadcasting Orchestra, directed by Robert Lawrence. The Paris audience liked the symphony, especially the slow movement.

Its first appearance in the United States was at a Los Angeles concert on 16 January 1947, with Alfred Wallenstein conducting the Los Angeles Philharmonic. It evidently captured the emotional temper of the time, a period when people longed to get back to normalcy. The audience responded positively. After years of existing in a state of tension, men and women welcomed a return to familiar and comfortable conditions. That was what the *Symphony in A Major* offered them. Subsequently other orchestras took it up—the NBC Symphony did so in May 1947, and the New York Philharmonic in February 1948.

The composition is usually denominated as Moore's Symphony No. 2, since he had written a *Symphony of Autumn* in 1930. This earlier work, though, is not as capably put together. The orchestration sometimes lacks clarity. The style wavers between conventional romanticism and impressionism. By the time he came around to composing the *Symphony in A Major* he had gained a great deal of experience in musical composition. He had become secure in his own style and saw plainly what he wanted to accomplish within a symphonic framework—nothing heavy and portentous but something to delight the senses. Throughout the composition one gets the sense of a relaxed creator skilled in his craft and confident that he can achieve the goals he has in mind.[4]

The audience hears Moore in an outgoing frame of mind. The music radiates a feeling of nonconfinement, a mood of elation. These are the symphony's most engaging attributes. Unambiguously, it suggests the American rural landscape and plain folk so effectively rendered in *Farm Journal* and *Cotillion*. The work, as might be expected, conforms to long-established musical norms.

The first movement has a sonata-allegro structure. It begins with a pensive *Andante con moto*. The winds sing quietly and lyrically. The strings enter. Sudden loud chords are heard but last only a moment. A cheery *Allegro guisto* abruptly starts off with a principal subject based on the introductory material heard earlier in the violins. No clearly defined dramatic climaxes ensue. No long melodies emerge. Much of the movement is dedicated to the manipulation of brief, good-humored melodic-rhythmic motifs. Every now and again the music bursts forth with country-dance rhythms and melodic stop-and-go as if responding to dancing feet. The development section gives a listener the curious feeling of traveling along a country road. Most loud spots serve as punctuations in the musical texture rather than true climaxes. Scarcely any contrapuntal complexity interrupts the essentially homophonic texture. However, some intricacy takes place when different motifs are heard simultaneously. They are so skillfully combined, varied, and recombined that they give only a suggestion of contrapuntal intricacy. Transparent scoring allows these passages to come across cleanly. Several passages seem cinematic—as if meant as a soundtrack for a folksy movie.

Next comes a slow *Andante quieto e semplice*. It is certainly a tranquil, agreeable movement. A solo trumpet starts a melody. The melody is then handed around to an assortment of instruments and acquires a variety of orchestral colorings. Brief expressive motifs make up the melodic line. A Joyce poem may have been the music's springboard; however, the impression the movement leaves of serene streams and meadows is distinctly American. The pastoral feeling is most acute in the middle of the movement, when high violins intone the melody and hand it on to a solo flute. Eloquence and volume increase for a while, but the music soon dies away. The ending is calm, assuring the listener that all is right with the world.

Again, the effect is almost cinematic. Interestingly, the one thing this and the other three movements lack are full-blown song-like tunes that are several measures long and have a beginning, middle, and end. Moore instead offers lyrical lines, to be sure, but these lines can be cut into melodic snippets that one may hear separately or stitched into a loose whole. The listener may wish that Moore had slipped in a hummable tune like Baby Doe's "Willow Song" or "Letter Song."

The third movement, a brief, sparkling *Allegretto*, reminds the listener of a playful scherzo despite the contrapuntal interplay in its parts. The chatter of woodwinds in the opening immediately grabs the listener's attention. The chatter continues in the background as thematic fragments are subjected to expert manipulation. In the middle, Moore inserts an effective passage for muted trumpets. The result almost resembles the effect of the muted trumpets in the second movement of Bartók's *Concerto for Orchestra,* only without the dissonance and intimations of instability. Moore says, "This is a polyphonic piece, somewhat resembling a minuet, and if there is any elegance about it, it is of the rural rather than the court variety."[5] As one might expect, the music is vivid, breezy, and easy on the ear. Distinctive and recurring figures zigzag through the measures and come together into a distinguishable overall design.

An energetic *Allegro con spirito* completes the symphony. The movement opens with a sudden, loud three-note trumpet call-to-attention. Moore's purpose is to offer a final scrap of recreation rather than a summation and serious culmination of the work. Nothing introspective appears. Chromaticism increases. Harmonic clashes intensify and operate in tandem with biting rhythmic patterns. They are meant to add spice to the proceedings, nothing more. Now and again the music breaks out with extroverted, even raucous, passages that parallel those in a march by John Phillip Sousa. The composition remains constantly outgoing and gregarious. Moore addresses the side of Americans that fancies a social rather than a solitary existence.

Attempting to explain the symphony's wide success, Jay Harrison wrote in the *New York Herald Tribune* on 27 October 1954: "Douglas Moore's Symphony in A is an open-air number, a latter day 'Pastoral,' which spins its larking tunes without self-consciousness or effort. Throughout it darts and chortles pictures, hilly places and country dances and has for itself a bouncing and breezy time. It is a happy piece, a random collection of happy ideas, and its moods, diverse as they are, suggest nothing so much as contentment. It is undarkened by worldly woe and no sadness hovers near it. It tells a pleasant tale and narrates it with a grin."[6]

After the *Symphony in A Major,* Moore would write nothing more for full symphony orchestra. Although Moore was a zealous advocate for the orchestral music of other composers, he failed to be the same for his symphony. Perhaps he sensed the times were changing and felt out of step with his colleagues. This led to a feeling of uncertainty about his symphonic abilities. He had more confidence in his writing for the musical stage. Thereafter he would concentrate most of his energies on writing operas. He died in 1969.

To the end, he felt keenly that composers were too preoccupied with questions of musical language and artistic philosophy. He said that they lived with the fear that what they composed might be insufficiently modern or much too modern. Moore saw his colleagues torn between writing as a reflection of America or as a part of an international style, not knowing what faction to please. He says of himself, "The particular ideal which I have been striving to attain is to write music which will not be self-conscious with regard to idiom, and will reflect the exciting quality of life, tradition, and country which I feel all about me." Moore adds, "If we happen to be romantically inclined, if we like a good tune now and then, if we still have a childish love for atmosphere, is it not well for us to admit the fact and try to produce something which we ourselves like?"[7]

THE DYNAMIC SYMPHONY: MENNIN

One feature strikes the audience most when listening to Peter Mennin's Symphony No. 3—its dynamic properties. Whatever the symphonic movement, one hears continuous forward motion and expansion on ideas stated at the beginning. The expression is usually forceful and energetic. The artist behind the music has an active mind that does not incline toward musical nationalism. No folk or popular sounds figure in his planning. Although he is of Italian extraction, no operatic lyricism enters his measures. He carefully and inventively lays out his structures. Melody is paradoxically both cosmopolitan and individual. One is tempted to speak of an international manner, but this description would be incorrect. The style is individual. The music, like that of other contemporary American composers, shows a native spirit, vigor, and rhythmic approach that come across as fresh.

He was named Peter Mennini at birth, but later changed his name to Peter Mennin in order to distinguish himself from his older brother, Louis Mennini. Both were composers and educators. Peter was born in Erie, Pennsylvania, in 1923. His Italian-born father, Attilio Mennini, was a restaurateur who loved music. The Mennini home was constantly filled with music supplied from phonograph records and radio broadcasts. By age seven, Peter was showing a definite inclination toward music and had composed his first piece. Four years later, he tried to write a symphony. At age sixteen, he was studying musical composition with Norman Lockwood at Oberlin Conservatory. However, the war interrupted his studies and, like Barber and Blitzstein, he found himself in the U.S. Army Air Forces. After his discharge, he entered the Eastman School of Music, studying with Howard Hanson and Bernard Rogers. Here, he earned bachelor's and master's degrees in 1945, and a doctorate in 1947.

When Peter Mennin began his artistic efforts, he witnessed the Federal Music Project acting to support the production of native works in the prewar years. The encouragement continued during the war, even though the Music Project had ended. He observed how American composers were courting the general public with compositions couched in an assimilable language that often made use of home-grown material.

With the war's conclusion, he witnessed the end in a number of quarters of the need to reach a broad public with a widely understood musical language. On the rise was a fresh interest in composing music using twelve-tone and other atonal techniques. Tonal centers were absent; repetitions remained at a minimum; consonance went by the board. Karlheinz Stockhausen, one of the influential European leaders of this trend, described the new serialism as follows:

> Serial thinking is something that's come into our consciousness and will be there forever: it's relativity and nothing else. It just says: "Use all the components of any given number of elements, don't leave out individual elements, use them all with equal importance and try to find an equidistant scale so that certain steps are no larger than others." It's a spiritual and democratic attitude toward the world. The stars are organized in a serial way. Whenever you look at a certain star sign you find a limited number of elements with different intervals. If we more thoroughly studied the distances and proportions of the stars we'd probably find certain relationships of multiples based on some logarithmic scale or whatever the scale may be.[8]

Unfortunately, the various explanations of the new trends were difficult either to understand or to accept. A small minority of the music public had the inclination to try something novel. A less adventurous but open-minded group tolerated the innovative directions music was taking. However, the resultant compositions were found incomprehensible and ugly by the general music public, which promptly turned its back on most contemporary productions. Nevertheless, by the fifties and sixties such writing would characterize the most influential composers. A few would remain faithful to a more traditional approach but would find themselves out of fashion and ignored. Mennin was somewhere in the middle.

He was an advocate neither for "a people's music" nor for serial writing. The young composer went his own way, selecting from the musical procedures offered him whatever he found congenial. He refused to succumb to the avant-garde trends. He favored the creation of big, solely musical works, uncluttered with programs, and gave his greatest creative attention to the writing of his nine symphonies. The resultant music was never trivial, insubstantial, or excessively romantic. Nor was it completely cerebral. The comic mode had little place in his output. To be more precise, he strove to portray the unrest within him and that affecting the world about him. The expertise that he brought to bear when composing music was enormous, and he employed it with the greatest attention to detail.

The composer had completed a First Symphony, in 1942, which was almost an hour long. He heard it performed at Eastman following his release from the military, and subsequently had it withdrawn. His Second Symphony, completed in 1944, went on to receive the Gershwin Memorial Prize (for one movement) and the Bearns Prize in Composition in 1945. He was at that time a student and his career was still in the future. He added to his laurels by composing the *Folk Overture* in that same year. It was less a work employing folk material and more one kept uncomplicated, comfortable to listen to, and filled out with melodies that appeared to be folk-like. It succeeded with audiences and was soon being performed throughout the country.

The summer of 1946 was spent at the Berkshire Music Center of Tanglewood, where he studied conducting with Serge Koussevitzky. All the while, he continued composing music, in particular his Symphony No. 3. By then, the course of his creative activities had become clear— he would be a composer primarily for symphony orchestra, secondarily for voice and chamber ensembles, and never for the operatic stage. He studied thoroughly the contrapuntal practices of the Renaissance composers. This is the one impact on his music that Mennin acknowledged. An early work such as the Symphony No. 3 may make the listener think of the dignity in Hanson's Third Symphony, the lofty seriousness in Diamond's Second Symphony, and the contrapuntal bustle in Schuman's Third Symphony. It reflects the prevailing musical direction of its decade, which was to write assimilable works that made bold statements delineated in brisk, syncopated patterns and well-defined modal lines.

This Symphony No. 3, Mennin's doctoral dissertation, premiered on 27 February 1947, with the New York Philharmonic directed by Walter Hendl. Shortly after, the Eastman School had it recorded. Virgil Thomson reviewed the music in the *Herald Tribune*, writing that it was "an accomplished work, in the sense that its shape holds together and that its instrumentation is professional. Its expressive content is eclectic, ranging from a Sibelius-like sadness to a syncopated animation suggestive of William Schuman." What Thomson neglected to add was that it does not persistently brood, as does a Sibelius symphony, nor does it rush about too busy to make its expressive point, as is apt to happen in a Schuman symphony.

The work caught on. Other conductors took it up, among them musicians with international reputations: Dmitri Mitropoulos, Artur Rodzinski, George Szell, and Fritz Reiner. It gained performances and fame in America and abroad. Like the young Samuel Barber before him, the young Peter Mennin found himself emerging out of the pack of American composers. Already, at age 23, he had acquired a style distinguished by persistent tension, emotional forcefulness, and intricate polyphony. He liked to employ modal rather than the traditional major and minor arrangements of the scale. From time to time he would employ the unstable Locrian mode.[9] Although he had a thorough grasp of orchestration, he did not seek after instrumental color, preferring to bring out and adjust individual lines with all the orchestral skill at his command. His symphonies offer serious music meant for careful listening, not music desirable for unwinding after a day's work or for background sounds for reading.

Mennin contributed a short analysis of the music for the first performance of Symphony No. 3:

The first movement, *Allegro robusto,* makes use of two ideas which are developed polyphonically. Rhythmic and melodic extensions finally lead to a canon for full orchestra. The first movement ends quietly.

The second movement, *Andante moderato,* is an extended song which moves along expressively, making use of sustained voice-weaving.

The third movement, *Allegro assai,* is a movement of full rhythmic impulse and with broad lines set off by polyphony of the orchestra.[10]

The motif out of which the first movement grows is an arresting and syncopated five-note subject introduced at the beginning. It will recur in different shapes in this and the other two movements. At first, the motif is just repeated. Next, after a build-up by the entire orchestra, the strings enlarge upon it briefly. Other subjects evolving out of the motif sound in the horns, winds, and later the violins. After that, persistently repeating figures support canonic passages that thrust the music forward in determined fashion to reach a magnificent peak of intensity. When the flare-up ends, tension lessens, texture lightens, and the movement closes. "*Robusto*" indicates something or someone strong and sturdy. It implies courage and indomitability—appropriate sentiments for the time. The potency and strong feeling that the music generates may be, I suspect, in remembrance of the war now ended, or they may be the intensified rhetoric appropriate to a symphony's first movement. Mennin does not say.

The second movement moves along at a reasonably slow pace. The "song" that Mennin refers to is tripartite and begins with a sorrowful singing in the strings. A variant of the motif is intoned. Woodwinds continue the song and elaborate on the motif for a while. Soon, an unassuming rising-and-falling repeated-bass figure underpins a polyphonic fabric. The music reaches a passionate peak of sound. The music quietens considerably at the close and only the muffled tone of strings is heard. If the view about the war connection of the first movement is accepted, then the plaintive slow movement may signify mourning over the death and destruction caused by the war.

The finale moves quickly and even impetuously. Motif-derived lyricism prevails, whether the texture is homophonic or polyphonic. Recollections of passages from the previous two movements enter. The melodic lines twine and untwine in convoluted motion. A breathtaking coda concludes confidently on a major harmony. If the symphony is at all related to current events, then this is a fittingly optimistic conclusion that offsets the tragic and mournful commentary on war in the first two movements.

The symphony proves that Mennin had evolved into a composer with a respect for time-honored practices and structures, although he subjected them to liberal interpretation. Early on, he was proving to be completely free from current vogues in music and steadily holding fast to his own artistic principles. As he grew older, his music would grow more chromatic, more rhythmically irregular, more severe and unyielding, and less oriented to a tonal center. It would sound eloquent and expressive in most of its measures.

He tried to explain himself in an interview by saying, "Individuality is an inevitable precondition for music of lasting value. Individuality does not mean novelty for its own sake, since novelty, once familiar, becomes a cliché. It does mean a strong musical thrust, unconcerned with convention, or with conformity either to the past or to the fads of the moment. It is concerned with the drive of the composer's musical ideas; it is having one's own voice, one's own face. . . . I don't think any real composer ever aligns himself with a group. . . . A composer has to travel alone." [11]

On graduation, Mennin went on to teach at the Juilliard School of Music in New York, remaining there for ten years. He completed his Symphony No. 4, *The Cycle,* for chorus and orchestra, in 1948. Its three movements are captioned *Allegro energico, Andante arioso,* and *Allegro deciso.* He composed for it a setting of his own poetry. After Virgil Thomson heard Robert Shaw conduct it with the Collegiate Chorale in New York City on 18 March 1949, he wrote in the *Tribune,* "The symphony's force lies . . . in its treatment of the choir as a section of the orchestra capable of rivalry with the instrumental body in loudness and in musical interest. I don't think I've ever heard a choral symphony in which the vocal and instrumental forces are so well equilibrated in the whole expressive achievement. . . . He had resolved a hitherto unsolved problem and created by that fact a musical work of genuine originality." [12]

In 1950, the University of Rochester showed it thought enough of his work to grant him a centennial citation for distinguished service to music.

A Fifth Symphony was finished in 1950. An impetuous first movement rushed on in toccata fashion. The slow second movement is a passacaglia. The third movement, appropriately labeled *Allegro tempestuoso,* weds rhythm to counterpoint. When he contributed to the program notes for its 2 April 1950 premiere, given by Walter Hendl and the Dallas Symphony, he outlined his basic approach to his writing—he was concerned with expressivity and, for that reason, placed greater emphasis on the broad melodic line and less on orchestral color.

Three years later a wiry Sixth Symphony followed. It was in the usual fast-slow-fast three-movement structure. Also, in 1952, he finished the *Concertato Moby Dick.* ("Concertato" is a term from the early-musical Baroque that indicates a style typified by the interaction of two or more groups of instruments or voices.) The title denotes the Melville novel, but the one-movement piece is not programmatic. The composer's emotional reaction to Melville's tale is given a musical voice.

Beginning in 1958 and for four years, Mennin acted as director of the Peabody Conservatory of Music in Baltimore. He then returned to Juilliard, becoming its president after William Schuman resigned. His Symphony No. 7, *Variation-Symphony,* was completed in 1963; the Symphony No. 8, in 1973; and the Symphony No. 9, in 1981. In addition, he composed three admirable concertos—for cello (1956); for piano (1958); and for flute (1983).

From 1962 until his death in 1983, Mennin labored to enhance the reputation of Juilliard. He supervised its move to Lincoln Center and won it an international standing. Not least was the establishment of a Theater Center, an American Opera Center, and a Conductor's Training Program. He also saw to an annual Contemporary Music Festival. As an administrator, Mennin had an unruffled, competent approach to carrying out the school's business. In his public appearances he was always well dressed and groomed. The outward show belied his complete commitment to his creative activities.

Before he died, he witnessed the decline of the American symphonic tradition that had looked so promising during his youth. His own nine symphonies, however impressive their qualities, would become strangers to the concert hall. No longer was an audience able to hear Mennin's indisputably substantial and skillfully made music—on occasion gracefully refined, more often dignified, always rhythmically active, and invariably solidly built. Mennin's harmonic language at its most daring had remained only cautiously contemporary. On the whole, he had shown no interest in the most up-to-date innovative practices. Here and there, one does find works containing noticeably discordant harmonies. Otherwise he remained faithful to his own beliefs. All things considered, Mennin's music deserves a major place in the concert repertoire.

THE PLAIN-SPOKEN SYMPHONY: THOMPSON

Although born in New York City, Randall Thompson (1899–1964) laid claim to a New England ancestry. He and his forebears were plain-speaking Americans, who disapproved of expressing things in a roundabout way. Their speech was clearcut; their dealings were straightforward. So it was in Thompson's music. Whatever else is said of it, it was always plain-spoken. His compositions are aimed at and meant to speak directly to the listener. He explained in an address called "Music, Popular and Unpopular," given at Princeton University in 1946, that "a composer's first responsibility is, and always will be, to write music that will reach and move the hearts of his listeners in his own day."[13]

He, like Douglas Moore, preferred to cultivate an idiom disposed to maintaining long-established values. Both were practiced hands at writing for voice. However, Thompson was not, like Moore, a romantic idealist who consistently looked back at American history for inspiration. Nor was he a cantankerous Yankee like Charles Ives, whose contentious nature found expression in the challenging disharmonies he wrote into his music. In life, Thompson was known for his waggishness, delightful traits, and love of good food and drink. As a composer he was always self-assured.

Thompson wrote about what he saw, what he believed, and what he felt, as in his deliciously satirical *Americana* for chorus and piano or orchestra (1932), the emotional declarations of *The Testament of Freedom* for men's chorus and piano or orchestra (1943), and the universally loved *Alleluia* for a cappella chorus (1940), respectively. All three compositions are embedded in contemporary times. Yet I can occasionally detect a wistful yearning for some things in the past. His orchestral music, too, is of the present in its generous helpings from ragtime, jazz, dance patterns, blues, spirituals, and popular song.

He was educated at the Lawrenceville School, located midway between Princeton and Trenton, New Jersey, where his father was an English teacher. The Thompsons spent summer vacations on a family farm in Kennebec County, Maine. Randall's musical tastes were first formed in Maine, where he, family, and neighbors amused themselves of evenings with the singing of time-honored ballads around a wheezy melodeon. One guest, a local woman, awakened his interest in music by teaching him some of the basics. He began his study of organ and piano with Francis van Dyke while at the Lawrenceville School. He took up composition after he enrolled at Harvard College (B.A., 1920; M.A., 1922), studying with Edward Burlingame Hill. Thompson would also take instruction from Ernest Bloch, in New York City, during the brief interim period between the granting of his B.A. and his returning to Harvard for his M.A. Later he received a three-year fellowship at the American Academy in Rome.

When Thompson returned to the United States in 1925, he took on teaching positions at Wellesley College (1936–37), the University of California, Berkeley (1937–39), the Curtis Institute (1941–46), Princeton (1946–48), and Harvard University (1948 until his retirement in 1965). He was devoted both to education and to music composition. With regard to education, witness his *Catalogue of the College Music Set* (a catalogue of a set of equipment for use in music study in liberal arts colleges, 1933) and *College Music: An Investigation for the Association of American Colleges* (1936).

His music works were chiefly choral. Their contents appealed to performers and audiences alike. They were consistently comfortable for amateur choruses to sing, and rewarding for listeners to hear. As Nicolas Slonimsky aptly put it, Thompson in his choral music "preserved and cultivated the melodious poetry of American speech, set in crystalline tonal harmonies judiciously seasoned with euphonious discords, while keeping resolutely clear of any modernistic abstractions."[14]

His choral compositions occupied prominent positions in the repertoires of American singing groups—not only the ones cited previously, but also *The Peaceable Kingdom* (1936), *The Last Words of David* (1949), *The Passion according to St. Luke* (1965), and *Frostiana* (1965). For the stage, he composed the opera *Solomon and Balkis* (1942) and *The Nativity according to St. Luke* (1961). Almost all of his compositions were composed on commission from some group or institution. Singing societies continue to enjoy performing his compositions; their audiences continue to love hearing them. His tunes appear with total clarity, translucent as gemstones. Our awareness of this music, especially its urbanity, humor, and humanity, comes through in passage after passage. One finds self-assurance and a unique mingling of rhythms and resonances on page after page.

These comments hold true for the three symphonies that he wrote. Everybody familiar with them will find the same recognizable ingredients as found in the choral music. One gets out of them a confirmation of the values that meant so much to the composer. Thompson cares about communication, particularly in the absence of words. Obvious is his love of the rhythms of jazz and American dance, and of the tunes in ballads, blues, and psalmody. One admires the assimilation of melody, rhythm, and harmony that one structure after another manifests. All of these traits together encompass this composer's strength.

His Symphony No. 1 (1929): *Allegro brioso, Poco adagio, Allegro,* boasts a blend of melodies pleasant to hear, rhythms close to the American land, and harmonies to hold the attention. The clear textures and guarded sentiments owe something to French composers and Stravinsky. The refined simplicity comes from Thompson himself. Actually, the symphony was a reworking of previous material: two sketches from his *Odes of Horace* for chorus and piano or orchestra. When premiered at Rochester on 20 February 1930, the symphony won enthusiastic approval. Thompson had tested the symphonic water, found it welcoming, and come across encouragement to write another symphony.

On the heels of this premiere, he received a Guggenheim commission to write his next symphony. The four-movement Symphony No. 2, one of the most popular American symphonies ever written, was composed during a sojourn in Gstaad, Switzerland, in 1930–31 and received its premiere on 24 March 1932, with the Rochester Philharmonic conducted by Howard Hanson. Its simplicity, forthright lyricism, and suggestions of popular music kept the work in the affections of audiences. Before the decade was over it would receive countless performances throughout America. Its movements are *Allegro, Largo, Scherzo-vivace, Andante moderato—Allegro con spirito—Largamente.* Critics appreciated the symphony's cheerful mood and melodic beauty. When he heard it in New York City, Lawrence Gilman wrote in the *Herald Tribune,* "Mr. Thompson was present last evening and after the resounding conclusion of his symphony he was acclaimed by the audience with a fervor that is seldom bestowed upon an American composer—unless, of course, he happens to be Mr. Gershwin."[15] Audience and critics declared his music, like Gershwin's, to be quintessentially American.

A constant undertone of criticism from those trying to move forward an advanced agenda gathered strength. Thompson was censured for lacking originality. From this critical point of view, the enthusiasm of audiences proved that his music smacked of pandering and diminished whatever stature he may have had. After the premiere of *The Peaceable Kingdom,* the naysayers irked him considerably, as is evident in a letter that he sent to Douglas Moore on 22 April 1936. Imagining himself addressing one of his critics, Thompson wrote, "Come now, are you a tune detective? And did you trap me in 30 minutes of unmitigated plagiarism? Won't you provide me with a key to my sources, if you did? Or did you mean 'originality' in some other sense? And if so, did you attach importance to it? And if you attached importance to it, how are you able to accept any of the classics? Are any of them 'original' in the sense that they bear no resemblance to previous works?"[16] Fortunately, Thompson would not be deterred, and he forged ahead with his work.

Thompson's Symphony No. 3, commissioned by the Alice M. Ditson Fund of Columbia University, failed to garner the marked admiration accorded the Second Symphony, perhaps because it was not relentlessly cheerful and was less obviously indebted to vernacular idioms. Nevertheless, it was devised in similar fashion to its two predecessors and contains its own admirable qualities. The composition was begun in 1944, while World War II was still raging, and not completed until 1947. He would continue to tinker with it until its first performance, on 15 May 1949, given by the CBS Symphony Orchestra under Thor Johnson. The occasion was the Fifth Annual Festival of Contemporary American Music at Columbia University.

The four movements have as directions, *Largo elegiaco, Allegro appas-*

sionato, Lento tranquillo, and *Allegro vivace.* The composer's own clarification of the symphony's contents is lucid and concise:

> The first movement (in A minor, common time) is in sonata form, with only one principle theme and one principal rhythm. The prevailing mood is one of sadness. The second movement (in D minor, alla breve) is full of action and defiance. The form is a modified rondo in which the final statement of the principal theme is presented more slowly. Allusions to the theme of contrast, also greatly augmented, bring the movement to a desolate conclusion. The third movement (in F major, with lowered seventh, in three-half time) is introduced by a phrase in the horn which later grows into a melody. The principal theme is song-like, and its three presentations are set off by plaintive passages in the woodwinds alone. The Finale (in A major, six-eight time) is in sonata form, and all the material is cheerful. There is no apotheosis of themes nor any heroic peroration. The serious and even tragic elements of the earlier movements are dispelled in exuberance.[17]

Unquestionably, the Third Symphony is a "war" symphony; that is to say that it has, among other things, a higher coefficient of seriousness than his previous two orchestral compositions. Cheerful it could not be. Drafts of the symphony were worked on during the peak of the fighting.[18] Thompson's descriptions, "sad" and "action and defiance," in movements one and two respectively, set the work into a context of mourning for the dead, conflict between nations, and bold confidence in the outcome of the conflict. The concern over the warfare is genuine. However, belligerent nationalism is absent. Dissonances, key clashes, and the subordination of popular elements distinguish this work from the previous two. The Third Symphony would be his most intensely experienced, eloquent, and thoughtful instrumental work.[19]

The first movement begins quietly enough, but it is the ominous quiet that prevails before disaster strikes. The dominant motif is built on two stepwise ideas, a descent of a quarter and two eighth notes followed by an ascent of four eighth notes. Three minutes later, the same motif bursts out in melancholic protest and anger. For a little more than two minutes the full orchestra rages loudly, gratingly, and bitonally. Eventually the quietness returns, but with it comes a greater feeling of unease, despite the "elegiac" label of the composer.

The second movement opens with a crash. Brass and percussion engage in a loud and powerful chant. A rush of strings follows. Soon the music gets softer and a chug-along rhythm propels the strings along. As in the previous movement, the full orchestra, dominated by stentorian brass, engages in sudden and violent interruptions. Once more the sound becomes muted. Fragmentary melodic phrases appear in the woodwinds, above a marching bass. Finally, the music turns extremely soft. The phrases above the marching bass are given longer notes. The movement dies down to a whisper.

The "plaintive" third movement vacillates between melancholy and wistfulness. Again and again poignant interpolations interrupt the pastoral singing. With the opening horn call, Thompson summons up a plein air atmosphere. After the horn announcement, strings intone a folkish modal song. The lyricism sounds like that of a composer who wants to pay final honors to the dead. This idea is brought home by the woodwinds and brasses that thrice interpolate a grief-stricken commentary and then allow the strings to continue their song.

The final movement's "exuberance" comes from unrestrained joy, possibly felt because of the end of the violence. The composer does not exalt over the Allies' triumph. He finds nothing noble in the thought of warfare. Moreover, this sprightly finale does not sum up the meaning of the composition. Thompson deliberately chooses a different route. He counters the previous uneasy moods with a superabundance of straightforward cheer. A gay country dance begins the proceedings and keeps on returning, despite the three contrasting sections, which are given a strained quality. At the close, the dance figure gains the upper hand and closes the symphony.

The fans of his Second Symphony were disconcerted by the moments of polytonality and unresolved added notes, in the first two movements especially, and unhappy because few whistleable tunes were offered them. The reemerging modernists were angry that the piece was tonal, the harmonies triadic, and the dissonances secondary. Boulez pontificated in 1950: "All non-serial composers are superfluous." Nevertheless, Thompson's Third was one of the finest symphonies composed in the forties, in both its musical ideas and its overall design. Noel Straus, music critic of the *New York Times,* reviewed the work enthusiastically, finding it to have "nobility, real depth of feeling.... Tragic in its implications, this was music that was at once markedly sincere, spontaneous, and moving," with its four movements "welded into a logical unity which made the symphony one of Mr. Thompson's major creations to date."[20]

Unfortunately for Thompson, the postwar years were not kind to him. Militant critics, academics, and young composers of radically different stylistic persuasions continued to attack him. His music was criticized as excessively old-fashioned, overly anxious to please the public, and insufficiently "serious." His persistent popularity was *prima facie* evidence that he had sinned. Soon, his commissions vanished. It was as if a vendetta was being conducted against him. He was excluded from the most important new histories of American music—those of Gilbert Chase, Wilfrid Mellers, Charles Hamm, and Richard Crawford. Although born in New York City, he has no entry in the *Encyclopedia of New York City.*

Only from the end of the twentieth century has a reassessment of Thompson's contributions to American music commenced.

THE AUGUST SYMPHONY: COPLAND

It is a constant source of amazement that a person born in Brooklyn to Lithuanian-Jewish parents could grow up to be not only one of America's most talented composers but also an artist who could speak for all America in his music. This person was Aaron Copland, born in 1900 in a home where nobody was especially musical or devoted to classical music. By the eighties he had earned the sobriquet "dean of American composers." Copland would die in 1990 having won widespread admiration for his compositions, his nurturing of young composers, and his services to the United States as musical ambassador to the world.

The musical public would esteem, in particular, those works of his written during the "American" period that began in 1936 with the play-opera *The Second Hurricane* and the symphonic poem *El Salón México.* What is more, he would compose a Third Symphony between 1944 and 1946 that would win the approval of composers, conductors, orchestral players, and the public for its supreme dignity and sense of monumentality—hence its description as "august." For several years, a debate would rage among various music critics over whether Copland's Third Symphony or Harris's Third Symphony deserved the inscription "the greatest American symphony."

On his own, encouraged by neither family nor friends, Copland had turned to music when an adolescent. He began his music studies by taking piano lessons with Leopold Wolfsohn between 1914 and 1918. Toward the end of 1917, he took lessons in theory and composition with Rubin Goldmark. Goldmark had studied with Antonín Dvořák and would become chairman of the composition department at the Juilliard School of Music at its founding in 1924.

In 1921, Copland made the crucial decision to study music at the American Conservatory at Fontainebleau, close to Paris. Mutual acquaintances introduced him to Nadia Boulanger, who became his and many other American composers' teacher in composition and orchestration. He remained with her until 1924, absorbing her appreciation of the music of Igor Stravinsky and her neoclassical approach to composition. He also learned about the modernistic musical theories boiling up among the young French composers. While a student in Paris, he grew conversant with percussive effects, ever-shifting meters, the simultaneous employment of sharply contrasting rhythms, the use of nontriadic harmonies, tone-row constructions, and the most up-to-date management of orchestration. On 11 January 1925, he made his American debut as a composer with his Symphony for Organ and Orchestra, performed by the New York Philharmonic with Walter Damrosch conducting, and Nadia Boulanger as soloist. The occasion prompted the often-quoted Damrosch remark: "If a gifted young man can write a symphony like this at 23, within five years he will be ready to commit murder!"[21] Later, Copland would arrange the work for an orchestra without the organ and name it Symphony No. 1. This was soon followed by his surrealistic ballet *Grohg;* excerpts from it were later incorporated into his *Dance Symphony.*

After his return to New York, Copland thought over what sort of American composer he wanted to become. He decided he wished to write music that the public would immediately recognize as "American in character." He chose jazz as his distinguishing language. The young composer was fascinated by jazz's melodic flexibility, driving rhythms, and harmonies ranging from diatonic to extremely chromatic. He wanted to incorporate its liveliness into his own compositions. The two principal works in this idiom are the *Music for the Theatre* suite (1925) and the Concerto for Piano and Orchestra (1926).

He also joined the League of Composers and began his long career as a writer, contributing articles to the League's *Modern Music*. He would be a cofounder of the Yaddo Music Festivals, the Arrow Press, and the American Composers Alliance. Finally, he authored three influential books: *What to Listen for in Music* (1939), *Our New Music* (1941, revised and enlarged in 1968 and retitled *The New Music, 1900–1960*), and *Music and Imagination* (1952, the published form of the Charles Eliot Norton lectures delivered at Harvard University, 1951–52).

After 1926, he decided that staying with a jazz-derived idiom was too limiting and turned away from it. His music grew denser, more intricate, more jarring to the ear, and more demanding of the listener's attention. Highlights of this period are the piano trio *Vitebsk* (1929), the *Symphonic Ode* (1927–29), the *Piano Variations* (1930), and *Short Symphony* (Symphony No. 2, 1932–33). The last was afterward arranged as a sextet for clarinet, piano, and string quartet. These four pieces were vital compositions, but difficult for instrumentalists to perform and problematic for many listeners to follow and understand.

The Great Depression descended on the United States. Copland's select audience dwindled to nothing; monetary support disappeared. Performances of his music decreased. For example, the *Short Symphony* waited until 1944 for a performance, given by Leopold Stokowski and the NBC Symphony Orchestra, and then was left to sit again on the shelf. Writing whatever music he pleased became a luxury Copland could not afford.

Franklin Delano Roosevelt was elected President of the United States and called on all American citizens to take courage and pull together to overcome the Depression. The Federal Music Project started operations. Copland, alongside most composers, painters, writers, and intellectuals, carried himself leftward, impelled toward a popular goal. His sympathies and those of many other artists were toward communism and social and economic equality. In 1934, he wrote a song to a text by Alfred Hayes, "Into the Streets, May First," for a contest sponsored by the *New Masses*, a prominent Marxist magazine of the thirties. The action would come back to haunt him during the years of the McCarthy witch hunt.

Arthur Berger reports that Copland and the others "who had formerly been escapist became aware of politics and economics" and wanted to come out of their shells. They fastened their aspirations on Roosevelt's New Deal, as "the vein of optimism and patriotic sentiment ... became *the thing* in the ranks of the *avant-garde*."[22] Copland realized an important audience was out there with whom he sympathized and whom he wished to cultivate—the general music public. The question he asked himself was: how could he reach this audience without sounding patronizing and compromising artistic integrity?

He simplified his harmonies, scrubbing away excessive dissonance and anchoring it within an intelligible tonal system. Rhythms no longer reached for the extremes and often turned into recognizable American dance patterns, traditional and otherwise. His melodies were appropriated from, or had a kinship to, American hymnody and traditional song. His textures acquired an unusual transparency; orchestration was spaced widely for lucidity. In sum, Copland resorted to an approach parallel to the unadorned language of ordinary Americans, yet one that remained peculiarly Coplandesque.

Virgil Thomson has claimed that Copland changed to a musical style akin to his own. Copland has acknowledged that debt. Copland was impressed by Thomson's ability to infuse his music with American speech rhythms and hymnbook harmony, within lucid and straightforward contexts. Yet Copland managed to retain an individual identity that is discernable in most of his compositions from whatever period.

Copland admitted, "It is a delicate operation to put fresh and unconventional harmonies to well-known melodies without spoiling their naturalness; moreover, for an orchestral score, one must expand, contract, rearrange, and superimpose the bare tunes themselves, giving them something of one's own touch. That is what I tried to do, always keeping in mind my resolve to write plainly—not only because I had become convinced that simplicity was the way out of isolation for the contemporary composer, but because I have never liked music to get in the way of the thing it is supposedly aiding. If it is a question of expressing the deepest ideas of one's own soul, then you write a symphony. But if you are involved in a stage presentation, the eye is the thing, and music must play a more modest role."[23]

On several occasions during the late thirties and throughout the forties, Copland said that his objective was to articulate and transmit his sentiments and convictions through music. These, of course, could not help but be influenced by contemporary events. He expressed his feelings and beliefs by means of musical techniques that were abreast of the time and designed to reach the men and women of his own time. When properly realized, he thought, such music was given contemporary and universal meaning.

He was convinced that a musical composition could be made to speak with a force and frankness that no other artistic medium could convey. He said in 1951, "What, after all, do I put down when I put down notes? I put down reflections of emotional states: feelings, perceptions, imaginings, intuitions. An emotional state, as I use the term, is compounded of everything we are: our background, our environment, our convictions. Art . . . gives meaning to *la condition humaine*. . . . It necessarily has purpose . . . moral purpose."[24]

This venture into the vernacular caught on with the public. The music became quite well liked. Hitting it off with audiences were *El Salón México* and the school play-opera *The Second Hurricane* (1936), the ballets *Billy the Kid* (1938) and *Rodeo* (1942), concert arrangements of the film tracks to *The City* (1939), *Of Mice and Men* (1939), and especially *Our Town* (1940), and individual concert pieces including *Music for Radio* (1937), *An Outdoor Overture* (1938) for high school instrumentalists, and *Quiet City* (1939).

None of these works expressed intense feeling; passion was not in Copland's vocabulary. In general, the music remained understated and unpretentious. His compositions could be said to reflect his artistic inclinations. They originated in a personality marked by restraint in words and actions. All things considered, whatever his artistic predilections and public persona, he believed in himself as an artist. He knew that what he was trying to do was essential to a composer whose efforts were meant to be meaningful for his own time. His self-belief enabled him to work creatively in the only way possible given the era he lived in. Alongside modesty in his relationship to colleagues, he harbored confidence in his abilities and awareness that what he did carried weight. Copland retained a sense of his own worth as an artist during most of his adult life.

The musical Americanisms now present in his music were so well received and imitated by other composers, they became fundamental to the sounds that defined America to the public. His vernacular style soon took on connotations of an industrious citizenry, of village and country places, and of the spacious Great Plains. Some claimed it framed the image of America's democratic soul. Overlooked was the fact that he was really "the kid from Brooklyn," and what he felt was, as Arnold Dobrin described it, an *urban longing* for a pastoral life of a different period and a nostalgia for the peace and gentleness of the natural world. Despite this, Copland never ceased to love city life and had no wish to live in the country or to cultivate the soil.[25]

Copland would also note that, after some decades when such interest was lacking, the writing of symphonies, particularly of a heroic or majestic nature, was again capturing the attention of the music world. World War II had spurred this interest on. American composers had made a great effort to link their music to the war effort. They believed that their new music would advance the cause of democracy. Copland contributed *Fanfare for the Common Man* (1942), *Lincoln Portrait* (1942), *Appalachian Spring* (1944), and, as a culmination of this period, the Third Symphony (1944–46). As successful as the two works of 1942 and the one of 1944 were, one could argue that they were preparations for the writing of the symphony.

The *Fanfare* is a brief but thrilling passage for brass and percussion, one of ten fanfares commissioned by conductor Eugene Goossens for the Cincinnati Symphony Orchestra. Goossens was attempting to promote the spirit of patriotism during wartime. It took a while for Copland to settle on a title, but Goossens's reaction to its final form merits mention: "Its title is as interesting as the music, and I think it is so telling that it deserves a special occasion for its performance. If it is agreeable to you, we will premiere it 12 March 1943 at income tax time." Copland put in, "I was all for honoring the common man at income tax time." Of the ten fanfares, only Copland's has remained constantly in the repertoire. It has been performed again and again, year after year, probably owing a little to the broad coverage of the title, more to the grandeur of its subject, and most to the affective impact of the music on large numbers of people. Copland would take up the *Fanfare* once more, expand the music, and integrate it into the last movement of his Third Symphony.

A *Lincoln Portrait* for speaker and orchestra, Copland's musical tribute to Abraham Lincoln, was the result of a commission from André Kostelanetz, who wanted a composition "to mirror the magnificent spirit of our country." Kostelanetz gave its first performance on 14 May 1942 in Cincinnati, with the Cincinnati Symphony Orchestra and with William Adams as speaker. *Lincoln Portrait* had its New York premiere at Carnegie on 1 April 1943, with Serge Koussevitzky conducting the Boston Symphony Orchestra and with Will Geer as speaker. The composer began the *Portrait* soon after the attack on Pearl Harbor, trusting that the music would heighten patriotism and boost morale during the weeks when America's misfortunes appeared overwhelming. He decided to draw on Lincoln's own words, spoken, not sung. Orchestral music surrounded the narrator's speech. The music, as Copland explained, would "draw a simple but impressive frame around the words of Lincoln."

Copland thought of A *Lincoln Portrait* as a *pièce d'occasion* and never expected it to live on. Nevertheless, the composition has become one of his most admired works. In it, he inserted Stephen Foster's "Camptown Races" and the traditional "Springfield Mountain" tune, which gave the piece a decided nostalgic flavor. The reading presents quotations from Lincoln's speeches that reveal the brave and compassionate man underneath. Despite the fact that several other composers held it in little regard,[26] the *Lincoln Portrait* became a work much valued by the public. Virgil Thomson described it as a pastorale, scherzo, and melodrama when he heard Koussevitzky and the Boston Symphony Orchestra perform in April 1943. "The first is plain but pleasant; the second, a sort of country-fair scene made up of phrases out of Stephen Foster, is brilliantly picturesque. Lincoln himself comes into the portrait only by quotation."[27] Charles Mills's assessment, in *Modern Music*, was, "With great economy, the score projects a conception of its subject that is noble but tempered with reason and minus the pomp and bombast generally associated with musical pictures of that great statesman. Carl Sandburg's simple, unpretentious reading was gratifyingly effective."[28] One adds that *Lincoln Portrait* helped Copland to arrive at the grandeur of expression so necessary in the symphony.

Finally, there is the *Appalachian Spring* ballet written for the Martha Graham Dance Company, on commission from the Coolidge Foundation. Graham sent Copland a scenario without a title; Copland recommended a few modifications. The writing began in June 1943 and was completed in June 1944. The title was then supplied by Graham without consulting the composer. On 30 October 1944, the premiere took place at the Library of Congress. At first composed for thirteen instruments, *Appalachian Spring* was later reorchestrated for a symphony orchestra.

The scenario involves a marriage in rural nineteenth-century America, set among people of strong faith and firm principles. The theme would remind Americans of the values they were fighting to preserve. The expression is pastoral; the atmosphere is serene and joyful. The harmonies, based on open fourths and fifths, evoke "our sparse and dissonant rural traditions rather than the thick suavities of our urban manner," according to Virgil Thomson. The instrumentation was "plain, clean-colored, [and] imaginative . . . designed to express the moods of the story and amplify the characteristics of the *dramatis personae*." Thomson found the work to be "poetically effective, theatrically functional, [and] musically interesting." The composition is predominantly static, "giving us . . . that blithe Elysian-Fields note that is ideally the pastoral manner."[29]

A slow introduction sets the rural scene, followed by a burst of unison strings, indicating the start of the activities. The bride and her intended engage in a tender dance, followed by the revivalist preacher and his flock, whose fast dance is folk-like and whose music takes on the square-dance sound of country fiddlers. After an allusion to the introduction, a tranquil and smoothly unfolding set of variations on the Shaker tune "Simple Gifts" fills out the scenes of the daily activities of the bride and her farmer-husband. At the end, husband and wife abide in their new home to music that recalls the introduction and leaves the listener feeling awe and admiration for what has transpired.

Appalachian Spring caught the fancy of the American public, especially after the composer extracted a concert suite from the ballet, and in this form made it available for concert performance. Not only was *Appala-*

chian Spring admired, but also it solidified the new *lingua Americana* manner that Copland had developed and would utilize in his symphony.

In March 1944, Serge Koussevitzky offered Copland a commission
for a major work. He accepted. For the next two years, composing the
Third Symphony would be his chief concern. Musical associates including Elliott Carter, David Diamond, Arthur Berger, and Samuel Barber
pressed him to complete the work. Copland created the first movement
in Mexico during the summer of 1944; the second in Bernardsville, New
Jersey, in the summer of 1945; the third movement in Ridgefield, Connecticut, by April 1946; and the finale at the MacDowell Colony and
Tanglewood during the summer of the same year. He completed the entire composition just before its first performance by Koussevitzky and the
Boston Symphony, on 18 October 1946. The score bore a dedication to the
memory of Natalie Koussevitzky, who had died in 1942.[30]

Around the months Copland was writing the Third Symphony, other
composers were also busy bringing their own symphonies to completion. In addition to the American symphonies already cited, European
symphonies proliferated, including Igor Stravinsky's *Symphony in Three
Movements,* Dmitri Shostakovich's Ninth Symphony, Sergei Prokofiev's
Sixth Symphony, Paul Hindemith's *Symphonia Serena,* Arthur Honegger's
Third Symphony, *Liturgique,* and Darius Milhaud's Second Symphony.
Copland's instincts were correct—the writing of symphonies of an exalted nature had become an international phenomenon.

Copland's Third Symphony is a forty-minute composition and calls
for a large orchestra (fourteen woodwinds, eleven brasses, a huge percussion section, piano, two harps, and strings). It is his longest and most ambitious instrumental work. The symphony also marks his return to writing orchestral music without benefit of a program or descriptive title. The
composer said he did his "darndest to write a symphony in the grand
manner." To accomplish this, he might well have looked over the symphonies of Gustav Mahler and Dmitri Shostakovich as well as those of
his American colleagues. Moreover, he used his own *Fanfare* in the finale
because he "wanted a noble finale that would reflect the war's victorious
struggle."[31]

The Third Symphony is without question imposing. It moves effort-
lessly among oration, invocation of emotion, and conjuring visions of an

ideal America. Themes remain simple, tonal, and singable. Textures stay open. Orchestral timbres are clear. A seasoning of jazz rhythms and sharp harmonies is sometimes added. No conscious quotation of traditional or popular music occurs anywhere in the music. Although Copland claimed no ideological basis for the symphony, the use of the *Fanfare for the Common Man* in the last movement indicates the direction of his thinking. He conceded, "After all, it [the symphony] was a wartime piece—or more accurately, an end-of-war piece—intended to reflect the euphoric spirit of the country at the time. It is an ambitious score, often compared to Mahler and to Shostakovich and sometimes Prokofiev, particularly the second movement."[32]

He gave the composition an arch construction. At one end of the arch is the poignant first movement, *Molto moderato.* It opens on a note of contemplation not unlike that of *Appalachian Spring,* or, perhaps more accurately, in the spirit of American hymnody. The opening contrasts with a more militant theme allotted to the brasses. No real development of his themes transpires. The central portion of the symphony is the lively scherzo, *Allegro molto,* and the moderately paced *Andantino quasi allegretto.* At the other end is the finale, *Molto deliberato (Fanfare)—Allegro risoluto.* Both the first and second themes of the first movement recur in later movements.

The scherzo proceeds along a customary symphonic path. Its musical ideas are derivations from materials heard in the previous movement. In the middle of what could be considered the trio, a waltz theme enters that would not have been out of place in *Rodeo.* The third movement starts off with a reference to the second subject of the first movement before sounding the theme for the ensuing variations. These are built sectionally. Each section blends into the next, ringing changes on expressions that the listener experiences profoundly.

The longest movement is the finale, which the composer thought of as an "extended coda, presenting a broadened version of the opening material." It starts with a magnificent version of the *Fanfare* before going on to the principal subject. The music then progresses somewhat in sonata-allegro fashion. However, an extensive coda, bringing back many of the ideas that went before, is substituted for the expected recapitulation. The closing peroration is dramatic and electrifying, particularly when it combines the opening theme of the first movement and the principal subject of the finale with the fanfare.

The symphony was greeted enthusiastically by music reviewers and audience at its premiere. It won the New York Music Critics Circle Award. Yet some contemporary composers wondered whether it was too grandiose, and whether the composer was too eager to make it sound imposing. Copland wondered also, and he made a few deletions in the last movement to satisfy himself and, he hoped, the detractors.

Popularity acted as a stigma with people of advanced tastes. One critic, writing in *Time,* claimed the symphony contained stolen material and thought that it had achieved a public esteem that kept Copland "too popular to be a great composer." [33] The English writer Wilfrid Mellers, in his *Music in a New Found Land* (1964, rev. 1987), found neither the *Fanfare,* nor *A Lincoln Portrait,* nor the Third Symphony worthy of discussing at all. Gradually, however, after the stretch of decades, most critics and listeners who had reacted negatively at first were able to grasp fully what Copland had attempted and appreciate the work's quality and significance. I will never forget a stirring performance of the Third Symphony given by Leonard Slatkin and the National Symphony Orchestra at Wolf Trap in the summer of 1997. I and the audience were so carried away by the work and the vital and exciting rendition that we gave the performers a prolonged standing ovation. The verdict was unanimous—the Third Symphony was a great work.

William Schuman has given an insightful evaluation of the symphony's significance: "The characteristics by now recognized as American are simple traits developed and shared by our strongest composers, the ones whose personal idioms reflect America to its people just as the characteristics of what the world knows as Finnish music are manifest in the personal idiom of Sibelius. As for Copland himself, I must say that, to me, his music is just as 'American' in the *Third Symphony* as in *A Lincoln Portrait.* One assumes, of course, that the *Lincoln Portrait* is 'American' because of its use of folk tunes and other Americanisms and because of the specific nature of the work, while the symphony has no illustrative title or declared programmatic significance. But the question is not whether the *Third Symphony* could have been written by anyone but an American. The point in question is that it could have been written by no one but Copland, who proclaims himself in that work, no less than in *Billy the Kid,* an American composer."[34]

No more symphonies would come from Copland. Nevertheless, he continued with a people-friendly agenda in works such as *In the Beginning* (1947), for a capella chorus, and the music for the film *The Red Pony* (1948). The suite carved from the film's soundtrack became a widespread (and Copland's own) favorite. The Concerto for Clarinet and String Orchestra (1948), written for Benny Goodman, revisited his jazz idiom but did not include the French-Stravinsky modernisms of the twenties. The *Twelve Poems of Emily Dickinson* for voice and piano (1950) is one of the finest song cycles composed by an American. Although accessible, these songs do not offer quite the easy listening of, say, *Billy the Kid* or *Rodeo.* In 1952, he veered to the opposite side with the completely assimilable *Old American Songs* for baritone and piano or orchestra. They are delightful and make no demands on the listener. Traditional comic and sentimental ditties, a century or more old, were arranged so as to have a maximum effect on an audience. An opera, *The Tender Land* (1954), tells a story rich in feeling and meaning and lets audiences rediscover America's past and way of life. Its setting is the open spaces and farmlands of the Midwest. Its music hews to simplicity and discloses a folkish underpinning.

In the fifties, Copland had to confront another, less savory side of the American character—its occasional manifestation of superpatriotism to the point of arrogant nationalism, and a worrisome responsiveness to the radical right. Senator Joseph McCarthy, who was fueling the "Red Scare," had come upon the composer's leftward leaning during the thirties and accused him of being a Communist. McCarthy also set out to destroy Copland's career and reputation, despite the contrary evidence of the several major works that celebrated America. Copland was investigated by the FBI and found guilty by association. He saw himself blacklisted.

In 1953, *A Lincoln Portrait* was removed from President Eisenhower's inaugural concert, owing to the prevailing political attitudes. Ironically, Copland was the most famous American composer at that time. The U.S. State Department had sent him to Europe and South America as musical ambassador. The investigation was put on hold in 1955 and brought to an end in 1975.

The charge infuriated most members of the musical world. It also prompted Copland to look inward and compose works of a private rather than public nature. In addition, aggressive younger composers of serial-music persuasion were penetrating into concert life and academia and condemning musical popularism and any appeal to the common man and woman. They and the many foreign-born orchestra conductors, who with the war's end felt little pressure to perform American compositions, caused the works of Copland and other composers of like persuasion to appear less frequently in concert halls.

Somewhat tentatively, Copland decided to conform to the latest imperatives, although he claimed that he was trying only to enrich his style with new chords. He began to compose using serial techniques in 1950, with his Quartet for Piano and Strings. A principal tone-row of eleven pitches (A-natural was left out) was designed so as to get two whole-tone scales. This strategy allowed him to avoid severe dissonances and even hint at tonality. Nevertheless, the composition was austere, intended for music connoisseurs, and not fashioned to appeal to the general public.

His next big venture in a similar direction was the *Orchestral Variations* of 1957. It provided evidence that the turn to complexity and de-emphasis of tonality was nothing new for him. In 1931 he had composed his *Piano Variations*—dissonant, gloomy, jittery, and stripped of ornament. The *Piano Variations* turned out too austere for most listeners. Piano soloists shunned it. Copland rewrote the work as the *Orchestral Variations,* in response to a commission from the Louisville Orchestra. A four-note motif-cluster formed the basis for the composition. It won no support from the general music public and few adherents from the pro-serialist minority.

His next and last major orchestral work was *Connotations* for orchestra, the result of a commission from Leonard Bernstein and the New York Philharmonic and intended for the celebration of Lincoln Center's opening in 1962. Like the Piano Quartet, *Connotations* was a twelve-tone work but with more pronounced atonality. Audiences found little to like about it. Dedicated serialist composers slighted it and portrayed Copland as a Johnny-come-lately who was trying to climb onto their bandwagon.

He tested the waters again in 1964 with his *Music for a Great City,* a suite in four movements: I. "Skyline"; II. "Night Thoughts"; III. "Subway Jam"; IV. "Toward the Bridge." Its music was extracted from the soundtrack to the film *Something Wild,* which had been a box-office disaster. This twenty-four-minute piece is suggestive of jazz, to be sure, but is also atonal and dissonant. Few listeners chose to meet its challenge. Again he tried with the twelve-tone *Inscape* for orchestra, completed in 1967, with the same results. It was not long before the discouraged composer composed scarcely anything at all. In addition, he was showing the first signs of Alzheimer's disease by the seventies. He died 2 December 1990 at North Tarrytown, New York.

On balance, no matter what the style, Copland's compositions were well made, had something significant to say, and remained profoundly musical. Experienced listeners could detect elements uniquely Copland's own in all of his compositions, whether jazz-oriented, dissonantly atonal, folk-related, or twelve-tone. Leonard Bernstein summed him up with "He's the best we have."

Without question Copland determined the essential qualities of American music as most concertgoers thought of American music. He was neither a romanticist nor a slave to European conventions. He did take direction from native folksong, traditional ditties, country dance, jazz, and blues. An Americophile, he wrote works that were spare and un-sentimental. They said what they had to say as directly and succinctly as possible. His music has profited every music-lover.

THE SELF-RELIANT SYMPHONY: CRESTON

Paul Creston (1906–1985) was largely a self-taught composer, at first owing to necessity and later by choice. He would come to believe that successful composers stood out not because of, but in spite of their formal musical training. Creston had confidence in himself and insisted on exercising his own judgment in evaluating all external resources toward his educa-tion in theory and composition. Normally, help or support from teachers and colleagues was neither needed nor desired. Whatever he composed, he wanted free of anyone else's authority. "Self-reliant," when applied to a symphony of his, indicates independence, an ostensibly autonomous composition relying only on Creston for its realization.

He was born Guiseppe Guttoveggio in New York City, the son of a poor Sicilian house-painter. He first ventured into music by taking piano lessons with a second-rate teacher, which left him unhappy. Later, he would study keyboard with two fine instructors, the Belgian organist Gaston Dethier and the Italian organist Pietro Yon. He would also change his name to something more comfortable to pronounce and remember, spurred on by his high-school nickname of "Cress." After two and a half years in high school, he was forced to quit school and go to work. Errand boy, bank clerk, and insurance-claim adjustor were three of the jobs he had. Yet he had the firmness of character to teach himself, both in general subjects and in music.

Creston studied music theory and composition without direction from others and learned from the music of the most eminent composers, past and present. The composers he most admired were Johann Sebastian Bach, Domenico Scarlatti, Frédéric Chopin, Claude Debussy, and Maurice Ravel. In addition, acquiring skill in the handling of instruments was of the greatest importance to him and took precedence over vocal techniques.

Music, to him, was meant to express and effectively convey feeling to the general listener. For this reason, he rejected extremes—the ultramodernism of post-triadic atonality and the ultraconservatism of a style conforming to a bygone age. Moreover, music had to make known its own meaning without the crutch of a program. A composition, no matter what the expressive aim, had to show consistency and unity through a clear ordering of its melodies and rhythms, so that they left no doubt in the audience's mind that they formed a coherent whole.

The importance of rhythm was brought home to him after he married Louise Gotto, a dancer in the Martha Graham Dance Company. Song and dance would be the guiding principles behind the music he would write later. He was then earning a livelihood by playing the organ, whether in theaters (1926–29) or for special occasions. At first, his leisure time was limited. His financial burden was great. It did not occur to him to devote himself to musical composition until the early thirties. By then, he had gained the position of organist at St. Malachy's Church, New York City, where he remained for many years. His last position, first held in 1975, was that of professor of music at Central Washington State College.

Creston's opus 1 was the *Dances* for piano of 1932. He thought enough of his seven *Theses* for piano (1933) that he showed them to the musical experimenter and composer Henry Cowell, who immediately took up the young composer's cause and continued his advocacy of Creston's music for years. After several chamber works and songs, Creston ventured into writing for larger ensembles with his *Partita* for flute, violin, and strings (1937), *Threnody* for orchestra (1938), and *Two Choric Dances* for orchestra (1938).

During the thirties, he solidified his style and enhanced his reputation with musicians, critics, and the music public. Once hit upon, his approach to composing remained mostly the same until the end of his career. He remained opposed to the radical changes evidenced in the more modern compositions, though he added up-to-date touches in his music, including atonal passages, when he felt the need for them. Tonal centers are normally present in his compositions, though often treated in an open and flexible way. Homophony prevails over polyphony in his textures. Creston's rhetorical gestures, especially when grand, are romantic in nature and colorful, if not gaudy, in effect. When he writes for orchestra, individual solos and open spaces in the orchestration are infrequent. Two or more instruments often thicken each line. Doubling of notes precludes transparency. Solid sounds strike the ear. In all of these aspects, Creston is the opposite of Copland.

Rhythm is a leading component of his compositional approach. It is sometimes marked, as in the manner of Stravinsky, and sometimes less pronounced but still present, as in the manner of Ravel. It may be articulated in short, repeated designs or in continually changing micro-units of the basic beat. Usually the rhythm accompanies and sustains a melodic line, which can be lengthy and occasionally ornate even though spawned from a motif. Creston's devotion to rhythm was such that he would eventually write several volumes of rhythmic studies for piano, entitled *Rythmicon*. In 1964 he would publish the *Principles of Rhythm*.

Creston's harmony is rich, sensuous, and meant to evoke subjective and sensory moods or impressions (again, the opposite of Copland's approach). Sometimes this ampleness is too much of a good thing. The incessant fullness of the chords can grow wearisome. Harmonic motion does not always signify a functional progression of chords meant to help define the structure. Triadic construction frequently piles third on third, resulting in dissonant seventh to eleventh layouts that do not resolve into consonances but just thicken the sound. Yet the total organization is curiously lucid and to-the-point. Creston's idiom takes a positive view of life. The music may be passionate and insistent; it is rarely gloomy or nostalgic.

Creston believed that composing music was a "spiritual practice." Mystic philosophies fascinated him. He said, "My philosophic approach to composition is abstract. I am preoccupied with matters of melodic design, harmonic coloring, rhythmic pulse, and formal progression; not with imitations of nature or narrations of fairy tales or propounding of sociological ideologies." He was not a conscious nationalist. Americanisms are not introduced into his measures. Tunes of a folk or popular character are absent. He declared, "I work to be my true self, which is American by birth, Italian by parentage, and cosmopolitan by choice."[35]

Over his career, he would compose several concertos, some for unusual instruments, dance-related pieces and tone poems for orchestra, and six symphonies. He also wrote compositions for band, vocal pieces, most of them with religious points of reference, and a number of chamber works. He was the author of two analytical studies, *Principles of Rhythm* (1964) and *Rational Metric Notation* (1979).

The Symphony No. 1, op. 20, was destined to establish his reputation as a composer. Completed in 1940, its first performance took place in New York City, given by Fritz Mahler and the NYA Symphony Orchestra, on 22 February 1941. When Eugene Ormandy and the Philharmonic presented it again on 23 March 1943, it won the New York Music Critics Circle Award, despite competition from Harris's Fifth Symphony, Copland's *Lincoln Portrait,* Schuman's *Prayer 1943,* and Gould's *Spirituals.*[36] Critics found Creston's composition to be sunny and spirited, just the music to buoy up morale in the gloomy days of the war. Textures were dense, but their richness came through effectively. It bothered no one that the harmony did not move functionally and that tonal centers were elusive. Auditors were supplied with plenty of fine melody. Nowhere was the music allowed to drag. Lasting a little over twenty minutes, it did not overstay its welcome.

Each movement conveys a specific mood tersely and convincingly. The first movement, in a sonata-allegro structure, is entitled "With Majesty." The second movement bears the label "With Humor." "With Serenity," the center of the symphony, comes next. The finale, a rondo, proceeds "With Gaiety," closing the composition with teasing rhythms, vivacious syncopations, snatches of melody in the woodwinds, and majestic brass episodes. It is a display of the composer in his most energetic and exciting manner—that is to say, in a manner approaching jazzy abandon.

The music was too rich in feeling to make a dedicated neoclassicist such as Arthur Berger happy. He reviewed the 1943 concert, writing that Creston's

> reputation is now soaring to a level out of proportion to the quality of his work. The competence of his *Threnody,* his *Choric Dance, Number 2,* and the *First Symphony* seem much less exceptional when his goal so far is recognized as little more than an immediate gloss. If the symphony maintained the level of the vigorous opening and interesting trumpet themes it would be much better, but it quickly degenerates and reaches a low point in the saccharine slow movement, which suggests a Mark Warnow arrangement.[37]

However, the impersonal sort of musical expression favored by Berger had few takers. The music public and most reviewers welcomed Creston's emotive take on music. From the First Symphony on, he climbed swiftly to countrywide recognition.

Shorter pieces for orchestra came between the First and Second symphonies. His Concertino for Marimba and Orchestra, op. 21, was completed in 1940 in response to a commission from Frederique Petrides and the Orchestrette Classique, an all-women thirty-member ensemble. Ruth Stuber was the soloist at the 29 April 1940 premiere. The soloist was kept busy coping with the showy syncopations. The audience was delighted with the unusual orchestral colorings, the snippets of melody, and the impressionistic flow of harmony. A Concerto for Saxophone and Orchestra, op. 26, followed in 1941, and a *Fantasy for Piano and Orchestra,* op. 32, in 1942. Written in 1943, the *Chant of 1942* is dark, moving, and weighted down with the disasters of the time—the abominations inflicted by the Nazis on Greece, Poland, and particularly on Lidice, Czechoslovakia.

Creston turned from the war to a look at America's roots when he composed *Frontiers,* op. 34, in 1943 on a commission from André Kostelanetz, who led its first performance, in Toronto, on 14 October 1943. The ten-minute composition contains his feelings about the epic western migration in the nineteenth century, which he says was "achieved through the vision, constancy, and indomitable spirit of the pioneers." The three main musical ideas recall the vision, trek, and achievement of these hardy Americans. Scored for large orchestra, the musical depiction is emotionally powerful, opulently delineated, and convincing all the way through.

The Symphony No. 2, op. 35, was finished in 1944 and given its premiere on 15 February 1945 by Artur Rodzinski and the New York Philharmonic. It proved to be one of the most notable and admired symphonies of the forties. The symphony's attractiveness arose from its skilled orchestration, telling melodies, and concise construction.[38] The symphony is an assertion of Creston's artistic belief that song and dance are the most basic elements in music, with all other elements subordinate to them. In Creston's own words, the symphony contains "an apotheosis of the two foundations of all music: song and dance."[39]

The composition is in two movements: "Introduction and Song" and "Interlude and Dance." The whole piece is put together from a melodic idea that goes from cellos, to violas, to violins at the beginning of the "Introduction." An important element in the symphony's attractiveness is the several striking treatments of this lengthy, rather chromatic theme. It transmutes into the warm, sympathetic, and sinuous "Song" that takes on a shape of its own—a set of open variations with the theme often presented in fragments. The melody becomes heated, sheds some of its chromaticism, and rises in ardent melodiousness to reach an imposing peak, after which it quiets down.

The second movement is a marked contrast to the first. It begins with a bold, portentous "Interlude" based on the main theme from the "Introduction." It heads immediately toward the lively "Dance." The latter is cast around a single subject, also derived from the "Introduction." This "Dance" experiences an assortment of seemingly spontaneous modifications. Beneath the lyric lines are sharply contrasted and syncopated rhythmic designs in recurring phrases. Strong rhythms with variable accents propel the "Dance" along. The "Dance" reaches its highest point in a decidedly original restatement of all the major ideas in the symphony.

The Symphony No. 3, op. 48, bears the subtitle *Three Mysteries* and was composed in 1950. It represents the religious side of Creston, with its three movements entitled "Nativity," "Crucifixion," and "Resurrection." Medieval plainchant furnishes the subject matter, which is thoroughly and reverentially developed. The first movement paints an innocent and blissful picture that leaves the listener elated. The second movement is particularly moving, centering around two plainchant melodies over a ground bass that climax in a gripping moment of peak intensity. The last movement aims at dignified magnificence in delivering its message of affirmation. The use of modality and harmonies that generate an ancient ambiance transports the listener to a moment beyond time and place. The music conveys a great deal of power. Curiously, the total effect is more visceral than spiritual. Elemental emotions predominate rather than contemplations of the divine Spirit.

In 1951, Creston completed his Symphony No. 4, op. 52; in 1955, his Symphony No. 5, op. 64; and in 1981, his Symphony No. 6, op. 118. All three exhibit sections where the composer is at his finest. However, as Creston grew older, one began to find redundancy, histrionic expression, and measures where inspiration is absent in his music. He died in 1985.

THE KNOTTY SYMPHONY: SESSIONS

In a way, it is appropriate for Sessions to be taken up last, since his idiom is like a weathervane pointing to the immediate future in American music. Many discriminating listeners who enjoy music with appreciation of its subtleties have praised the music of Roger Sessions. On the other hand, the general music public finds it difficult to understand a typical Sessions composition. His convoluted music has more layers of meaning than average music-lovers can penetrate. The combined attempts of music theorists, historians, and advocates for modernity have failed to clear the mystification produced by a performance of a Sessions symphony.

Yet he was a composer with great artistic integrity. A study of one of his scores reveals a formidable intellect at work. A complicated arrangement of harmonies, rhythms, melodic lines, and interrelated units characterizes the music. The logic is impeccable. However, the sound lacks charm, sensuous appeal, and any hint at euphony. Chromaticism remains high, and dissonance incessant. At times pandemonium seems to cut loose, and even a knowledgeable audience cannot entirely take in the extraordinary skill and meticulous attention to detail that infuse the measures.

Some writers claim that he demands too much of his listeners. Sessions said his music expresses what he is, and the listener must take it or leave it. In short, the composer will dance to nothing but his own pipe. A majority of listeners have elected to leave it. In a *New York Times* article, Sessions wrote that he once asked the Italian composer Alfredo Casella about reducing the technical complexities in his Violin Concerto (1956) and got the reply that he could do nothing because all of his music was born difficult.[40]

Nevertheless, admirers claim that Sessions's music is distinguished by its vital rhythms, solid structures, magnificent melodies, and deep emotions. Although it presents huge technical and communicative difficulties for performers and audiences, the music makes known its strength and value after the intelligent listener continually listens to it over weeks or months. Admirers state that his compositions communicate crucial and thoughtful perceptions, but can do so only if the listener gives complete attention to the music and makes a real effort to grasp what meets the ear.

Aaron Copland admired the fine quality of Sessions's workmanship and said that his feelings were most evident in his slow movements: "At such times Sessions creates without aid of surface mannerisms a music profoundly his own: music of ineffable pessimism—resigned, unprotesting, inexpressibly sad, and of a deeply human and nonromantic quality." The music of Sessions, Copland admitted, did not make friends easily and was perhaps needlessly complex. It required the fullest attention and showed an indifference to "audience psychology." Sessions's works presented "a certain stern, grim, dour aspect, as if the pieces dared you to like them."[41] Peter Korn comments that "the predominant impression [given by the music] . . . is one of restlessness, of nervous tension, conjuring up the image of the 'tortured composer' who is himself in need of consolation, rather than having the ability to console."[42]

Roger Sessions (1896–1985) was born in New York City to parents whose forebears were New Englanders. He grew up in Hadley, Massachusetts, at his family's ancestral home. Owing to his intellectual accomplishments, he entered Harvard College at age fourteen and graduated four years later. He then studied music theory and composition with Horatio Parker (who taught Charles Ives and Douglas Moore) and Ernest Bloch (who taught George Antheil, Randall Thompson, and Douglas Moore). At twenty years of age, he began his long teaching career with a faculty position at Smith College.

In 1923, he composed his first major work, the incidental music to the *Black Maskers,* a senior-class production of a play by the Russian playwright Leonid Andreyev. From it, he extracted music for a four-movement suite for large orchestra in 1928. This colorful orchestral suite, an example of romantic and symbolic expressionism, shows the influence of Bloch. It is one of his most accessible and most often played compositions. He would write nothing like it again.

For eight years beginning in 1925, Sessions lived in Europe, supported by two Guggenheim fellowships, the Prix de Rome, and a Carnegie grant. He would return to America after viewing with alarm the Nazi rise to power. While abroad, he absorbed the neoclassic viewpoint of the Stravinsky-Boulanger set and the twelve-tone principles of the Schoenberg-Berg circle. He also came to reject nationalism, fearful that it could lead to Nazi-like fascism. Speaking to the American Musicological Society in Pittsburgh in December 1937, he insisted that American composers had to give up the too-easy exploitation of American traits in their work, and critics and musicologists had to cease insisting on national expression from composers. Composers had to discover their own genuine musical impulses and follow them, no matter where they led.[43] Three years later, he was worrying about "fascist-like demands" that music patriots were making about expressing national feeling and reflecting the American scene.[44]

The central part of Sessions's creative activity is his nine symphonies. His well-regarded Symphony No. 1 dates from 1927. Its music sounds full-bodied and powerful. Composed in Europe, this composition is in a style that reveals a paradoxical mix of influences. One hears Bloch's richness of expression, Stravinsky's devotion to impersonal rhythm, and intimations of the serial-music approach that would become prevalent later. The first movement drives forward at a phenomenal rate and generates an uneasy restlessness. It features spirited woodwind and brass segments and scattered percussive interruptions. The slow movement sounds almost hymnic, especially when the strings try to sing. Devotees hear warmth and poignancy in its measures. The last movement is forceful, sharply defined, and, according to some enthusiasts, flecked with humor. When Koussevitzky and the Boston Symphony Orchestra first performed it on 22 April 1927, the audience greeted the music with hisses. Nevertheless there is much to admire, and even enjoy, in the music.

Not long after his return to the United States, Sessions joined the faculty at Princeton University, where he remained for most of the next fifty years (interrupted by stints at Boston University and at Berkeley). Like Piston, he was one of America's most significant educators. Among his students were the composers David Diamond, Milton Babbitt, Ralph Shapey, Leon Kirchner, Vivian Fine, Andrew Imbrie, Ellen Taaffe Zwilich, and John Harbison. He also was an inveterate writer of articles and letters—commentaries on the musical world and on musical composition. Five books of his appeared: *The Musical Experience of Composer, Performer, Listener* (1950, rev. 1962), *Harmonic Practice* (1951), *Reflections on the Music Life in the United States* (1956), *Questions about Music* (1971), and *Roger Sessions on Music: Collected Essays,* ed. E. T. Cone (1979). He played an influential role in the League of Composers. In 1928, he cofounded the short-lived Copland-Sessions concert series.

Much of his Violin Concerto was composed in Europe, starting in 1931. He completed it in 1935, and not long after finished his First Quartet for Strings (1936), *From my Diary* for piano (1940), and the Duo for Violin and Piano (1942). As the thirties and early forties rolled by his music grew increasingly dense, intricate, chromatic, and technically demanding to play.

Already, in the Violin Concerto, one discovers extremes of complexity, avoidance of a tonal center, tremendous demands on orchestra players and listeners, and a fiendishly difficult part for the soloist. Even Aaron Copland found the texture too complex, the melody too involved, the structure too gargantuan, and the thought too condensed.[45] The four movements are labeled *Largo e tranquillo, Scherzo (Allegro), Romanza (andante),* and *Molto vivace e sempre con fuoco.* The absence of violins in the score is meant to call attention to the solo instrument. Because of the technical burdens placed on the violinist and orchestra, the concerto's premiere was delayed and finally took place in 1940. As was by now usual at a Sessions concert, the audience reacted negatively.

Sessions responded to the refusal of concert audiences to accept his music with a lament over the reluctance of listeners to exert themselves. He presented them with music to contemplate, not sounds to wallow in. He wrote to John Duke from Princeton University on 30 July 1944, saying: "The most serious danger today is that we offer the people 'Panem et circenses' [bread and circuses] and encourage them to demand no more than that. Should this demand become general and really compelling—if people demand no more of art and of culture in general than what is immediately acceptable to the majority, with a minimum of effort, then Fascism is around the corner whether we like it or not."[46]

Almost twenty years after his First Symphony, Sessions completed his Symphony No. 2 (1944–46). The premiere took place on 9 January 1947, with Pierre Monteux conducting the San Francisco Symphony Orchestra. The composition came into existence in the midst of a situation considerably far removed from that of the First Symphony. The Great Depression and then World War II had followed the Jazz Age. The composer's attitude toward his music had altered. However, his style had not taken the same direction as that of the composers discussed earlier. The tonal references still perceivable in the First Symphony are much less in evidence in the Symphony No. 2. In reality, he offers no tonal anchor whatsoever for most of the symphony. He is well on his way to incorporating a twelve-tone approach into his writing. Therefore, at the very end, when one hears a seven-measure D-A pedal, and the unadulterated blaze of a D major triad to close the work, one is astonished.

World War II hides in the symphony's measures, as does an awareness of President Franklin D. Roosevelt's last illness and death. The first page of the score bears the dedication "To the Memory of Franklin Delano Roosevelt." Yet the listener must understand that Sessions wanted to write absolute music, never a composition with programmatic references. The ear is subjected to an unusually heavy barrage of conflicting sounds, which is driven home by a huge orchestra—twelve woodwinds, eleven brasses, timpani, percussion requiring three more players, piano, and strings.[47] The effect is sometimes frightening. The last movement culminates in a final shattering climax and a D major shout of victory. Indeed, if there is any hint at a tonal center in the music, it is to the tone D. The first movement opens on a D minor triad, thickened with the note G, and closes on the note D. The finale begins with a D major triad plus an added D-sharp, and ends on a D major triad.

About this composition, Sessions said later, "I feel the Second Symphony is a point towards which I had been moving in a number of previous works, and one which forms, as it were, a point of departure for the music I have written since. Those who desire a clue to the 'emotional content' of the symphony, I would refer to the indications at the head of the various movements and sections, though the hearer may perhaps find the *Adagio* predominantly dark in color and mood and feel the finale at its climax acquires a character to which the indication *Allargamente* no longer corresponds. . . . My music is always expressive in intent."[48]

The symphony's first movement, *Molto agitato*, in five sections (A B A¹ B¹ A²), moves back and forth between disturbed and quieter (*tranquillo e misterioso*) segments. Ultimately, the disturbed passages calm down a little and take on some of the quieter sections' characteristics. Although there is nonstop chromaticism, the music suggests the key of D minor. The meter starts with a 4/4 time signature but constantly changes throughout the movement. At the start, the orchestra is very loud. Violins scurry about in sixteenth notes against a held chord (G-B-D-F-A) in the woodwinds and brasses. The quiet section that follows is slower in tempo and commences with a solo violin playing high up in range, followed by a solo flute. After the two sections alternate again, a final allusion to the beginning leads to a close of the movement, which is furnished with the label *più tranquillo*. A muted viola solo, playing sixteenth-note figurations in smooth and connected fashion, plays very softly for fourteen measures in 3/4 time and stops when all of the strings pluck the note D.

The sardonic second movement, *Allegretto capriccioso*, is a curtailed scherzo that marches rhythmically along in an off-kilter manner. A phrase given to an oboe and an English horn sets the prevailing character of the movement within three measures. The notes swing up and down, legato and with wrong-note inflections, followed by an equally brief staccato continuation, which then abruptly cuts off. The music that comes next is just as quirky, beginning to end. The change in expression is especially welcome after the perturbed first movement and before the bleak slow movement.

The third movement is a desolating *Adagio* that focuses on the flatted notes, especially the tone B-flat. Sessions asks that the *Adagio* be played *tranquillo ed espressivo*. Yet the music is anything but calming. Misery is more the picture painted. Muted strings set the atmosphere. At measure 10, a long oboe solo begins. Here, and in the measures that follow, the ceaseless chromatic tones invoke feelings of angst, of dread over some impending doom.

The massive finale keeps to a constant 5/4 meter. The key signature of two sharps points to a D major tonality. The movement is marked *Allegramente* and calls for a rapid tempo. But the term also suggests cheerfulness—an attribute not present in the music. What is almost constantly present is the repeated rhythmic pattern of an eighth note, followed by two sixteenths—a rhythmic combination much favored by Dmitri Shostakovich. This finale is assertive, even boldly aggressive, and, like the second movement, rhythmic.

Discerning men and women of the music world, including the composers Copland and Stravinsky, have praised the work. Audiences have found little to like in it. Virgil Thomson's commentary, made on 17 March 1947, takes the audience's side. He writes that Sessions's compositions, such as the Second Symphony, are "difficult to play and not easy to listen to. They are learned, laborious, complex, and withal not strikingly original. They pass for professor's music, and the term is not wholly unjustified. Because the complexity and elaboration of their manner is out of all proportion to the matter expressed. Nevertheless, they are impressive both for the seriousness of their thought and for the ingenuity of their workmanship. . . . Though they have unquestionably quality, they have just as certainly almost no charm at all. And we have no place in our vast system of musical distribution for music without charm. . . . [There is] no direct melodic or harmonic appeal."[49]

Sessions himself had considered revising the music before deciding against it. The work stands in extraordinary opposition to the American symphonies from the same period. It sounds neither audience-friendly nor Americana-oriented in idiom. If it is to be likened to any previous work, then Arnold Schoenberg's *Five Pieces for Orchestra,* of 1909, may serve as a precedent. However, the symphony has a more definite rhythmic backbone and meanders less.

This said, Sessions's symphony has maintained a unique position for itself in the American orchestral repertoire. It sounds earnest, intellectual, and determined to travel its own path. Its careful and thorough working-out of ideas reveals the inventive composer. Perhaps the music bears too great a load of learning. This encumbrance results from trying too hard for excellence. The composer's intention is praiseworthy and therefore pardonable.

Certain of the piece's failings are not easy to accept—its lack of melodic attractiveness, indifference to an audience's ability to process the sounds, and overwhelming technical difficulties for the players. Sessions's sincerity is patent. His seriousness of purpose is unquestionable. The extra effort needed to understand the symphony should be made. The listening difficulties it imposes are admittedly greater than those presented by any of the other symphonies taken up in this study. Nevertheless, when and if comprehension comes, it can be gratifying.

Serial techniques permeate the symphonies that came after the Second. Interestingly, the Third Symphony of 1957 sounds close to its predecessor in style. The music in the first movement can become forceful and does achieve big climaxes. However, it never sounds abandoned; the composer keeps a tight control over every measure. The second movement is the expected scherzo. Like the scherzo of the Second Symphony, it is given a definite rhythmic profile and sardonic bite. Dark memories and severe beauty reside in the slow movement. The finale progresses with the usual Sessions expression of stouthearted decisiveness. As part of a program note to this symphony, Sessions once wrote: "My third symphony is larger in conception and scale than the first and does not contain the sharp and even violent contrasts of the second. In saying this, I am simply noting a difference in character, not implying a fundamental change of artistic direction. I regard this symphony as belonging very definitely among a series of works which began with my second string quartet. It contains new elements, however, even with respect to these works."[50]

Symphony No. 4 dates from 1958 and contains a muscular, idiosyncratic "Burlesque," a choppy, abstracted "Elegy" with an agitated and strident middle section, and an austere, intellectually imagined "Pastorale." The Symphony No. 5 is a more concentrated work. Its parade of motives moves along swiftly throughout the three sections, labeled *Tranquillo—Lento—Allegro deciso*. Otherwise the symphony exhibits the expected tight planning, extreme intellectualizing, and indifference to the capacities of the music public.

Sessions composed the icily glistening Sixth, the abrasive Seventh, and the smoothly proportioned Eighth Symphony during the era of the Vietnam War—a war he hated and an era whose domestic disturbances he found greatly upsetting. These works continue in the international serial-technique style that Sessions had adopted with his Third Symphony. The contrasts of loud vehemence and quiet unease are frequent. The expected erudition is always evident. No new ground is broken. His final symphony, the Ninth (1978), seems more subdued, or perhaps a better word is resigned, than the previous symphonies. In it, he appears to have withdrawn from the life around him. The approach to symphonic writing is still the same. From all that has just been said, it is clear that Sessions remained without question artistically consistent throughout his creative life.

He wrote important works other than symphonies, of course, among them the opera *Montezuma* (1963), the *Rhapsody for Orchestra* (1970), the cantata *When Lilacs Last in the Dooryard Bloom'd* (1970), the Concerto for Violin, Cello, and Orchestra (1971), and the Concerto for Orchestra (1981). Their musical characteristics are similar to those of the symphonies. None ever succeeded with an audience.

After I heard Sarah Caldwell present *Montezuma* in Boston, during March 1976 (I have also heard *When Lilacs* at Harvard's Sanders Theater), I had to conclude that Sessions was happier with instruments than with voices. Voices are treated as if they were instruments. To most listeners, the music that he writes for singers fails to mirror the expressive needs of the text or the dramatic situation of the vocalists. Boredom is the consequence. The opera's libretto is flabby; the drama remains static. With Sessions, a vocal part cannot be delivered distinctly or given any resemblance of tunefulness. Singers are fortunate just to stay on pitch.

Sessions's standing as a composer, therefore, centers mainly on his instrumental writing, especially his nine symphonies. Newspaper reviewers have been critical or guardedly respectful; none have been honestly captured by the music. Audiences have made clear their antipathy. The music will find trouble gaining widespread public recognition. Performers hesitate over the difficulties that confront them, even in scores that they admire. In addition, they believe that playing intricate and inharmonious works to a reluctant public is like knocking on a deaf man's door. As a result, after their premieres, his works are rarely scheduled for performance.

Certainly his symphonies, at least, deserve better. However complex the symphonies are, an artist of integrity and high ability has produced them. Conductors should offer them as *pro bono* presentations that they provide especially for the public good.

This chapter provides final proof that no two American composers wrote symphonies that are the same. One cannot confuse the music of one composer with that of another. The works of each composer have their own characteristic mode of activity and distinctive manner of expression. Moore's compositions are easy to like. Sessions's symphonies almost defy you to like them. Thompson's candid and direct language is a contrast to Mennin's energetic and forceful idiom. Copland's Third Symphony occupies its own place—one of supreme dignity and grandeur that inspires admiration. Inspired ideas abound in all of the symphonies. They are there to be shared with the willing listener.

5

AMERICAN
SYMPHONIES
AFTER 1950

Most composers of the thirties and forties had incorporated generally enjoyable, communicative, and intelligible combinations of melody, harmony, and rhythm into their symphonies. They had given a clear overall organization to each movement. Within each movement, the relationship between beginning, middle, and end was meant to be unambiguous. The writing was usually idiomatic to each instrument and exploited its most telling musical range. Along with facilitating understanding, they had wanted their symphonies to present sounds that conveyed the hope that humankind could curb its baser urges and produce a more civilized society. The end result was music that, they anticipated, would bond them to performers and audiences. For a while these symphonies pushed American music into the limelight, winning it worldwide artistic respect and importance.

Regrettable to say, a cultural movement leads often to its own downfall, not only because the initial inclinations, however noble, are soon marred by compromise, cliché, and decreased energy, but because of the unforeseen—and in the fifties, the unforeseen was the evolving contention between nations, ethnic groups, and ideologies. Self-centered people grew even more self-centered. To employ reason and remain open to new ideas came under public suspicion. Conformity and superficial ways of life dominated the American scene. A majestic design like Hanson's or Copland's Third Symphony would now be seen as an anomaly.

Thus, the united world to which the composers of the Roosevelt years had looked forward never materialized after World War II. Instead, nations, societies, and ethnic groups worked to destroy whatever unity there was between and within them, politically, socially, and culturally. The Cold War between the United States and the Soviet Union brought on a division that provoked conflict. The Berlin blockade began. The atomic bomb, and then the hydrogen bomb, possessed by the United States and the Soviet Union, threatened vast populations with annihilation.

The Korean War (1950–53) was America's first bid to stop the spread of communism. (The Vietnam War, coming a decade later, would be the second.) McCarthyism pressed forward the practice of accusing liberal-thinking Americans of disloyal, pro-Communist activity based on doubtful or no evidence. Racial conflict, grating youthful lifestyles, and other social disturbances tore the United States apart. To write music extolling the universal human spirit started to seem incongruous. Young artists, though not all, began to close the window on the disturbing outside world and directed their gaze inward at their own private world for inspiration. Trying to reach the general public appeared of no consequence.

Most of Europe's leading composers had come to the United States during the thirties and forties owing to European fascism and World War II. A few of them became permanent residents. They turned into sought-after teachers of the next generation of American composers. Some of them, along with other important European musicians who visited America after the war, cast suspicion on American society, culture, and musical creations. Most of them were indifferent to lending a hand in developing the emerging American symphonism. Unfortunately, America's adamantly Europhilic cultural leaders dominated symphony boards of trustees. They aided in downplaying the importance of things American in classical music.

One or two Americans became quite irritated, as did Paul Turok, at the visiting Luciano Berio, in 1972. Turok writes that when Berio arrived in America from Italy, he received a great deal of admiration and promotion in the media. He profited more from his music during his brief stay in the United States than did most American composers during their entire professional lives. Nevertheless, Berio persisted in denouncing America's free-enterprise system and calling attention to its poisonous effect on American music. "In a not-very-subtle way," Turok writes, "this is saying, it is safe to ignore American music, because the system . . . etc. In fact, the aggressive behavior Berio attributes to American composers best fits that of Boulez, also no friend of American music. European artists are for internationalism, so long as they come out on top."[1]

An extremely influential German philosopher and musicologist, Theodor Adorno, busied himself denouncing the laziness of American audiences and the composers who pandered to these audiences.[2] Younger American composers took note of his advocacy of serialism and his declarations that audiences were to be challenged, not pacified. In part to remain *de rigueur,* some deliberately wrote obscurantic compositions that they knew would utterly confuse or put off the listening public. Other emerging American composers, also feeling the foreign influences, felt that the old order represented by the accommodating styles of the thirties and forties had to be assailed in order to make way for fresh thinking.

These attacks were continuations of the unsympathetic mindset among European intellectuals and artists that had prevailed over two centuries. One recalls an observation that Louis Moreau Gottschalk, an astute and talented American composer-pianist, made in 1862: "There certainly is an intelligent class who read and who know the truth; but it is not the most numerous, nor the most interested in doing us justice. . . . From Talleyrand, who says that '*l'Amérique est un pays de sales cochons et de cochons sales*' [America is a country of dirty and filthy swine], to Zimmerman, director of the piano classes at the Paris Conservatoire, who without hearing me refused to receive me because '*l'Amérique n'était qu'un pays de machines à vapeur*' [America was only a country of steam engines] there is not an eminent man who has not spat his petty spite upon the Americans."[3]

To look askance at the American compositions of the thirties and forties grew to be the fashion. The most popularly accepted composers—including Barber, Thompson, Moore, and Hanson—were held to be of no account. The dominant cutting-edge style turned into the serial music first promulgated by Arnold Schoenberg, Alban Berg, and Anton Webern. Serialism was now advanced in the United States through the example of works by Webern, the teaching of Schoenberg, the militant advocacy of visitors such as Luciano Berio, Karlheinz Stockhausen, and Pierre Boulez, and the paths followed by American musicians including Roger Sessions and Milton Babbitt. Its proponents were soon occupying dominant positions in academia. These composers believed in exercising complete control over every aspect of composition: dynamics, rhythms, tempos, vertical organization, and horizontal organization. Except for Sessions, a great many nontonal composers considered a symphony to be the last thing they wished to write. It became fashionable to proclaim that the symphony was dead.

At the same time, experiments were going on in writing "chance" or "aleatoric" compositions and using electronic contrivances. John Cage was leading a special group of composers in a different direction from the serialists. Silence, random sounds, uniquely "prepared" instruments, and performers allowed to play anything they chose were some of the directions followed. On the horizon were appearing colleagues of Cage who would find room for every sort of random sound imaginable—compositions based on brain waves, geographical formations, and patterns of stars in the sky. Nihilism, for them, was a supreme virtue. It would prove not to be a virtue for the general music public.

However, for a time, the ascendant contemporary music was atonal, of which serialism was a part. Compositions in which the material was organized without reference to a tonal center, and in which chromatic tones were used without emphasis on any one, found an open path onto the programs of ensembles dedicated to the new, and that crowded out the rest. This took place first in New York City, and then spread to Boston, Chicago, and other large cities. Since New York City was the headquarters for major periodicals and newspapers and the center of the music publishing, recording, and media industries, its influence was immense. Most of the atonalists were academics and admirers of the ways of science, particularly mathematics. Several of the composers were unquestionably

204 · *The Great American Symphony*

sincere and gifted—among them Milton Babbitt, George Perle, Charles Wuorinen, Gunther Schuller, and Leon Kirchner. Connoisseurs who understood the details, methods, and principles of nontriadic compositions did enjoy and appreciate the subtleties in the modern compositions produced by these men. A special sensitivity honed by education and frequent exposure to these more disconcerting works was required if one hoped to assimilate them.

Unfortunately, this new music has proved more and more unacceptable to the great majority of music lovers. They will make no effort to take it in and absorb it as something of their own. They refuse to intellectualize about music or to be subjected to insistent discords, apparent lack of melody, disconnection between measures, and odd rhythms that come from nowhere. Soon, the announcement of the premiere of any contemporary work caused them to flee the concert hall. With them fled tolerance. All new music was quickly tarred by the same negative brush.

One must conclude that, in most instances, the post-1940s younger artists rejected or waved aside any leaning toward cultural democracy and practiced arts that were exclusive rather than inclusive. Without question, they found uncongenial the musical movements of the years 1935 to 1950. Cultural hegemony no longer belonged to the American symphonists; it clustered around the anti-symphonists.

Meanwhile, Serge Koussevitzky had died, and most foreign-born conductors, who as usual headed the major symphony orchestras, felt no pressure and had less inclination to perform American symphonies. If they played a contemporary work at all, it was most likely to be one from the conductor's own country. Whenever American symphony orchestras took trips abroad, it was a miracle if they scheduled an American work.[4]

To be sure, American symphonies were still being written and played, but they were reluctantly performed. A work premiered in one city often failed to make its way to other cities and had few, if any, repeated performances by the orchestra that gave it a first airing. At the same time, the hinterland remained adamantly conservative in its tastes and showed a preference for music composed prior to the twentieth century. Its regular diet included heavy doses of symphonies from long-gone composers such as Mozart, Beethoven, Brahms, and Tchaikovsky. What orchestras played in places beyond the metropolitan centers, even when they included the first performance of symphonies of more traditional orientation, rarely made the headlines. Such works did not merit serious consideration by the national media.

THE SYMPHONY IN THE LEANEST YEARS

The leanest years for American symphonies were from 1950 to around 1990. This was a period when composers had to choose between one of two approaches for their continued creative existence: either they originate a style that has hardly ever been promoted previously, or they take up and master a style developed by previous twentieth-century composers.[5] The former would categorize the manner adopted by John Cage and other practitioners of indeterminacy and by the electronic composers; the latter, Roger Sessions, Milton Babbitt, and other practitioners of atonalism who followed in the footsteps of Arnold Schoenberg, Alban Berg, and Anton Webern. The latter approach would, of course, also describe composers who followed in the footsteps of the American symphonic composers from Hanson to Copland.

However critics might disparage them, symphonies continued to be written and performed, even in Chicago, Boston, San Francisco, and New York City. Almost all of the composers already discussed in this study kept on writing them in the postwar years. Other composers would come to the fore who wrote substantial compositions that valued and used the recent past as a foundation. In spite of everything, this music made possible some sympathetic interchange with listeners. The more recent compositions, while honoring those of their predecessors, also contained stylistic modifications in response to the changing times. Dissonance did increase; tonality loosen; chromaticism multiply. Even so, these adjustments were introduced judiciously and a tonal focus was preserved so as not to alienate the audience.

Several composers who persisted in writing symphonies did gain some sort of national recognition. In what follows, five of them are selected for mention in order to indicate the stylistic variety in these compositions. Whatever else they were doing, symphonic composers were not standing still.

A first case in point, Robert Ward, has written seven symphonies. The

Seventh Symphony was premiered in 2005. He is best known for his operas, especially *The Crucible,* which won the Pulitzer Prize in 1962. Born in Cleveland, Ohio, in 1917, he began his formal music studies with Howard Hanson and Bernard Rogers at the Eastman School of Music and finished them with Aaron Copland at the Berkshire Music Center. His living came mostly from teaching. Eventually, he established himself in the South—at the North Carolina School for the Arts and at Duke University.

His instrumental music tries to communicate clearly in order to elicit an emotional response. "I've failed if I don't achieve that," he has said. Robert Ward's music has rhythm, life, and color. It affords a brilliant reflection of our own musical heritage. It grows out of folk, blues, jazz, traditional song, popular music, and the sort of openness affected by Harris and Copland. In his symphonies, he proves to be an honest and competent musical artist who has created conspicuously native music drawing on European antecedents. He utilizes the late-Romantic devices of Dvořák and Brahms plus shadings of Debussy and Ravel, but gives them an American inflection. Strings receive full-throated melodies. Individual woodwinds sing of rustic delights. Brasses turn out stentorian flourishes. Variety abounds. Ward speaks with feeling, even at times verging on the sentimental. The aim is to address the listener directly and hold on to his attention. Ward only occasionally ventures beyond the parameters set by, say, Barber and Copland. Nevertheless, his symphonies are of his own minting and are not splinters off compositions of earlier composers.

Bolder than Ward in the use of nontraditional harmony, Vincent Persichetti composed nine symphonies before his death in 1987. His symphonies demonstrate his talent for contrapuntal writing. They also reveal a fine level of craftsmanship, especially in the integration of warm lyrical lines with more contemporary harmonizations. Like the two other Italian-American composers already discussed, Mennin and Creston, he shows little interest in consciously introducing Americanisms into his music. His expression may go from noncommittal objectivity to emotional subjectiveness. Persichetti is a cosmopolitan artist.

Especially worth knowing is his Symphony No. 9, *Janiculum,* composed in 1970. Here he brings together both types of expression and manages to give universal significance to individual feeling. The one-movement work begins and ends on music derived from the chimes of the Chiesa de San Pietro sul Giacolo of Rome. Persichetti needs a full orchestra with a large percussion section in order to ponder life's meaning. The ancient god Janus, after whom the Janiculum Hill is named, has two opposite faces—male-female, active-passive, comic-tragic—which the music tries to capture. The melody tends to the diatonic; the harmony builds oftentimes on the dissonant structures introduced in the twentieth century.

More adventurous than Ward and Persichetti in using a modern idiom, Benjamin Lees allows his five symphonies to speak in a more individual way. No two are exactly alike. In a very general way he utilizes classical structures and retains a vaguely perceived concept of tonality. He has a talent for introducing excitement into his measures, as well as just enough conflict to command the listener's attention. His is the opposite of cerebral music. To give an instance, his Symphony No. 3 (1968) imparts an impression of tragedy, perhaps owing to the Vietnam War, which was raging at the time. A torrent of emotion flows from the first to the last note. Mixed together are traditional harmonies, bitonal passages, and strident chords.

Lees's Symphony No. 5, *Kalmar Nyckel* (1988), was commissioned by the Kalmar Nyckel Committee to honor the 350th anniversary of the founding of Wilmington, Delaware, by the first Swedish settlers in America. The committee's name and the symphony's subtitle refer to the ship the settlers traveled on. Although Howard Hanson's Third Symphony of 1936 had commemorated the same event, Hanson's idiom is vastly different from that of Lees. Hanson is a Romanticist and follows traditional ways. Lees is more daring. His harmonies are bolder, rhythms tenser, melodies less conventional than those of Hanson. Connections between Lees's symphony and the event it celebrates are hard to find.

The Fifth Symphony is in one movement, but in three sections corresponding to three movements of a symphony. The first section is speedy in tempo and brilliant in effect. The second section is slow and melancholic. Strings swell with feeling as they lead to the last division. The final section defies characterization. Brasses and percussion mark a change in pace. Rhythms are unsettled and alter frequently. The music continues high-spirited, but on edge underneath. Some hymning and a bizarre interlude offer contrast. The symphony finishes on a dazzling outburst of sound.

The kinds of expression that Lees brings forward are unique, unlike those of any other composer. However sharp and tense his music, he wants sincerely to reach his audience. On balance, he seems to have succeeded.

A political radical in his youth and a staunch musical Americanist during young adulthood, Elie Siegmeister began to compose with displays of dissonant harmonies, unsettled if not unsettling rhythms, and oddly progressing melodies after World War II. He was always an American populist and artist of strong convictions, which he voiced with confidence and certainty. His music sounds completely different from that of the three composers previously mentioned.

He grew up in New York City, studied composition abroad with Nadia Boulanger, and returned to New York City, where he pursued a distinguished career as a composer. At first, Siegmeister included facets of folk tradition, music, and dance in his works. Blues, jazz, and popular music were also elements he integrated into his measures. Siegmeister's early style was unabashedly tonal, melodious, jaunty, and extroverted. Audiences found his offerings easy to get at and enjoy.

In the fifties and sixties, Siegmeister's style changed. Although his works still recall folk music, blues, jazz, and popular music faintly, they now feature increased impetuosity, show an absence of key centers, and appear gradually more *sui generis.* The listener hears a curious mix of sound that resembles the music of Charles Ives, Aaron Copland, and Béla Bartók. Dissonance is prominent; melody tenuous; and rhythm untamed. Yet his music remains individual.

Although Siegmeister continued to maintain that he was concerned about reaching a wide audience, his followership decreased rapidly. His First Symphony came out in 1947. By 1957 and his Third Symphony much of the stylistic change was on display. The work, in free variation form, is cast into one movement divided into three sections. A preliminary *Moderato* makes known three germinal motifs that will dominate the rest of the symphony. Americanisms are barely perceptible and enter, possibly, without the composer's awareness. The first part, for example, has simi-

larities to the early *Western Suite*. However, the previous extroversion is
now replaced by powerful personal emotion. By 1970 and the Fourth Symphony, he had veered closer to the hammered-out music of Bartók and the
jumbled-up, devil-take-the-hindmost approach of Ives. His Ninth (and
last) Symphony, *Figures in the Wind,* was finished in 1990. Nothing quite
like Siegmeister's music has been composed by anyone else.

George Rochberg provides a final example of a symphonic composer
active principally before 1990. He is selected for discussion because he was
willing to change with the times, try out a variety of procedures in composition, and attempt a reconciliation between music of the older and more
recent past (Beethoven to Mahler) and that written in twentieth-century
modes. In all three aspects he can be seen as a bridge to the composers
active after 1990. Rochberg, born in 1918, attended the Mannes College
of Music. He later joined the faculty of the music department at the University of Pennsylvania, remaining there until 1983.

At first he tried out serialism in his compositions. However, he de-
serted the serialist camp after 1963 and the death of his son. Rochberg
had found serialism too confining for expressing his emotion and, in particular, his anguish and anger at the loss of his son. Within a few years
Rochberg was much debated in musical circles because of his mixing
tonal with atonal music and employing musical collage. His String Quartet No. 3 (1972) incorporated a set of variations in Beethoven's style. The
String Quartet No. 6 (1978) includes a set of variations on Pachelbel's
Canon in D. *Contra Mortem et Tempus,* for violin, flute, clarinet, and piano
(1965), has pasted into it musical quotations from Ives, Varèse, Boulez,
and Berio. His veering toward a more comprehensible style and confron-
tation with serialism reverberated from the seventies to the end of the
century. Gradually, the musical world caught up with his use of fragments
from earlier compositions as pastiches in his own and with his intelligible
emotionalism. He helped to alter the shape of new music into a configu-
ration that during the fifties seemed impossible.

The first two of his six symphonies are serial works composed with
skill, a talent for fabricating parts that fit neatly together, and a mastery
of lyrical discourse in the slow movements. They show spirit and potency.
At the same time, they are gloomy and nervous works. Despite their atonalism, they almost make the listener believe he hears music organized

around a tonality. Rochberg departs from serialism with the Symphony No. 3 for Double Chorus, Chamber Chorus, Soloists, and Large Orchestra (1969), which includes snippets of other composers' works treated in a way to make them appear fresh. These he integrates into his own music. With the Symphony No. 4 (1976), this time for orchestra alone, the music becomes more melodious, the orchestration more colorful, and the composer unreservedly a Romantic. He does not shirk introducing large helpings of discordant tones. Somehow he makes them seem to belong, like sizing to firm up the musical fabric.

His Symphony No. 5 (1984) continues in a similar vein to the Fourth. Even more than the Fourth, it is technically well organized and emotionally cohesive. The listener discovers passionate feeling, forcefulness, and Mahler-like passages in its seven sections. His last symphony, the Sixth, was completed in 1987 and is beautifully crafted, airs ideas of substance, and is clearly a striking, strongly felt, and authoritative work.

There is a tentative quality to Rochberg's symphonies. In them, he experiments with broadening the boundaries of expression. What he composes does possess superior merit, but seems provisional; fine as far as he has gone, but not the final word in his search. He died before he could arrive at a conclusion.

THE SYMPHONY AFTER 1990

After the eighties, the stigma connected with the writing of symphonies diminished. More composers, writing in a variety of styles, made contributions to the genre than had in the previous thirty years. The realization had grown among them that modern composers were again painting themselves into a corner. No one needed or wanted challenging works any more. The disturbingly provocative composition no long provoked. It was ignored.

In most instances, the reforms in music meant turning tonal and becoming more or less accessible. Several reformers were older music practitioners such as Alan Hovhaness, who wrote sixty-seven pieces that he called symphonies from 1936 to 1992, Ezra Laderman, who wrote eight symphonies from 1964 to 1994, and Lou Harrison, who wrote four from 1964 (his much-discussed *Symphony on G*) to 1990. A younger group commenced writing symphonies in the eighties, including Christopher Rouse with two from 1981 to 1994, John Harbison with four from 1981 to 2004, Ellen Taaffe Zwilich with four from 1982 to 2000, John Corigliano with two from 1988 to 2000, and Aaron Kernis with two from 1989 to 1991. These composers feel that they can go in any stylistic direction, depending on what they think they need in order to construct a composition. They mingle tonality and atonality, consonance and dissonance, conventional melody and unsingable linearity, and regulated tones and randomness. At one moment the music can sound as if it is emerging from a rock-music concert, at another as if it is harking back to the Renaissance, and at still another quite chaotic. Among the more recent contributors are two composers who, early on, were described as minimalists: Philip Glass with eight symphonies from 1992 to 2005, and John Adams with his prototype symphony, entitled *Naive and Sentimental Music* (1999), and his *Doctor Atomic Symphony* of 2005.

A new crop of American composers who find value in writing symphonies are now making an appearance. Among them are John Beall (b. 1942), Stephen Dankner (b. 1944), Jim Cockey (b. 1947), Dan Lockair (b. 1949), Steve Heitzeg (b. 1959), and Kevin Beaver (b. 1973). Their teachers may have been serial, aleatoric, or electronic composers. Nevertheless, after embarking on their creative careers they have gone their own way. To them, the symphonic structure is very much alive. They are pouring a rich, diverse, and listener-friendly content into it.

These composers, in both their pronouncements and their styles, seem to believe that to sustain any culture an artist needs to take into account the collected knowledge and experience of artists from earlier periods. They profess a trust in the symphonic genre—building on the viewpoints of its former masters, refurbishing its rhetoric and structures, and confident they have the ability to make everything sound new. Nevertheless, theirs is an uphill struggle.

They are shaping their compositions in a cultural democracy that puts forward a denial of hierarchical division of society according to class and that advances the idea that no musical idiom, whether classical or popular, and whether American, European, Asian, or African, is any more valuable than another. Popular music is no longer an entertainment more agreeable than otherwise. It now has become promoted as "Art"—a designation encouraged by the media, music vendors, performers, and leaders who now dominate all the publicity channels and propound what is acceptable. Whether it is deserving of the designation is not the issue; that the powerful forces behind popular music are contributing to the crowding out of classical music is.

Coverage of classical music has mostly disappeared from newspapers and magazines. Arts sections at best have become living-style sections aimed mainly at youths and featuring rock-music groups and movie stars. There is nothing necessarily wrong with this trend. However, it gives no coverage to mature tastes and crowds out references to classical music, let alone any serious discussion of it. The same goes for teaching in the public schools. Music classes have vanished or, if they still exist, turn almost exclusively to any music but classical. Publicly funded television increasingly dilutes its classical-music offerings.

Americans have a mounting consciousness of the diversity in the world and of the abundant musical cultures from which they can select— owing to travel, radio, film, television, printed sources, the Internet, and music available through a recorded medium. The public can give its approval to anything it wishes, and it does.[6] No longer can cultural democracy mean, as it did in the Roosevelt years, the providing of access to and participation in whatever a consensus of members of a society deems worthwhile. Consensus can no longer be arrived at. In the United States of the twenty-first century, the American public has become too culturally fragmented to achieve any semblance of unanimity. In most people's minds cultural authority vested in a select few has been disallowed or done away with.[7] As Bernard Holland observed, in January 2003, classical music is no longer a pinnacle of culture but one alternative among many.[8] Art exists, even under the most favorable circumstances, in a cultural marketplace, to be bought and sold like any other product.

Whether the consequences are for good or ill, America still struggles to maintain the importance of classical music—that is to say, to keep it at the top of its values and Europeans' regard. Lots of Americans have not been won over to classical music. The penchant to flatten cultural levels has also aided in the decline of classical music. For the moment, our musical legacy, including our symphonic tradition, seems to be less enthusiastically supported. Scarcely ever does one of our major orchestras schedule one of the magnificent symphonies of the thirties and forties.

Change integrated with an accommodation of the past is a characteristic of all civilizations. Whatever the outcome of our present situation, one thing is certain—there will always be more complex and more uncomplicated sorts of music. Classical music may not disappear, but it will indeed change. At the same time, it must cultivate a willing audience. Whether symphonies will continue to be written is ultimately up to the composers who manage to win the support of consenting performers and an approving music public. Meanwhile, it is to be hoped that music lovers will find reason to cherish and enjoy the symphonic bounty already provided by our American artists of the thirties and forties.

We should keep in mind that musical art does not progress; it just alters. The worthiness of fine compositions of the past is the equal to the merit of those of the present or future. What changes are the mandates placed on the composer and the aesthetic and expressive needs of the public. For these reasons, the symphonies of the thirties and forties may yet again prove deserving of the music world's attention. To those who cherish these works, it is their fondest hope.

NOTES

Preface

1. For further discussion of the relation of music, composers, and audiences in the thirties, see Nicholas Tawa, *American Composers and Their Public* (Metuchen, N.J.: Scarecrow, 1995), 116–128.

2. Ibid., 116.

1. Preliminaries

1. Arthur M. Schlesinger Jr., *The Disuniting of America,* rev. and enlarged ed. (New York: Norton, 1998), 43.

2. James Truslow Adams, *The Epic of America* (Boston: Little, Brown, 1931), 214–215.

3. These interpretations are discussed in an essay provided by the Library of Congress; see "What is the American Dream?" http://memory.loc.gov/learn/lessons/97/dream/thedream.html, accessed 11 March 2007.

4. Alexis de Tocqueville, *Democracy in America,* vol. 2, trans. Henry Reeve, rev. Francis Bowen and further corrected by Phillip Bradley (New York: Vintage, 1954), 36–37, 50.

5. I have written extensively on this subject. See, especially, Nicholas E. Tawa, *Art Music in the American Society* (Metuchen, N.J.: Scarecrow, 1987).

6. Jacques Barzun, *The Culture We Deserve* (Middletown, Conn.: Wesleyan University Press, 1989), 64.

7. Virgil Thomson, *Music Reviewed, 1940–1954* (New York: Vintage, 1967), 169.

8. Lawrence Morton, "American Conductor and Works for L.A.," *Modern Music* 21 (November–December 1943): 37.

9. Winthrop Tryon, "First in Boston," *Modern Music* 20 (May–June 1943): 260.

10. Bruce Archibald, "Patronage and Composer," notes to the CD *Walter Piston: Symphony No. 6; Leon Kirchner: Piano Concerto No. 1* (New World NW286), 2.

11. Aaron Copland, "Serge Koussevitzky and the American Composer," *Musical Quarterly* 30 (1944): 255.

12. Moses Smith, *Koussevitzky* (New York: Allen, Towne and Heath, 1944), 302.

13. *Life,* 12 December 1938, 27–38.

14. See Hans Heinsheimer, "Challenge of the New Audience," *Modern Music* 16 (November–December 1938): 30, 32; Minna Lederman, "Star-Spangled Orchestras," *Modern Music* 17 (March–April 1940): 194.

15. Heinsheimer, "Challenge of the New Audience," 30–31.

16. Aaron Copland, "From the '20's to the '40's and Beyond," *Modern Music* 20 (January–February 1943): 82.

17. Arthur Berger, *Reflections of an American Composer* (Berkeley: University of California Press, 2002), 277–278.

18. Aaron Copland, *The New Music,* rev. and enlarged ed. (New York: Norton, 1968), 161–162.

19. Kenneth J. Bindas, *All of This Music Belongs to the Nation* (Knoxville: University of Tennessee Press, 1995), 65.

20. *The Federal Music Project* (Washington, D.C.: Works Progress Administration, 1936).

21. Ibid., 28–29.

22. Otto Luening, *The Odyssey of an American Composer* (New York: Charles Scribner's Sons, 1980), 384.

23. Barbara B. Heyman, *Samuel Barber* (New York: Oxford University Press, 1992), 194.

24. These composers are discussed in Nicholas E. Tawa, *Mainstream Music of Early Twentieth Century America* (Westport, Conn.: Greenwood, 1992).

25. Kenneth Clark, *What Is a Masterpiece?* (New York: Thames and Hudson, 1981), 10–11.

26. David Ewen, ed., *The Book of Modern Composers* (New York: Knopf, 1950), 453.

27. Peter Jona Korn, "The Symphony in America," in *The Symphony,* vol. 2, ed. Robert Simpson (Baltimore, Md.: Penguin Books, 1967), 2:244.

28. They may be read in *Roger Sessions on Music,* ed. Edward T. Cone (Princeton, N.J.: Princeton University Press, 1979), 271–329.

29. Ibid., 294.

30. Berger, *Reflections,* 21.

31. William Schuman, "Americanism in Music: A Composer's View," in *Music in American Society, 1776–1976,* ed. George McCue (New Brunswick, N.J.: Transition Books, 1977), 23.

32. Ashley Pettis, "The WPA and the American Composer," *Musical Quarterly* 26 (1940): 101–102.

33. Eugene Goossens, "The Public—Has It Changed?" *Modern Music* 20 (January–February 1943): 76.

34. John H. Mueller, *The American Symphony Orchestra* (Bloomington: Indiana University Press, 1951), 23.

35. Alfred Frankenstein, "How to Make Friends by Radio," *Modern Music* 21 (November–December 1943): 9.

36. Virgil Thomson, *Selected Letters of Virgil Thomson,* ed. Tim Page and Vanessa Weeks Page (New York: Summit Books, 1988), 127.

37. Ellen Dissanayake, *What Is Art For?* (Seattle: University of Washington Press, 1988), 192.

2. Symphonies of the Mid- to Late Thirties

1. Franklin D. Roosevelt, "Radio Address to the Young Democrats Clubs of America," 20 April 1940, *The American Presidency Project,* www.presidency.ucsb.edu/ws/index.php?pid=15940, accessed 16 March 2007.

2. Franklin D. Roosevelt, "Address on the Occasion of the Fiftieth Anniversary of the Statue of Liberty," 28 October 1936, *The American Presidency Project,* www.presidency.ucsb.edu/ws/print.php?pid=15210, accessed 16 March 2007.

3. Franklin D. Roosevelt, "Roosevelt's address on The Museum of Modern Art as printed in the *Herald Tribune* on May 11, 1939," Museum of Modern Art Research Resources/Archives, http://www.moma.org/research/archives/highlights/04_1939.html, accessed 16 March 2007.

4. Nathan Broder, *Samuel Barber* (New York: Schirmer, 1954), 30.

5. Walter Simmons, *Voices in the Wilderness* (Lanham, Md.: Scarecrow, 2004), 265–266.

6. Broder, *Samuel Barber,* 19.

7. Richard Jackson and Barbara Heyman, in *The New Grove Dictionary of American Music,* vol. 1, ed. H. Wiley Hitchcock and Stanley Sadie (New York, 1938), s.v. "Barber, Samuel."

8. Broder, *Samuel Barber,* 35.

9. My comments on the music are based on the score: Samuel Barber, *First Symphony (In One Movement)* (New York: Schirmer, 1943).

10. Otto Luening, *The Odyssey of an American Composer* (New York: Scribner's Sons, 1980), 270.

11. Morris C. Hastings, "Entr'acte. Dr. Hanson and Americanism," an interview reprinted from the *Musical Key* (15 October 1939) in the Boston Symphony Orchestra Program Notes for the concert of 3 November 1939: 156, 158, 160.

12. Nicolas Slonimsky, in *Dictionary of Contemporary Music,* ed. John Vinton (New York: Dutton, 1974), s.v. "Hanson, Howard."

13. Ibid.

14. Howard Hanson, preface to the orchestral score, *Symphony No. III* (Rochester, N.Y.: Eastman School of Music of the University of Rochester, 1951).

15. The quotation is reproduced in John N. Burk's Boston Symphony Orchestra Program Notes for the concert of 3 November 1939.

16. Elliott Carter, "American Music in the New York Scene," *Modern Music* 17 (January–February 1940): 97.

17. Simmons, *Voices in the Wilderness*, 132.

18. Howard Hanson, *Symphony No. 4* (Rochester, N.Y.: Eastman School of Music of the University of Rochester, 1955).

19. Hugo Leichtentritt, *Serge Koussevitzky* (Cambridge, Mass.: Harvard University Press, 1946), 42.

20. Luening, *The Odyssey of an American Composer*, 280.

21. Dan Stehman, *Roy Harris* (Boston: Twayne, 1984), 32.

22. Arthur Berger, *Reflections of an American Composer* (Berkeley: University of California Press, 2002), 22–23.

23. A month before the premiere of the Third Symphony, Charles Ives's seminal First Piano Sonata (*Concord*) had been given its initial performance.

24. Roy Harris, *Third Symphony, in One Movement* (New York: Schirmer, 1940).

25. Reproduced in Stehman, *Roy Harris*, 64–65.

26. Ibid., 66.

27. Ibid., 67. The "acidic satire and brittle smartness" were far more characteristic of the ten years before 1935 than of afterwards.

28. Herbert Elwell, "Harris' Folksong Symphony," *Modern Music* 18 (January–February 1941): 113–114.

29. Quoted in Dan Stehman, *Roy Harris: A Bio-Bibliography* (Westport, Conn.: Greenwood, 1991), 151.

30. Review, "Music from Chicago," 21 November 1940, of a performance of Harris's *American Creed*, in Virgil Thomson, *Music Reviewed, 1940–1954* (New York: Vintage, 1967), 15–16.

31. Aaron Copland, *The New Music,* rev. and enlarged ed. (New York: Norton, 1968), 120.

32. Michael Steinberg, *The Symphony* (New York: Oxford University Press, 1995), 495.

33. Elliot Carter, in *Modern Music* 16 (November–December 1938): 37.

34. Peter Jona Korn, "The Symphony in America," in *The Symphony,* ed. Robert Simpson (Baltimore, Md.: Penguin Books, 1967), 2:256.

35. "List of Instruments," prefacing the score, in William Schuman, *Symphony No. III in Two Parts* (New York: Schirmer, 1942).

36. Nathan Broder, "The Music of William Schuman," *Musical Quarterly* 31 (1945): 22.

37. Ibid., 17.

38. I was a student in his composition seminar.

39. Steinberg, *The Symphony*, 498.

40. Flora Rheta Schreiber and Vincent Persichetti, *William Schuman* (New York: Schirmer, 1954), 93.

41. Ibid., 21. I was in the audience when the symphony was first performed.

42. I am aware of the statement made in 1980 by Christopher Rouse: "As taut and concise as the Symphony No. 3 is expansive and majestic, the Fifth Symphony remains one of Schuman's most popular works, representing at its best his early dynamically affirmative style"; see K. Gary Adams, *William Schuman: A Bio-Bibliography* (Westport, Conn.: Greenwood, 1998), 10. I have found little real evidence of its popularity with audiences.

43. Joseph Machlis, *American Composers of Our Time* (New York: Crowell, 1963), 143–144.

44. Steinberg, *The Symphony*, 496.

45. Joan O'Connor, *John Alden Carpenter* (Westport, Conn.: Greenwood, 1994), 203.

46. Ibid., 358.

47. Howard Pollack, *Skyscraper Lullaby* (Washington, D.C.: Smithsonian Institution Press, 1995), 358.

48. Francis Perkins, "Dr. Stock Leads Musicians in New Symphony," New York *Herald Tribune,* 23 November 1940, 9.

3. Symphonies of the War Years

1. William O'Neill, *A Democracy at War* (Cambridge: Harvard University Press, 1993), 430.

2. John Peatman, "Non-Militant, Sentimental . . . ," *Modern Music* 20 (March–April 1943): 153.

3. Arnold Dobrin, *Aaron Copland* (New York: Crowell, 1967), 159–160.

4. Douglas Moore, "Young Composers after the War," *Modern Music* 21 (November–December 1943): 23–24.

5. Aaron Copland, "From the '20's to the '40's and Beyond," *Modern Music* 20 (January–February 1943): 80.

6. Arthur Berger, "Spring Season, 1943," *Modern Music* 20 (May–June 1943): 254.

7. John H. Mueller, *The American Symphony Orchestra* (Bloomington: Indiana University Press, 1951), 277.

8. George Antheil, *Bad Boy of Music* (Garden City, N.Y.: Doubleday, Doran, 1945), 29.

9. Virgil Thomson, *Virgil Thomson* (New York: Knopf, 1966), 75, 78.

10. Nicholas Tawa, *American Composers and Their Public* (Metuchen, N.J.: Scarecrow, 1995), 66–67, 120.

11. Linda Whitesitt, *The Life and Music of George Antheil, 1900–1959* (Ann Arbor, Mich.: UMI Research Press, 1983), 45, 50. The quotation is from page 75.

12. Quoted in the notes to the CD *George Antheil, Symphony No. 3 "American"; Tom Sawyer, Hot Time Dance, McKonskey's Ferry, Capital of the World* (CPO 777 040-2), 19.

13. Quoted in the notes to the CD *George Antheil, Symphony No. 4. Morton Gould, Spirituals for Orchestra, Formations* (Bay Cities BCD-1016).

14. For example, Copland certainly envied Shostakovich's musical successes, which created a strong desire in him to emulate them, and would allow the Russian's musical style to seep into his Third Symphony—see *The Virgil Thomson Reader,* ed. Richard Kostelanetz (New York: Routledge, 2002), 178; and Elizabeth Bergman Crist, "Critical Politics: The Reception History of Aaron Copland's Third Symphony," *Musical Quarterly* 85 (2001): 232–263.

15. Quoted in Whitesitt, *The Life and Music of George Antheil,* 62.

16. Reprinted in Victoria J. Kimberling, *David Diamond: A Bio-Bibliography* (Metuchen, N.J.: Scarecrow, 1987), viii.

17. Ibid., 32–33.

18. Quoted in the notes to the CD *David Diamond, Volume III: Symphony No.1, Violin Concerto No. 2, The Enormous Room* (Delos DE 3119), 7.

19. Kimberling, *David Diamond,* 12.

20. Charles Mills, "Over the Air," *Modern Music* 22 (November–December 1944): 65.

21. Program notes to the New York Philharmonic concert of 10 January 1958, reprinted in Kimberling, *David Diamond,* 24.

22. Aaron Copland, *Copland on Music* (Garden City, N.Y.: Doubleday, 1960), 173.

23. One of Bernstein's greatest disappointments was the failure to win the appointment of conductor to the Boston Symphony Orchestra.

24. Humphrey Burton, *Leonard Bernstein* (New York: Doubleday, 1994), 123.

25. The quotation is reproduced in Jack Gottlieb, notes to the CD *Bernstein Conducts Bernstein: Symphony No. 1 "Jeremiah"* (Deutsche Grammophon CD 415 964-2).

26. The details about the symphony are found in Gottlieb, notes to the CD *Bernstein Conducts Bernstein: Symphony No. 1 "Jeremiah."*

27. See Lamentations 1:1–4,8, 4:14–15, 5:20 (KJV).

28. I witnessed both his intellect in action and the depths of his knowledge when I was his student in theory and composition.

29. Walter Piston, *Harmony,* 3rd ed. (New York: W. W. Norton, 1962), 329–330.

30. Quoted in the notes to the CD *Walter Piston: Symphony No. 2 and 6; Sinfonietta* (Delos DE 3074).

31. Bruce Archibald, in *The New Grove Dictionary of American Music,* vol. 3, ed. H. Wiley Hitchcock and Stanley Sadie (New York, 1938), s.v. "Piston, Walter (Hamor, Jr.)."

32. These comments are based on the local newspaper reviews of the premiere.

33. Walter Piston, "The Composer Speaks," in *The Book of Modern Composers,* ed. David Ewen (New York: Knopf, 1950), 496–497.

34. Reprinted in Hugo Leichtentritt, *Serge Koussevitzky* (Cambridge: Harvard University Press, 1946), 116–117.

35. When I first went to him as a student, I mentioned how much I enjoyed *The Incredible Flutist.* He responded with a grimace and refused to say a word about it.

36. Elliott Carter, "Piston," in *The Book of Modern Composers,* ed. David Ewen (New York: Knopf, 1950), 502–503.

37. Howard Pollack, *Walter Piston* (Ann Arbor, Mich.: UMI Research Press, 1982), 74.

38. Pollack is wrong when he claims that the Second Symphony expresses the heroic struggle of America in World War II—see Pollack, *Walter Piston,* 82.

39. Michael Steinberg, *The Symphony* (New York: Oxford University Press, 1995), 420.

40. Pollack is wrong again when, on page 83, he asserts that the finale "is a call to arms."

41. I should admit to having been a student of Piston (1949–1951), admiring the man and composer, and having a longstanding love for the symphony.

42. Reprinted in Pollack, *Walter Piston,* 111.

43. See Don A. Hennessee, *Samuel Barber* (Westport, Conn.: Greenwood, 1985), 310.

44. Samuel Horan, "Samuel Barber," *Modern Music* 20 (March–April 1943): 162.

45. Barbara B. Heyman, *Samuel Barber* (New York: Oxford University Press, 1992), 206.

46. Reprinted in Michel Fleming's notes to the CD *Samuel Barber, Symphony No. 2, Adagio for Strings* (Chandos CHAN 9169).

47. The negativity would climax with the Metropolitan Opera presentation of his *Anthony and Cleopatra* in 1966. Except for the *Third Essay* (1966), no major works would be written after this opera.

48. Michel Fleming, notes to *Samuel Barber, Symphony No. 2, Adagio for Strings.*

49. The fiasco encountered at the premiere of *Anthony and Cleopatra* was attributable to the production designed and directed by Zeffirelli, not to Barber's music, which was solid in character and filled with attractive melody.

50. Richard Jackson and Barbara Heyman, in *The New Grove Dictionary of American Music,* vol. 1, ed. H. Wiley Hitchcock and Stanley Sadie (New York, 1938), s.v. "Barber, Samuel."

51. Eric A. Gordon, *Mark the Music* (New York: St. Martin's, 1989), 232.

52. Donald Fuller, "Airborne over New York," *Modern Music* 23 (Spring 1946): 116.

4. Symphonies of the Immediate Postwar Years

1. Otto Luening, in *Dictionary of Contemporary Music,* ed. John Vinton (New York: Dutton, 1974), s.v. "Moore, Douglas."

2. Aaron Copland, *Music and Imagination* (New York: Mentor Books, 1959), 101.

3. Eric Salzman, notes to the CD *Douglas Moore: Farm Journal, Cotillion Suite, Symphony in A Major* (CRI American Masters, CD 714).

4. The author wishes to thank David Kanzig for the information on Moore's *Symphony in A Major* that he made available, especially the pages of the Donald Joseph Reagan dissertation, "Douglas Moore and His Orchestral Works." Mr. Kanzig is proprietor of the website babydoe.org and Director of Programming for WVIZ/PBS television and 90.3 WCPN radio in Cleveland, Ohio.

5. Quoted in Donald Joseph Reagan, "Douglas Moore and His Orchestral Works," Ph.D. diss., Catholic University of America, 1972, 176.

6. Ibid., 169.

7. David Ewen, *American Composers: A Biographical Dictionary* (New York: G. P. Putnam's Sons, 1982), s.v. "Moore, Douglas Stuart."

8. Jonathan Cott, *Stockhausen: Conversations with the Composer* (New York: Simon and Schuster, 1973), 101.

9. The tones B to B on the piano's white keys, with this pattern of intervals: semitone-tone-tone-semitone-tone-tone-tone.

10. Jim Svejda, notes to the CD *Peter Mennin: Moby Dick, Symphonies 3 and 7* (Delos DE 3164), 6.

11. See Walter Simmons, "Peter Mennin: Biography," published in *American National Biography* (1993) and reproduced on Walter Simmons's website: http://www.walter-simmons.com/articles/346.htm, accessed 10 January 2007.

12. This and the previous quotation from a Thomson review may be found reprinted in Ewen, *American Composers: A Biographical Dictionary,* s.v. "Mennin, Peter."

13. Caroline Cepin Benser and David Francis Urrows, *Randall Thompson: A Bio-Bibliography* (Westport, Conn.: Greenwood, 1991), 29.

14. *The Concise Edition of Baker's Biographical Dictionary of Musicians,* 8th

ed., rev. Nicolas Slonimsky (New York: Schirmer Books, 1994), s.v. "Thompson, Randall."

15. Philip Kennicott, notes to the CD *Randall Thompson: Symphonies 2 and 3* (Koch International Classics 3-7074-2 H1), 2.

16. Benser and Urrows, *Randall Thompson*, 23.

17. Ibid., 5.

18. Randall Thompson's sketches for the Third Symphony may be found at Harvard University's Houghton Library, call number: bMS Mus 173 (28b). Interestingly, according to his penciled remarks on the sketches, he did not orchestrate the work until the four months before the performance.

19. Benser and Urrows, *Randall Thompson*, 29–30.

20. David Ewen, *American Composers: A Biographical Dictionary*, s.v. "Thompson, Randall"; Benser and Urrows, *Randall Thompson*, 122.

21. See Copland's letter to Howard Shanet, 13 December 1966, in *The Selected Correspondence of Aaron Copland*, ed. Elizabeth B. Crist and Wayne Shirley (New Haven: Yale University Press, 2006), 240.

22. Arthur Berger, *Aaron Copland* (New York: Oxford University Press, 1953), 29.

23. Aaron Copland and Vivian Perlis, *Copland, 1900 through 1942* (New York: St. Martin's/Marek, 1984), 279.

24. Copland, *Music and Imagination*, 117.

25. Arnold Dobrin, *Aaron Copland* (New York: Crowell, 1967), 194–195.

26. Arthur Berger, "Spring Season, 1943," *Modern Music* 20 (May–June 1943): 255; Colin McPhee, "Scores and Records," *Modern Music* 20 (May–June 1943): 277; Virgil Thomson, *Music Reviewed, 1940–1954* (New York: Vintage Books, 1967), 95.

27. Thomson, *Music Reviewed*, 95.

28. Charles Mills, "Over the Air," *Modern Music* 20 (November–December 1942): 63.

29. Written 20 May 1945 and included in Virgil Thomson, *The Art of Judging Music* (New York: Knopf, 1948), 162.

30. Aaron Copland and Vivian Perlis, *Copland since 1943* (New York: St. Martin's, 1989), 61–66.

31. Howard Pollack, *Aaron Copland* (New York: Henry Holt, 1999), 410, 412.

32. Copland and Perlis, *Copland since 1943*, 67–68.

33. Ibid., 68–69.

34. William Schuman, "Americanism in Music, A Composer's View," in *Music in American Society, 1776–1976*, ed. George McCue (New Brunswick, N.J.: Transaction Books, 1977), 22–23.

35. Walter Simmons, *Voices in the Wilderness* (Lanham, Md.: Scarecrow, 2004), 202.

36. Monica J. Slomski, *Paul Creston: A Bio-Bibliography* (Westport, Conn.: Greenwood, 1994), 20.

37. Arthur Berger, "Spring Season, 1943," *Modern Music* 20 (May–June 1943): 255.

38. Slomski, *Paul Creston*, 10.

39. Simmons, *Voices in the Wilderness*, 231.

40. Tim Page, notes to the CD *Roger Sessions: Symphonies 1, 2, and 3* (New World NWCR 573), 2.

41. Aaron Copland, *The New Music* (New York: Norton, 1968), 128–130.

42. Peter Jona Korn, "The Symphony in America," in *The Symphony*, vol. 2, ed. Robert Simpson (Baltimore: Penguin Books, 1967), 262.

43. Roger Sessions, *Roger Sessions on Music: Collected Essays*, ed. Edward T. Cone (Princeton, N.J.: Princeton University Press, 1979), 135.

44. Ibid., 289.

45. Aaron Copland, "Scores and Records," *Modern Music* 15 (1937–38): 244–245.

46. Roger Sessions, *The Correspondence of Roger Sessions*, ed. Andrea Olmstead (Boston: Northeastern University Press, 1992), 335–336.

47. Roger Sessions, *Symphony No. II* (New York: G. Schirmer, 1949).

48. Tim Page, notes to the CD *Roger Sessions: Symphonies No. 1, 2, and 3* (CRI CD 573), 9.

49. Thomson, *Music Reviewed, 1940–1954*, 211.

50. Tim Page, notes to *Roger Sessions: Symphonies No. 1, 2, and 3*, 10.

5. American Symphonies after 1950

1. Paul Turok, in *Music Journal* 32 (November 1974): 4. See also Harold C. Schonberg, *Facing the Music* (New York: Summit Books, 1981), 362.

2. See, for example, Theodore W. Adorno, *The Philosophy of Modern Music* (London: Sheed and Ward, 1973), for his views concerning contemporary music and the need to challenge the audience.

3. Louis Moreau Gottschalk, *Notes of a Pianist*, ed. Jeanne Behrend (New York: Knopf, 1964), 51–52.

4. These conclusions were reached after I had examined what was actually performed here and abroad by our major orchestras from the sixties to the nineties.

5. On this point, see Gary Taylor, *Cultural Selection* (New York: Basic Books, 1996), 46.

6. See Everett Helm, *Music and Tomorrow's Public* (New York: Heinrichshofen Edition, 1981), 12.

7. A discussion of the implications of cultural democracy is found in Michael Kammen, *American Culture, American Tastes* (New York: Basic Books, 1999), 37.

8. Bernard Holland, "Pleasure Dome for the Los Angeles Philharmonic," *New York Times,* 28 January 2003, http://query.nytimes.com/gst/fullpage .html?res=9D02E6D81239F93BA15752C0A9659C8B63&scp=1&sq= pleasure+dome+philharmonic&st=nyt, accessed 25 June 2008.

SELECTED BIBLIOGRAPHY

Adams, Don, and Arlene Goldbard. "Cultural Policy in U.S. History." *Webster's World of Cultural Democracies* (1995). http://www.wwcd.org/policy/US/ UShistory.html, accessed 21 December 2006.

———. "New Deal Cultural Programs." *Webster's World of Cultural Democracies* (1995). *http://www.wwcd.org/policy/US/newdeal.html*, accessed 21 December 2006.

Adams, K. Gary. *William Schuman: A Bio-Bibliography.* Westport, Conn.: Greenwood, 1998.

Antheil, George. *Bad Boy of Music.* Garden City, N.Y.: Doubleday, Doran, 1945.

Attali, Jacques. *Noise: The Political Economy of Music.* Trans. Brian Massumi. Minneapolis: University of Minnesota Press, 1985.

Barber, Samuel. *Symphony No. 1,* Opus 9. New York: G. Schirmer, 1943.

———. *Symphony No. 2,* Opus 19. New York: G. Schirmer, 1950.

Barzun, Jacques. *The Culture We Deserve.* Middletown, Conn.: Wesleyan University Press, 1989.

Becker, Howard S. *Art Worlds.* Berkeley: University of California Press, 1982.

Benser, Caroline Cepin, and David Francis Urrows. *Randall Thompson: A Bio-Bibliography.* Westport, Conn.: Greenwood, 1991.

Berger, Arthur. *Aaron Copland.* New York: Oxford University Press, 1953.

———. *Reflections of an American Composer.* Berkeley: University of California Press, 2002.

Bernstein, Leonard. *Findings.* New York: Simon and Schuster, 1982.

———. *Jeremiah: Symphony No. 1 for Mezzo-Soprano and Orchestra.* Corrected edition. New York: Boosey and Hawkes, 1992 [1943].

Bindas, Kenneth J. *All of This Music Belongs to the Nation.* Knoxville: University of Tennessee Press, 1995.

Blitzstein, Marc. *The Airborne; Symphony.* Piano score. Washington, D.C.: Library of Congress: *M1533.3.B55 A5,* n.d.

Border, Nathan. "The Music of William Schuman." *Musical Quarterly* 31 (1945): 17–28.

———. *Samuel Barber.* New York: Schirmer Books, 1954.

Brustein, Robert. "The Four Horsemen of the Anti-Culture." *Partisan Review* 69 (2002). *www.bu.edu/Partisanreview/archives/2002/4/Brustein.html.*

Burton, Humphrey. *Leonard Bernstein.* New York: Doubleday, 1994.

Carpenter, John Alden. *Symphony No. 2.* Revised version. Washington, D.C.: Library of Congress: *ML96.C274 (Case),* 1947.

Carter, Elliott. "Walter Piston." *Musical Quarterly* 32 (1946): 354–375.

Clark, Kenneth. *What Is a Masterpiece?* New York: Thames and Hudson, 1981.

The Concise Edition of Baker's Biographical Dictionary of Musicians. 8th edition. Rev. Nicolas Slonimsky. New York: Schirmer Books, 1994.

Copland, Aaron. *Copland on Music.* Garden City, N.Y.: Doubleday, 1960.

———. *Music and Imagination.* New York: Mentor, 1959.

———. *The New Music.* Rev. and enlarged edition. New York: Norton, 1968.

———. *Third Symphony.* New York: Boosey and Hawkes, [1966?], ca. 1947.

———. *What to Listen for in Music.* Rev. edition. New York: Mentor, 1963.

Copland, Aaron, and Vivian Perlis. *Copland, 1900 through 1942.* New York: St. Martin's/Marek, 1984.

———. *Copland since 1943.* New York: St. Martin's, 1989.

Creston, Paul. *Symphony No. 2, op. 35.* Washington, D.C.: Library of Congress: *ML96.C8335 (Case),* 1944.

Cuyler, Louise. *The Symphony.* New York: Harcourt Brace Jovanovich, 1973.

Diamond, David. *Symphony No. 3.* New York: Southern Music, ca. 1969.

Dissanayake, Ellen. *What Is Art For?* Seattle: University of Washington Press, 1988.

Dobrin, Arnold. *Aaron Copland.* New York: Crowell, 1967.

Downes, Edward. *Adventures in Symphonic Music.* New York: Farrar and Rinehart, 1949.

Downes, Olin. *Olin Downes on Music.* Ed. Irene Downes. New York: Simon and Schuster, 1957.

Ewen, David. *American Composers: A Biographical Dictionary.* New York: G. P. Putnam's Sons, 1982.

———. *The Book of Modern Composers.* New York: Knopf, 1950.

———. *The Complete Book of Twentieth Century Music.* New York: Prentice-Hall, 1952.

The Federal Music Project. Washington, D.C.: Works Progress Administration, 1936.

Finkelstein, Sidney. *Composer and Nation.* New York: International Publishers, 1960.

Fowler, Tommy. "Music, Politics, and the Future." *COMA* (2003). http://www.coma.org, accessed 20 October 2006.

Gordon, Eric A. *Mark the Music: The Life and Work of Mark Blitzstein.* New York: St. Martin's, 1989.

Hamm, Charles. *Music in the New World.* New York: Norton, 1983.

Hanson, Howard. *Symphony No. 3.* Rochester, N.Y.: Eastman School of Music of the University of Rochester, 1941.

Harris, Roy. *Third Symphony, in One Movement.* New York: G. Schirmer, ca. 1940.

Helm, Everett. *Composer, Performer, Public: A Study in Communication.* Florence: L. S. Olschki, 1970.

———. *Music and Tomorrow's Public.* International Music Council (UNESCO). New York: Heinrichshofen Edition, 1981.

Hennessee, Don A. *Samuel Barber.* Westport, Conn.: Greenwood, 1985.

Heyman, Barbara B. *Samuel Barber.* New York: Oxford University Press, 1992.

Howard, John Tasker. *Our American Music,* 4th ed. New York: Crowell, 1965.

Jacobs, Norman, ed. *Culture for the Millions?* Boston: Beacon, 1964.

Kammen, Michael. *American Culture, American Tastes.* New York: Basic Books, 1999.

Kimberling, Victoria J. *David Diamond: A Bio-Bibliography.* Metuchen, N.J.: Scarecrow, 1987.

Korn, Peter Jona. "The Symphony in America." In *The Symphony,* ed. Robert Simpson. Baltimore: Penguin Books, 1967. 243–267.

Larson, Gary O. *American Canvas.* Washington, D.C.: National Endowment for the Arts, 1947.

Lehrman, Leonard. *Marc Blitzstein: A Bio-Bibliography.* New York: Praeger, 2005.

Leichtentritt, Hugo. *Serge Koussevitzky.* Cambridge, Mass.: Harvard University Press, 1946.

Leppert, Richard, and Susan McClary, eds. *Music and Society.* Cambridge, England: Cambridge University Press, 1987.

Levy, Alan Howard. *Musical Nationalism.* Westport, Conn.: Greenwood, 1983.

Lipman, Samuel. *Arguing for Music/Arguing for Culture.* Boston: Godine, 1990.

Luening, Otto. *The Odyssey of an American Composer.* New York: Scribner's Sons, 1980.

Machlis, Joseph. *American Composers of Our Time.* New York: Crowell, 1963.

Martin, Peter J. *Sounds and Society.* Manchester, England: Manchester University Press, 1995.

McCue, George, ed. *Music in American Society.* New Brunswick, N.J.: Transaction Books, 1977.

Mennin, Peter. *Symphony No. 3.* New York: G. Schirmer, ca. 1984.

Moore, Douglas. *Symphony in A.* New York: G. Schirmer, ca. 1947.

Mueller, John H. *The American Symphony Orchestra.* Bloomington: Indiana University Press, 1951.

Mumford, Lewis. *The Conduct of Life.* New York: Harcourt, Brace, 1951.

Norton, Richard. *Tonality in Western Culture.* University Park: Pennsylvania State University Press, 1984.

O'Connor, Joan. *John Alden Carpenter.* Westport, Conn.: Greenwood, 1994.

Olmsted, Andrea. *Conversations with Roger Sessions.* Boston: Northeastern University Press, 1987.

———. *Roger Sessions and His Music.* Ann Arbor, Mich.: UMI Research Press, 1985.

O'Neill, William. *A Democracy at War.* Cambridge, Mass.: Harvard University Press, 1993.

Perone, James E. *Howard Hanson: A Bio-Bibliography.* Westport, Conn.: Greenwood, 1993.

Pettis, Ashley. "The WPA and the American Composer." *Musical Quarterly* 26 (1940): 101–112.

Pollack, Howard. *Aaron Copland.* New York: Henry Holt, 1999.

———. *Skyscraper Lullaby.* Washington, D.C.: Smithsonian Institution Press, 1995.

———. *Walter Piston.* Ann Arbor, Mich.: UMI Research Press, 1982.

Prausnitz, Frederik. *Roger Sessions.* New York: Oxford University Press, 2002.

Reagan, Donald J. "Douglas Moore and His Orchestral Works." Ph.D. diss., Catholic University of America, 1972.

Reimer, Bennett, and Jeffrey E. Wright, eds. *On the Nature of Musical Experience.* Niwot: University of Colorado Press, 1992.

Rorem, Ned. *Lies, 1986–1999.* Washington, D.C.: Counterpoint, 2000.

Rouse, Christopher. *William Schuman.* New York: Schirmer Books, 1980.

Schlesinger, Arthur M., Jr. *The Disuniting of America.* Rev. and enlarged edition. New York: Norton, 1998.

Schonberg, Harold C. *Facing the Music.* New York: Summit Books, 1981.

Schreiber, Flora Rheta, and Vincent Persichetti. *William Schuman.* New York: Schirmer Books, 1954.

Schuman, William. "Americanism in Music: A Composer's View." In *Music in American Society, 1776–1976,* ed. George McCue. New Brunswick, N.J.: Transaction Books, 1977. 15–25.

———. *Symphony No. 3 in Two Parts.* New York: G. Schirmer, 1942.

Secrest, Meryle. *Leonard Bernstein.* New York: Knopf, 1994.

Sessions, Roger. *The Correspondence of Roger Sessions.* Ed. Andrea Olmstead. Boston: Northeastern University Press, 1992.

———. *Roger Sessions on Music: Collected Essays.* Ed. Edward T. Cone. Princeton, N.J.: Princeton University Press, 1979.

Shepherd, John, and Peter Wicke. *Music and Cultural Theory.* Cambridge, England: Polity, 1997.

Simmons, Walter. *Voices in the Wilderness: Six American Neo-Romantic Composers.* Lanham, Md.: Scarecrow, 2004.

Slomski, Monica J. *Paul Creston: A Bio-Bibliography*. Westport, Conn.: Greenwood, 1994.

Smith, Moses. *Koussevitzky*. New York: Allen, Towne and Heath, 1944.

Stehman, Dan. *Roy Harris*. Boston: Twayne Publishers, 1984.

———. *Roy Harris: A Bio-Bibliography*. Westport, Conn.: Greenwood, 1991.

Steinberg, Michael. *The Symphony*. New York: Oxford University Press, 1995.

Suspičić, Ivo. *Music in Society*. Stuyvesant, N.Y.: Pendragon, 1987.

Taubman, Howard. *Music on My Beat*. New York: Simon and Schuster, 1943.

Tawa, Nicholas. *American Composers and Their Public*. Metuchen, N.J.: Scarecrow, 1995.

———. *Art Music in the American Society*. Metuchen, N.J.: Scarecrow, 1987.

———. *Serenading the Reluctant Eagle*. New York: Schirmer Books, 1984.

Taylor, Gary. *Cultural Selection*. New York: Basic Books, 1996.

Thompson, Randall. *Symphony No. 3*. Cambridge, Mass.: Houghton Library, Harvard University. A.MS.; [v.p.] 21 Aug. 1947–19 Mar. 1949. 27f. (53p.), pencil sketch, call number: bMS Mus 173 (28b).

Thomson, Virgil. *The Art of Judging Music*. New York: Knopf, 1948.

———. *Music Reviewed, 1940–1954*. New York: Vintage, 1967.

———. *The Musical Scene*. New York: Knopf, 1945.

———. *Selected Letters of Virgil Thomson*. Ed. Tim Page and Vanessa Weeks Page. New York: Summit Books, 1988.

———. *The State of Music*. New York: Morrow, 1939.

———. *Virgil Thomson*. New York: Knopf, 1966.

Tischler, Barbara L. *An American Music*. New York: Oxford University Press, 1986.

Tocqueville, Alexis de. *Democracy in America*. 2 vols. Trans. Henry Reeves, rev. Francis Bowen, further corrected by Phillips Bradley. New York: Vintage Books, 1954.

Tommasini, Anthony. *Virgil Thomson*. New York: Norton, 1997.

Vinton, John, ed. *Dictionary of Contemporary Music*. New York: Dutton, 1974.

Warner, W. Lloyd. *American Life*. Rev. ed. Chicago: University of Chicago Press, 1962.

Whitesitt, Linda. *The Life and Music of George Antheil, 1900–1959*. Ann Arbor, Mich.: UMI Research Press, 1983.

INDEX

accessibility, musical, 2; at century's close, 210
Adams, John, 211
Adorno, Theodor, 202
American Composers Orchestral Concerts, 45
"American Dream," 3–4
American Federation of Labor, 9
American Music Center, 45
American public, 2, 4; attitudes, 4–5, 13, 85, 86
Americanisms in music, 24–26, 47, 56, 122, 152–153, 176, 181
Antheil, George, 83; Airplane Sonata, 89; background, 88–90; *Ballet Mécanique*, 89–90; *Death of Machines*, 89; film composer, 91; *Helen Retires*, 90; *Jazz Sonata*, 89; musical style, 88–89, 90, 98; nonmusical activities, 90–91; Piano Concerto, 90; *Sonata Sauvage*, 89; *Symphonie en fa*, 90; Symphony No. 1, 90; Symphony No. 2, 90; Symphony No. 3, 92–94; Symphony No. 4 (*1942*), 91, 94–98, 145; Symphony No. 5 (*Joyous*), 98; Symphony No. 6 (*After Delacroix*), 98; *Transatlantic*, 90

antidemocratic activities in the United States, 12–13, 85–86, 182–183
"art for art's sake," 10
art in America, 4, 32
audience for classical music, 9, 10, 11–12, 26–27; new listeners, 8–9; why people listened, 4, 9, 28–29, 86, 160
avant-garde, 10

Barber, Samuel, 11, 16, 33, 82, 83; *Adagio for Strings*, xi, 15, 43; background, 34–36; *Dover Beach*, 38–39; *First* and *Second Essay* for orchestra, 43; *Knoxville, Summer of 1915*, 43, 135–136; *Music for a Scene from Shelley*, 38; *Medea's Meditation and Dance of Vengeance*, 43; musical style, 36–38, 39, 129, 131, 136; Overture to *The School for Scandal*, 35, 38; *Prayers of Kierkegaard*, 43; Symphony No. 1, xi, 39–43; Symphony No. 2 (*Airborne*), 43, 128–134, 145; Violin Concerto, 43
Bartók, Béla, x
Berio, Luciano, 202
Berkshire Music Institute, 111

NICHOLAS TAWA is co-founder of the Sonneck Society, now the Society for American Music. He is Professor Emeritus of Music at the University of Massachusetts, Boston.